Banded Together

THE WORKING CLASS
IN AMERICAN HISTORY

Editorial Advisors
James R. Barrett
Alice Kessler-Harris
Nelson Lichtenstein
David Montgomery

A list of books in the series appears at the end of this book.

Banded Together

Economic Democratization in the Brass Valley

JEREMY BRECHER

University of Illinois Press

URBANA, CHICAGO, AND SPRINGFIELD

Library of Congress Cataloging-in-Publication Data
Brecher, Jeremy.
Banded together : economic democratization in the Brass Valley /
Jeremy Brecher.
    p.   cm. — (The working class in American history)
Includes bibliographical references and index.
ISBN-13: 978-0-252-03612-5 (hardcover : alk. paper)
ISBN-10: 0-252-03612-3 (hardcover : alk. paper)
ISBN-13: 978-0-252-07806-4 (pbk. : alk. paper)
ISBN-10: 0-252-07806-3 (pbk. : alk. paper)
1. Social action—Connecticut—Naugatuck River Valley.
2. Deindustrialization—Connecticut—Naugatuck River Valley—
History. 3. Naugatuck River Valley (Conn.)—Social conditions.
4. Naugatuck River Valley (Conn.)—Economic conditions.
5. Brass Workers History Project. I. Title.
HN17.5.B713   2011
330.9746'1—dc22   2010040244

This book is dedicated to the people of the Naugatuck Valley, who have educated me, sustained me, and taken me unto them as their pet outsider. I can truly say of the valley, as Herman Melville's Ishmael said of his whale ship, that it has been my Yale College and my Harvard.

If all the people in a city are banded together to make it a better place to live, then it will be a better place to live. That's what the Naugatuck Valley Project is all about.

—Theresa Francis

Contents

Prologue   ix

Acknowledgments   xi

Introduction   xiii

1. Roots of Powerlessness in the Brass Valley   1

2. Banding Together   21

3. Buyout   35

4. Organizing   49

5. Century Brass   67

6. The Life and Death of Seymour Specialty Wire   84

7. Founding ValleyCare Cooperative   111

8. Taking Care of Business   130

9. The Demise of ValleyCare   149

10. Brookside Housing Cooperative   164

11. Economic Democratization from Below   186

12. Afterstories   203

Notes   219

List of Interviews   241

Index   243

Prologue

On a dreary day in April 1983, a hearse rolled through the little town of Thomaston in western Connecticut's Naugatuck Valley. Behind the hearse, four white-gloved factory workers carried a bier. On it was laid out a clock—a Royal Seth mantel clock manufactured by the Seth Thomas Clock Company. The procession halted at the green next to the 168-year-old Seth Thomas factory. Then laid-off workers from Seth Thomas stuffed the clock with paper towels, soaked it with gasoline, and set it ablaze. They announced they would send the ashes to executives of Talley Industries, a multinational conglomerate that had bought Seth Thomas and then, unexpectedly, shut it down forever.

Seth Thomas was not just a business; it was the basis for a way of life that typified industrial communities throughout America. For generations, local girls and boys had grown up expecting to work at the Seth Thomas Clock Company or the Plume and Atwood mill that Thomas had founded to supply his clock company with brass. Thomaston schoolchildren chanted:

> Ashes to ashes
> Dust to dust
> If Seth Thomas doesn't get you
> Plume & Atwood must.[1]

When Talley decided to close Seth Thomas, those who worked there were among the last to find out. Mary Tycenski, whose family had worked at Seth Thomas for many decades, recalls that one afternoon in 1982, "We were working and they just called a meeting. One of the executives from Talley Industries was there. He just said they were closing Seth Thomas down and moving to Georgia. Just everybody felt just terrible. It was a shock."[2]

The day Seth Thomas closed, James Wilson was the last one to leave the building. "It was eerie. We wished all the people from Seth Thomas goodbye. It was like a morgue."[3]

According to the local union president, Seth Thomas's ninety-two laid-off union members had together given 1,450 years of service to the company. The plant's closing left many of them facing long-term unemployment.

The closing also left a wound in the community's identity. Matthew Monahan, Thomaston postmaster and a former Seth Thomas employee, said, "It just seemed as though Seth Thomas *was* Thomaston. If you ever travel anywhere in the Navy or anywhere, they might not know where Thomaston was, but if you mention Seth Thomas clocks, they all had a Seth Thomas clock in their home. The Navy ships had Seth Thomas clocks. Even in Japan I saw Seth Thomas clocks. They were known throughout the world." Francis Kane, a retired Seth Thomas employee, said, "I figured Seth Thomas really belongs to Thomaston; that's where it originated."[4]

The demise of Seth Thomas was only one of dozens of plant closings that were decimating the clock, brass, rubber, and other industries of the Naugatuck Valley in the early 1980s—and only one of thousands occurring throughout industrial America. "Deindustrialization" was devastating life in the valley, but there was little effort to do anything about it. The reason was simple: a sense of utter powerlessness in the face of forces and decisions over which people in local communities had virtually no control.

It was that bitter feeling of powerlessness Seth Thomas workers sought to express by holding a funeral and cremating a clock. Former Seth Thomas employee Linda Turner called it "a symbolic gesture of ordinary people against something they cannot change." In a eulogy for the clock, Rev. Henry Cody of St. Thomas Parish in Thomaston said, "We mourn for the workers who served with dedication, loyalty, and skill. We ask for a resurrection here, that people may again have a chance to create."[5]

Acknowledgments

Hundreds of people have helped me on this project in one way or another over the past quarter century; I thank them all. I would like to acknowledge the leaders, staff, and participants in the Naugatuck Valley Project (NVP) who helped me with this work over the years, including Ken Galdston, Carol Burkhart-Lyons, Barbara Therrien, Theresa Francis, Janet Caggiano, and Rev. Elizabeth Rosa. Thanks also to the more than one hundred people who let me interview them for this research and the hundreds more who have let me interview them for other aspects of my research in the Naugatuck Valley.

I received help with the chapters on ValleyCare from Ruth Glasser and with the chapter on Brookside from Lucien Lafreniere. Among those who introduced me to the valley were Peter and Frances Marcuse, who have supported my involvement ever since, and my first valley collaborators, Jerry Lombardi and the late Jan Stackhouse.

The Mattatuck Museum has provided me a base for thirty years of research in the Naugatuck Valley and specifically helped with archiving my NVP materials and participating in the 2009 NVP History Project; I would like to acknowledge in particular Ann Smith, Marie Galbraith, Suzie Fateh, and Cynthia Roznoy. Sister Marie Michaud and another volunteer who has requested to remain anonymous made an enormous contribution by transcribing many of the interviews used in this book.

I would also like to thank those who have given me comments on all or part of the book, including Ken Galdston, Carol Burkhart-Lyons, Ruth Glasser, Jill Cutler, Charles Hotchkiss, and Peter Rachleff.

I would like to thank the Cooperative Charitable Trust, which nurtured the initial research project that gave birth to this book and provided support to finish it. I would also like to thank the members of the Cooperative Charitable Trust Forum, who individually and collectively provided a great deal of my knowledge and understanding of all matters connected with cooperatives and employee ownership as well as commentary on the original studies that resulted in this book. This project was also made possible by support provided to related work by the Connecticut Humanities Council, the Catholic Communications Campaign, the Ford Foundation, and the National Endowment for the Humanities.

Introduction

This book tells the story of a group of factory workers, housewives, parishioners, and organizers who tried to create an alternative to the economic powerlessness manifested in the closing of Seth Thomas and dozens of other factories in the Naugatuck Valley region. They sought ways to establish greater democratic control over the economic forces, institutions, and decisions that were devastating their communities, livelihoods, and ways of life. Starting in the early 1980s, they created a community alliance called the Naugatuck Valley Project to serve as a vehicle for their efforts; organized workers in dozens of companies to respond to the threat of plant closings; helped workers buy and run a failing brass mill; started an employee-owned home–health care company; organized tenants to create permanently affordable, democratically run cooperative housing; and addressed the education, transportation, health, and other crises that accompanied the devastation of the local economy. This book draws lessons from their efforts for those who experience the effects of economic powerlessness and want to band together to establish more democratic control over their economic lives.

Shortly before the demise of Seth Thomas, I was engaged in a community-based oral history project on the lives of working people of the Naugatuck Valley called the Brass Workers History Project.[1] Old-timers had told me and my collaborators of their arduous, dangerous, insecure, and oppressive work, but also of their pride in their own labor and in the communities it sustained. They described how they and their parents had built dense community networks and institutions and had used them to gain a degree of power over their conditions of life through unions, community action, and the political process.

As we were recording the experiences of the Naugatuck Valley's workers, the industrial economy that had sustained their way of life was collapsing around us. The unions and community institutions through which they had exercised some degree of collective power were being decimated. It was the start of the era of "Reaganomics," and most government leaders, far from trying to remedy the collapse, argued that government should stand back and let private business and the market provide the answer.

When my collaborators and I looked for someone to provide a positive vision of the future for the tens of thousands who had toiled in the region's factories, we found little more than advice to accept the inevitable, embrace the deterioration of wages and conditions, and hope that cheap labor might lure some new businesses into the region's decaying plants. I felt in my heart that we were writing an epitaph for the traditions of community building, mutuality, and labor solidarity we had found in the valley and that those traditions would have no inheritors.

But something I was not expecting arose almost as if from the ashes of the clock cremated by the Seth Thomas workers. A number of churches, unions, and community organizations decided they had to find a more positive way to address the economic problems of their members in the Naugatuck Valley. With guidance from an experienced organizer, they set up the Naugatuck Valley Project with the stated goal of helping workers and communities gain more control over the economic decisions that were affecting them. Because it identified economic problems as problems of power and control, the NVP promoted local, democratic ownership through such vehicles as employee-owned companies, cooperative housing, and a community land trust. Its strategy was to take the techniques of community organizations and citizen action groups and project them into the economic sphere. According to organizer Ken Galdston, "The idea of the project is that if you bring together the diverse groups in the community that are hit by these decisions made far away, and if you teach them how to organize, how to focus on an issue, how to bring their full pressure to bear, you can get those other people to sit down with you and start making decisions that you want."[2]

It made a difference. Less than a year after Seth Thomas closed, for instance, a local union leader at another Talley subsidiary attended an NVP briefing on the "early warning signs" of a plant closing. When he said those signs were already appearing in his shop, the NVP immediately pulled together a local coalition of union and church people. Confronted by a story in the newspaper and a call from a local minister, the president of the subsidiary agreed to meet with the NVP. Eventually, he agreed to an NVP proposal that

Talley give preference in any sale to buyers who would keep the jobs in the area; some, though not all, of the purchasers did so.

Where workers and residents had previously stood by, helpless to affect the forces that were eliminating their jobs and devastating their communities, now they had become players. They made the heads of corporations sit down and bargain with them. They influenced corporate policy—no doubt in a limited way, but enough to mean that the story did not always have to end with a funeral.

The NVP's goal was not just to save one or another set of jobs, but rather to build an organization that could help valley communities enhance their economic conditions on a continuing basis. It set out, therefore, to train leaders rooted in the congregations, unions, and community organizations of the valley who could mobilize these institutions to jointly address problems in the face of which they separately were powerless. The NVP became a vital force in the Naugatuck Valley, with sixty-five member organizations, chapters in six towns, hundreds of active supporters, and meetings almost daily in one or another part of the valley.

As this book was being completed in 2009, the NVP was celebrating its twenty-fifth anniversary. Its accomplishments over that quarter century have been substantial. It has trained hundreds of leaders and organized hundreds of campaigns around jobs, housing, health care, education, environment, industrial brownfield redevelopment, job training, neighborhood blight, community services, youth leadership training, and many other issues that affect the lives of ordinary people in the Naugatuck Valley. It has drawn participation from up and down the Naugatuck Valley; from the cities and the suburbs; from congregations, unions, small business organizations, and community groups; and from diverse ethnic, racial, and religious subcultures. It has been widely recognized as a national leader in efforts to train and empower community residents to address economic and social problems through their own action.

I was aware of the NVP from its inception, and as the self-appointed chronicler of Naugatuck Valley social movements, I began tracking and documenting its activities, attending meetings and conventions, and periodically interviewing staff and leaders. My relationship to the project was essentially that of a historian who could be drawn on for background about the valley and a sympathetic journalist reporting on some of its more noteworthy efforts.

As a historian, I found this an extraordinary opportunity to observe the emergence of a new kind of social enterprise—right in the middle of a social world I had spent the preceding years studying. It promised to illuminate the

NVP's Victories and Accomplishments, 1984–2009

General Time Controls (GTC)—organized employees and religious leaders to have one line of production sold to a local buyer when the Thomaston company was shut down

Uniroyal Rubber—organized congregations and employees of the Naugatuck company to protect retirement benefits, including health care and pension plans

Seymour Specialty Wire—organized an employee buyout to create the largest democratically owned industrial firm in the nation from 1984 to 1991

Reymond's Bakery—worked with the union to secure the "right of first refusal" for employees to purchase the bakery when it was sold, setting a national precedent

Bristol Babcock—the NVP's organizing campaign strengthened the union and prevented the workers from granting unwarranted concessions demanded by the company

Berkeley Heights Tenant Council—organized public housing residents to create a tenants' council and to secure complete renovations of the apartment buildings, eliminating common hallways so the housing was safer for all residents

Naugatuck Supermarket—organized congregations to secure a new supermarket to improve access to food for low-income residents in an area of town without a grocery store

Naugatuck Valley Housing Development Corporation—created a community land trust to pursue development of permanently affordable housing in the valley

Brookside Housing Cooperatives—organized to win the construction of 102 units of permanently affordable, cooperatively owned, democratically controlled, limited-equity cooperative housing in Waterbury

ValleyCare Cooperative—created an employee-owned home–health care company that provided high-quality, low-cost health care and employed more than eighty people

Waterbury Seniors/Grocery Committee—organized downtown residents to secure free van transportation to outlying grocery stores and later helped secure the new Shaw's Supermarket

Multi-Metals Training Center—worked with local manufacturers and Waterbury Adult Education to create a model job training program that has placed hundreds of workers in the eyelet and screw machine industries

Neighborhood Blight—through creative actions, including a "Badder Homes and Gardens Tour," secured a city blight officer and a new police precinct in Waterbury

UConn Torrington—organized to save this branch of the university from closure

Thomaston Area Youth Activities Council—organized to create a youth center with a variety of programs for area youth, spurring youth and parents into action

Naugatuck Valley Brownfields Pilot—led the effort to secure federal pilot status and funding for a regional effort to clean up and redevelop abandoned and polluted industrial sites, including the redevelopment of a brass factory in Thomaston, bringing brass production and jobs back to the community in 2000

Waterbury's Inner-City Neighborhoods—organized a network of religious, tenant, and neighborhood leaders in the inner-city neighborhoods of Waterbury concerned about critical community reinvestment issues such as abandoned housing, inadequate policies and services, and lack of recreational space

Waterbury Housing Coalition—the NVP partnered with Neighborhood Housing Services and Mutual Housing Association of South Central Connecticut to create the WHC to rehab 33 units of housing on Willow Street and Chestnut Avenue that is affordable, safe, and clean

Tax Relief for Low-Income Residents—provided the City of Waterbury with an Economic Impact Study prepared by Amadon and Associates, Professor John Clapp from the University of Connecticut, and Nicholas Carbone, retired president of the Connecticut Institute for Municipal Studies, to determine the impact of shifting the burden of taxes to residential property owners by examining residents' ability to pay the higher taxes by estimating the resulting increase in the number of delinquencies; the NVP empowered the City of Waterbury to create a $2.49 million tax circuit breaker, giving tax relief to low-income families

Latino Caucus and Volunteer Translation Office—created the Latino/Hispanic Resource Center (LHRC) in Derby, which provides referral interpretation services on a volunteer basis to one thousand people per year and is an important link between newer immigrants and local social service agencies

NVP Youth Empowerment—along with St. John of the Cross Church, in Middlebury, conducted Youth Leadership Trainings for three summers at Westover School in Middlebury, bringing together more than one hundred youth from diverse backgrounds and ten different towns in the valley

Predatory Lending/Unfair Trade Practices—brought more than seventy-five cases to the Connecticut attorney general, who then brought a suit against four major Waterbury predatory lenders and realtors, which resulted in more than forty-five cases charging predatory lending and consumer fraud; the suit settled for $750,000

Environmental Remediation Technician Training Program—worked to get an agreement from two district Workforce Investment Boards to create an environmental remediation technician training program at Naugatuck Valley Community College, to train valley residents in its first year to clean up the valley's 189 brownfield sites

Public Act 07-185—in collaboration with a statewide coalition won the passage of a health care bill by the Connecticut legislature that included $4.7 million in Medicaid reimbursement for medical interpretation services, as well as empowering this group to form an official Medical Interpreting Association of Connecticut to set statewide standards, inaugurated in June 2007

Medical Interpretation Services—won Griffin Hospital's hiring of a Radiology Department staff member to serve the Polish community, complementing the part-time Spanish-language interpreters previously hired by Griffin and Charlotte-Hungerford hospitals; won agreement from three of four valley hospitals to install videoconferencing medical interpretation services to further improve interpretation service for Limited English Proficient patients; reached at least seventy-five hundred LEP residents, in person and through public access television, through Health Care Navigation Training, which uses community volunteers to teach LEP speakers how to navigate the health care system and about their right to medical interpretation[3]

vexed historical problem of how new movements arise and their relation to what preceded them. It also whetted my growing interest in globalization, contemporary community-labor coalitions, and network-based forms of organization.

The NVP was not necessarily the kind of organization I would have envisioned as a solution to the problems of working people in the Naugatuck Valley. Nonetheless, I have utmost respect for what the NVP accomplished, and I believe its experience illuminates not just one policy or strategy but the entire problem of economic empowerment. I share the NVP's commitment to a more democratic way of organizing economic life, and I willingly appear as an advocate for the proposition that ordinary people need to organize themselves to challenge decisions that profoundly affect them but over which they have little power. I consider the NVP as a series of experiments in trying to do just that. Whether successful or unsuccessful, these experiments provide insight into the process of economic democratization.

It gradually became clear to me that I would have to write a book about the NVP. I conducted more than one hundred interviews with project leaders, staff, and other knowledgeable members of the local community; collected many file drawers of documentation; and attended upwards of one hundred events as a participant observer. I asked the project to formally approve the idea of a book; it agreed to cooperate, to give me access to staff and files, and to assist my fund-raising efforts. We agreed that I would be free to write whatever I pleased, but the project could append a "dissenting opinion" to the book if it wished. While I have received useful feedback from NVP participants, no dissenting opinion has proved necessary. I have worked on the book intermittently for more than twenty years, and I hope that it reflects the benefits of historical perspective and of what I have learned in studies of globalization, community-labor coalitions, and network organization that I have worked on in the interim.[4]

This book is first of all the story of particular individuals who faced a particular situation and had to decide how to respond to it. Each of them could have ignored what was happening in their community, or dealt with it solely as an individual, or even pulled up stakes and run away. Instead, each of them chose to act together with others, even if it meant making sacrifices and taking risks. Each found their own meaning in such action and changed their worlds and themselves through it. The story of the NVP is their story.

This is also the story of a very particular place, albeit one that shared many traits with other American industrial regions. I have spent thirty years interviewing, researching, writing, making movies, developing exhibit scripts, teaching classes, and organizing cultural festivals in and about the Naugatuck Valley, and this book is intended in part to present yet another aspect of its life.

This is also the story of a particular time in the life of the valley, industrial America, and indeed the world. It is focused on the crisis of deindustrialization from the mid-1980s to the early 1990s. The challenges posed by the sudden collapse of the valley's industry were different from the ongoing problems of a postindustrial region today. The NVP continues to this day as a significant part of the life of the Naugatuck Valley, but it has repeatedly reinvented itself to address the problems of a region in which there are few plants left to save. The NVP's history is brought down to the present in a 2009 exhibit at Waterbury's Mattatuck Museum and on the Web site http://www.brassvalley.org.

Looking back, we can see that the region's deindustrialization marked the start of the process we know today as economic globalization. But in the mid-1980s, the term had hardly been invented, and the phenomenon was understood not as a whole but only in its fragmented manifestations. Deindustrialization was bringing rapid change to industrial communities, but there was still a residue of local industry worth trying to save and strong local religious, union, and other organizations on which organizing efforts could draw. For a brief time in the mid-1980s, employee buyouts were facilitated by the flood of capital available for takeovers of all kinds. The lessons of that experience cannot be applied directly to the very different conditions of later times.

Despite its particularity, the NVP's experience is relevant to a basic unresolved problem of modern civilization: most people's lack of power over the economic forces and decisions that affect them. The NVP tried to address valley residents' concrete economic problems by organizing them to establish their own economic institutions and to assert greater power over businesses, markets, and public policy. It refused to accept that the only choice was between government and the market; instead, it sought to complement and transform both through forms of democratic cooperation. Its experience may therefore help illuminate the continuing worldwide pursuit of community-based economic democratization. Such illumination may be even more relevant today as—after a quarter-century experiment with unfettered free-market capitalism—the realities of poverty, job insecurity, and the economic destruction of communities become more and more evident worldwide.

There is also a universal dimension to this story. People everywhere are threatened by forces they do not control and have to decide whether to accept or resist them. People everywhere have to decide whether to pursue their interests alone or band together with others around mutual concerns. People everywhere have to decide whether to meet adversity with resolution and heroism. The tragedy of defeat by heartless forces is universal, but so is the struggle to make "a better place to live" in the face of those forces.

This book is the story of a road not taken. Sociologist Fred Perella, author of *Poverty in American Democracy*, former codirector of the Office of Urban Affairs of the Archdiocese of Hartford, and one of the godfathers of the NVP, noted prophetically in the mid-1980s that America's economic difficulties were already causing pain, "but it's nothing like the pain they are going to cause in the next twenty years. If we don't develop communitarian and collaborative ways of dealing with these problems, there's going to be a lot more pain. I think the Naugatuck Valley Project is an embryonic sign of what has to develop in the future on a much broader basis for this society to survive and be strong."[5]

Instead, that quarter century has been shaped by what was once called "Reaganomics" and is now often referred to as "neoliberalism." Private business and the market have been less and less constrained by any requirements of social responsibility. The results for the Naugatuck Valley have been very different from what was promised, however, even long after the initial "shock therapy" of deindustrialization. The number of employed residents of the

Central Naugatuck Valley Region shrank 5.8 percent between 1990 and 2001.[6] An increasing proportion of jobs were temporary, part-time, contract, or other forms of contingent work. In Connecticut as a whole, poverty grew during the 1990s from a 3.5 percent rate in 1987–88 to a 9.1 percent rate in 1997–98. Forty thousand more Connecticut children were living in poverty in 1998 than in 1989.[7] The increase in poverty was concentrated in deindustrialized regions like the Naugatuck Valley. Behind numbers like these lies the kind of pain that Fred Perella prophesied. If we do not want unending decades of further pain, we need to revisit the "communitarian and collaborative ways of dealing with these problems" of which he believed the NVP served as an "embryonic sign."

This book focuses on three elements essential both for local action and for a democratic economic vision: grassroots organization, democratically controlled enterprises, and supportive public policies. There are lessons from the NVP for each.

To influence economic decisions, people have to organize themselves. This book examines the NVP as an extended experiment in creating and running a democratic popular organization, bringing together different elements of a community, agreeing on strategies, developing leaders, strengthening the infrastructure of existing organizations, and where necessary creating new ones.

To sustain control of economic forces, people have to establish their own economic institutions. This book emphasizes the NVP's experimentation with community-, employee-, and resident-controlled enterprises and institutions.

To protect their rights and provide resources for the institutions they create, people need public policies that support their efforts. The NVP has advocated and sometimes won state and local policies that supported worker buyouts, public investment in locally owned businesses, cooperative housing, land trusts, and other democratic economic initiatives. In contrast to discussions of economic strategy, community development, and industrial policy that emphasize the role of government and the market and ignore the potential contribution of organized workers and communities, this book draws on the experience of the NVP to indicate how public policy can support those organizing on their own behalf.

The NVP's approach can be characterized as economic democratization from below. This approach starts with organizing people at the grassroots level, and it sees them as the agency of change. Such an approach may seem quixotic in an increasingly globalized economy. And indeed, economic democratization from below, by itself, is unlikely to solve the economic problems of the United States or the world. But such community-based approaches can provide crucial elements of a multifaceted process of economic democratization at multiple levels from the global to the local. Indeed, without economic democratization from below, efforts at change from above will always be in danger of creating new and undemocratic concentrations of power and resources.

As I was completing this book in 2008–9, the world was entering the worst economic crisis since the Great Depression of the 1930s. People in the Naugatuck Valley and, indeed, throughout the world were facing new hardships and threats to their well-being. They were also searching for new solutions. I believe the experience of the Naugatuck Valley Project has two important lessons to contribute to that search. First, by organizing themselves at the grassroots level across boundaries of race, religion, ethnicity, and culture, people can actually have an impact on the forces that affect their lives. Second, some of the harm that results from the exclusion of ordinary people from ownership and control of productive wealth can be overcome by directly connecting work that needs to be done and people who need work. I hope those lessons are spelled out throughout this book in ways that people in and beyond the Naugatuck Valley can adapt and test for themselves.

This book is intended not only for people with an interest in history but also for those who are grappling with how to address the economic problems of today and tomorrow. For that reason, it examines in considerable detail the nitty-gritty difficulties of organizing, creating, and running alternative economic enterprises. I suspect that for those trying to create alternatives today, the lessons of heartbreaking failures may be as useful as the inspirational success stories.[8]

This book tells the interrelated stories of the NVP as an organization and the specific projects it initiated. "Roots of Powerlessness in the Brass Valley" presents the historical background of Naugatuck Valley industry, the development of the working class, the impact of deindustrialization, and the reasons valley communities found the latter so difficult to combat. "Banding Together" describes the way diverse constituencies came together around common interests and shared fights to create the NVP. "Buyout" describes how the NVP helped one group of workers purchase the company they worked for and run it as "Seymour Specialty Wire: An Employee Owned Company." "Organizing" explores the many facets of the NVP's approach to organizing and the kind of organization that resulted from it. "Century Brass" describes an unsuccessful effort to buy a failing brass company. "The Life and Death of Seymour Specialty Wire" describes the seven-year life and ultimate demise of Seymour Specialty Wire. The next three chapters deal with

ValleyCare Cooperative, the employee-owned home–health care company founded by the NVP. "Founding ValleyCare Cooperative" describes how the company was created. "Taking Care of Business" describes how the company provided a needed community service and quality jobs for more than fifty women, most of whom had previously been unemployed or on welfare. "The Demise of ValleyCare" explains why the company did not survive. "Brookside Housing Cooperative" recounts how a group of low- and moderate-income tenants organized themselves and created their own cooperative housing development to provide permanent affordability through a land trust, sweat equity, and tenant management. "Economic Democratization from Below" analyzes the main elements of the NVP's strategy for countering the economic powerlessness of valley residents, their relation to similar efforts elsewhere, and their significance for future efforts. "Afterstories" brings the various threads of the NVP story down to the present.

In his eulogy for the cremated Seth Thomas clock, Rev. Henry Cody had asked that workers again have a chance to create. Naugatuck Valley workers did not receive a new chance to create brass, rubber, or clocks. But they did create a new and original social movement. One of them, a housewife and retired factory worker named Theresa Francis, put the meaning of their efforts this way: "You have to become involved and help with creating your community because if you don't, you are a victim, and God didn't make us victims; he made us cocreators. And that's what we're about, and that's what we're supposed to be about. That's my way of saying what the Naugatuck Valley Project is about."[9] Ultimately, that's what this book is about.

1. Roots of Powerlessness
in the Brass Valley

One day in 1982, I received a call from a recent graduate of the Yale School of Organization and Management named Ken Galdston. He told me he wanted to create an organization to save jobs in the Naugatuck Valley.

I was skeptical of Galdston's proposal. I had seen the existing strategies of governments, unions, and other institutions charged with representing the interests of local workers and communities prove futile in the face of corporations prepared simply to shut down and move away. I felt changing that outcome was a hopeless task and that people in the valley were almost as powerless to halt its decline as they seemed to feel. That powerlessness was rooted in three hundred years of the valley's history and in global economic forces that seemed to be in no one's control.

The Brazen Age

Talk about the rise of industrial civilization, and you are talking about places like the Naugatuck Valley. The Naugatuck River originates in the western Connecticut uplands and races due south through rocky hills toward Long Island Sound. Over the course of ten thousand years, Native peoples planted corn on its fertile banks and fished in its plunging falls. In the 1630s, Puritans from Massachusetts established towns along the Connecticut River and nearly exterminated the Pequot Indians, the most powerful tribe in New England, clearing the way for expansion of what became the Connecticut Colony. Settlers thereupon spread rapidly from Hartford into the Connecticut interior, reaching the banks of the Naugatuck River in 1673.[1]

The Naugatuck Valley's first colonial settlement, today's Waterbury, began as a corporation whose land was owned jointly, though in unequal shares, by the town's "proprietors." A town meeting (from which women, Indians, blacks, and those not in good standing in the church were excluded) governed the town. A church and a school, not to mention stocks and pillories, soon followed. Settlement gradually spread up and down the valley, with Waterbury remaining by far the largest town.

For their first century and a half, the Naugatuck Valley settlements were farm villages. Their basic unit was the household, whose labor was complexly divided among men, women, children, servants, and slaves. The villages produced a wide range of foodstuffs, building materials, and craft products they needed, but they lacked the capital, equipment, and skills to compete with English manufacturing. From the start, they had to be part of an intercontinental trading system. Farm and timber products—a 1679 list includes wheat, rye, barley, Indian corn, pork, beef, wool, hemp, flax, cider, pipe staves, and horses[2]—moved from the interior of the colony over the poor roads to Hartford or New Haven, whence merchants shipped them to Boston and the Caribbean islands to join the famous "triangular trade" of New England agricultural products, West Indian rum, and African slaves.

Even after the colonies became independent, manufacturing developed slowly due to the difficulty of competing with British-made goods. Nonetheless, in the face of growing population and declining agriculture, some Naugatuck Valley households began turning out buttons, clocks, and other handicraft products on a small scale for local consumption. When the War of 1812 cut off British imports, valley craftsmen for the first time could sell such manufactured goods in a wider domestic market,[3] but many failed in the face of "foreign competition" when international trade was restored.

The expansion of American settlement southward and westward and the improvement of roads and canals gradually expanded the "home market" for products made in the Naugatuck Valley and elsewhere in the Northeast. Waterbury merchants began investing in small manufacturing shops, each employing up to a dozen workers, and financing the famous "Yankee peddlers," who "set out with large wagons, loaded with dry-goods, hats and shoes, together with tinware," heading for the southern and western states.[4] This expanding market meant fortunes could be made from expanded production. The result was an American version of the Industrial Revolution.[5] In Waterbury, that revolution started with buttons.

In 1802, Abel and Levi Porter started producing metal buttons by hand. They formed a partnership that employed nine people; it eventually became Waterbury's largest employer, the Scovill Manufacturing Company. As the company grew, it subdivided the steps of button making into separate tasks, then replaced tools held and used by workers with machines that held and guided the tools and drove them by mechanical force—a force initially provided by the waterfall on a tributary of the Naugatuck River. By 1864, one machine could produce 216,000 buttons per day. Mass production by machine increased productivity and reduced the cost of products enormously, allowing a further expansion of the market.

In the late 1820s, Naugatuck Valley button manufacturers imported from the English midlands, home of the Industrial Revolution, the skilled workers and machinery needed to produce the brass (a multiuse alloy of copper and zinc) they used for buttons and hardware. As Pittsburgh became a city of steel and Troy, New York, the nation's preeminent producer of stoves, the Naugatuck Valley became an industrial complex specializing in brass and brass-related products and known as the "Brass Valley." By 1880, three-quarters of all rolling and manufacturing of brass and copper in the United States was done in Connecticut, mostly in the Naugatuck Valley. Brass products accounted for three-fourths of Waterbury's industrial production. The *Boston Commercial Bulletin* proclaimed in 1869, "Brass is the life of Waterbury; but for it the city would be no city. . . . You hear it, smell it, see it, feel it everywhere; in the button on your military cap, in the burner of your lamp, in the pin which you stick in your collar; the stairs of your hotel and public buildings are plated with it, your chair is mended with it, Bridget in the kitchen pushes her clumsy needle with it: it is the Brazen Age in Waterbury."

Thousands of new products and innovative ways to make them were invented in the Brass Valley. The Scovill Company claimed to have created an average of one hundred new products every year for sixty years. The brass masters helped finance the mass production of brass clocks. When Naugatuck's Charles Goodyear patented the process of vulcanizing rubber in 1843, Naugatuck became the center of the American rubber industry, producing millions of rubber boots and shoes that in turn used millions of clasps turned out by the brass industry. As lighting technology shifted from whale oil to kerosene to electricity, Naugatuck Valley producers pioneered first new types of lamps, then gas piping, and finally wire and electrical products. The valley's products changed the way people lived all over the world.

The rise of brass, clock, rubber, and related industries reshaped the Naugatuck Valley towns. Backyard workshops became block-long brick factories. Farm villages became mill villages and eventually industrial towns and cities. Waterbury's population grew from fewer than three thousand in 1800 to five thousand in 1850, ten thousand in 1860, forty-five thousand in 1900, and one hundred thousand in 1930.

The making and selling of clocks, buttons, rubber products, and brass made families like the Gosses, Sperrys, Chases, and Eltons wealthy dynasties. They formed a tight-knit entrepreneurial elite who socialized, intermarried, shared civic leadership, and dominated the boards of directors of the region's major corporations, banks, and civic institutions.

The early companies started as individual proprietorships or partnerships. After an 1837 law allowed the incorporation of joint stock companies as legal entities distinct from their owners, most companies took the form of limited liability corporations. The same families owned or controlled many of the valley's brass companies, and from 1851 on they divided their markets through trade agreements. As part of the national "merger movement" at the turn of the century, most of the valley's brass producers came together to form the American Brass Company, which produced two-thirds of all brass in the United States. It and two fast-growing rivals formed the "Big Three," which, a Waterbury labor leader would later recall, "ran this town lock, stock and barrel."[6]

When large western copper deposits were discovered in the 1890s, it was widely expected that the brass industry would abandon the Naugatuck Valley,[7] but economic forces and entrepreneurial decisions led it to remain. The valley's complex of skilled workers, suppliers, and manufacturers proved difficult to replicate elsewhere. Further, the brass masters had interests not only in local industry but in local real estate and banking; such interests encouraged them not to abandon the valley but instead to reinvest in local factories and railroads and in western copper supplies, helping ensure that the valley would remain the center of the brass industry for another half century.

Brass Valley industries had their greatest expansion during World War I, when plants ran day and night turning out cartridge cases, fuses, and other war matériel; the production and workforce of some companies doubled or tripled. In 1920, an estimated two-thirds of U.S. brass ingots, bars, plates, sheets, rods, and wire were made in Connecticut, mostly in the Naugatuck Valley.

During the 1920s, American Brass and Chase Brass were bought out by Anaconda and Kennecott, giant national copper corporations; other valley industries, such as the Seth Thomas Clock Company, also became subsidiaries of large national corporations. This did not lead to major changes in the valley, however. Only gradually were local magnates superseded by a professionalized and bureaucratized management cadre directed from national corporate headquarters. In effect, the Naugatuck Valley industrial complex was incorporated as a unit within a nationally integrated industrial system. Anaconda's slogan, "From the Mine to the Consumer," caught the spirit of this integration. While the complex was oriented toward the huge U.S. market, it also reached far beyond U.S. borders, using copper from Chile and selling watches in Bombay.

World War II placed this U.S. industrial system, and with it the Naugatuck Valley industrial complex, in a uniquely dominant global position. In 1950, the United States produced 40 percent of all the world's goods and services. In the aftermath of the war, an international system of finance and trade was established, based on the U.S. dollar and the United States' economic, military, political, and cultural dominance, which provided a growing global market for the Brass Valley industrial complex and its counterparts throughout the country. Brass Valley communities experienced relatively full employment and rising wages, due in part to the "Keynesian" fiscal and monetary stimulation provided by the federal government. *Time*'s Henry Luce proclaimed the era the "American Century," and the Naugatuck Valleys of America were its productive base.

Working People in the Brass Industrial Complex

From their founding by colonial settlers well into the nineteenth century, Naugatuck Valley towns had a highly homogeneous population, culture, and leadership. Nearly a century after Waterbury's first settlement, one-half of the town's eighty-two offices were held by lineal descendants of its original proprietors.[8] A few Native Americans and African Americans, often enslaved, lived in the area, but they were excluded from participation in nearly all public institutions. Like the rest of New England, valley settlements gradually evolved from Puritan communal villages devoted to a religious mission into Yankee towns where property was privately owned and individual and worldly pursuits were increasingly dominant.[9]

The rise of manufacturing transformed a community of largely self-sufficient households into one composed primarily of employees and their families.[10] Unlike the self-employed farmers and craftsmen of earlier eras, most factory workers did not own their own tools and materials. They faced unemployment during recessions and depressions; they could be fired by their employers; they had no way to make a living if jobs were not available. The growing class division was symbolized in the 1880s when a committee of prominent men decided to place Waterbury's Civil War memorial in the fashionable neighborhood at one end of the town green, notwithstanding a local newspaper's report that nine out of ten people it had polled preferred that the monument be placed in a working-class district.[11]

The burgeoning factories attracted thousands of immigrants, first from Ireland and northern Europe, then from southern and eastern Europe and French Canada. Immigrant settlements typically began with single individuals or families who made their way to valley towns, found work, built shantytowns, and sent for family members and acquaintances from home to join them. Ethnic colonies continued to grow around these nodes. Local or provincial associations proliferated. Households, neighborhoods, clubs, job opportunities, unions, and politics were all organized along ethnic lines. Churches, temples, and mosques generally formed the first and most important colony-wide institutions. From the late nineteenth century to the present, the great majority of Waterbury's people, like the lands from which they came, have been Roman Catholic.

Interethnic tensions were present from the first. In 1839, a plan by Waterbury nativists to drive the Irish from town was thwarted only when the Irish, supplied with weapons by other local Yankees, offered to resist. An uneasy coexistence of peoples was established, marked by ghettoized ethnic neighborhoods, separation of social life, and partial or complete exclusion of immigrant peoples from Yankee social institutions. Formal institutions associated with the government, on the other hand, were at least in principle based on "equality before the law"—immigrants generally could become citizens, vote, and send their children to the public schools.

During and after World War I, most immigration to the United States was cut off, and what had been immigrant colonies increasingly became American ethnic communities. Nonetheless, despite increasing intermarriage among white ethnic groups, ethnic identity remained strong in the Naugatuck Valley: even in 1990, the most common bumper stickers proclaimed, "It's Exciting to Be Polish," "Forever French," and other ethnic mottoes.

The Naugatuck Valley had African Americans from its founding, but in 1920 they represented barely 1 percent of the population of Waterbury. Prior to World War I, most black workers were excluded from the brass plants. When foreign immigration was cut off, Naugatuck Valley employers changed their policy and began hiring black men; factories excluded all black women until World War II. A 1923 study found that in Waterbury, "There are sections in close proximity in which over 90 per cent of the Negro population live. . . . The antagonistic sentiment of whites prevents them from moving outside of the narrow limits of a recognized 'Negro area.'"[12]

Despite discrimination, African Americans migrated to the Naugatuck Valley during and after World Wars I and II and formed settlements with institutions paralleling those of immigrants. The mass migration resulting from the destruction of the southern black peasantry reached the valley in the 1950s and led to the expansion of Waterbury's African American community to approximately 10 percent of the city's population. The 1960s saw the rise of a civil rights movement, ghetto riots, and an end to legalized segregation in valley towns.[13]

From the beginning of industrialization, a large proportion of the valley's factory workers were women—thirty-three of the fifty-two workers employed at the Scovill button shop in 1831, for example. In addition to their role in maintaining the household, many immigrant women worked in the factories. Many also helped support families by taking in boarders and performing industrial homework.

With the rise of industry, workers organized to gain greater control over their working and living conditions. The valley's first major union, the Knights of Labor, conducted the brass industry's first recorded strikes; it published a labor newspaper and elected a labor government in Naugatuck in the 1880s.[14] At the turn of the century, women brass workers had their own "Lady Brass Workers of Waterbury" local alongside a variety of male locals. By 1903, Waterbury had forty-five unions; a 210-day strike by trolley workers won wide support even from the business community until a violent incident led to the suppression of the strike by the state militia and election as mayor of an industrialist pledged to oppose unions. For the next thirty years, unions were not accepted by Naugatuck Valley factory owners. They hired labor spies and kept extensive files on labor activists. Labor meetings were suppressed, and organizers were periodically thrown out of town by local police.

In 1919 and 1920, more than fifteen thousand workers, mostly unskilled immigrants, conducted two general strikes that closed factories throughout the Naugatuck Valley. Workers organized by ethnic group, with sections for Italians, Poles, Russians, Portuguese, French, and other groups. Their goals included seventy-five cents per hour minimum pay, equal pay for women doing the same work as men, an eight-hour day, and recognition of workers' shop committees. Hundreds of strikers were arrested, one was shot dead by a policeman, meetings were forbidden, and the governor twice sent in machine gun battalions from the Connecticut State Guard. The 1919 strike ended when Naugatuck Valley employers granted a 10 percent wage increase. The 1920 strike ended in debacle for the workers, and the valley remained "open shop."

The burgeoning labor movement of the 1930s reached Waterbury by means of what might be termed "industrial unionism from below." Western miners who worked for large national corporations like Anaconda and Kennecott discovered that when they struck, the companies simply continued to produce, using stockpiles in their eastern brass mills. Western miners in the International Union of Mine, Mill, and Smelter Workers, one of the first affiliates of the Congress of Industrial Organizations (CIO), took up a collection and sent organizers east to the Naugatuck Valley to try to organize the brass workers. Former Mine, Mill organizers quipped to me, "It takes brass balls to organize in the Brass Valley." But by the early 1940s, most companies were forced by a series of strikes and representation elections to bargain collectively with their workers. Unions became an established part of life in the valley.

Within the expanding economy of the "American Century," unionized workers won job security, rising wages, pensions, health insurance, and other elements of a higher standard of living and far greater control over their conditions of life. Although few who examined the Naugatuck Valley would have accepted the common claim that the American working class had disappeared or become "middle class," there was a genuine economic enfranchisement based on the "good jobs" made possible by the combination of economic prosperity and working-class organization.

Yet there was a carefully drawn limit to workers' power. It was clearly articulated in federal labor law, which required employers to bargain with their employees over wages, hours, and working conditions but not over investment and other decisions that "lie at the core of entrepreneurial control."[15] Although workers in the shops sometimes informally challenged "management's right to manage," both unions and employers in the valley generally accepted the broad class compromise that allowed workers to demand a share of an expanding pie but left corporations free to make the basic managerial decisions.

The Era of Deindustrialization

Starting in the 1950s, a series of forces began to erode first the Naugatuck Valley industrial complex, then the U.S. dominance of world manufacturing, and ultimately the entire system of nationally based economies. The causes included a cascade of deliberate choices by economic and political decision makers and interactions and unintended consequences of those decisions that led to results that nobody planned or anticipated.[16]

In the mid-1950s, the valley's brass industry began to decline. Competing materials like plastics and aluminum cut into the market for brass. The development of highways and truck transportation made specialized industrial complexes less advantageous and a greater decentralization of industry possible. The continuing movement of markets westward and employers' desire to escape the strong working-class organization of northeastern cities led them to shift investment out of concentrated industrial regions like the Naugatuck Valley to nonurban areas in the South and West.

Meanwhile, reviving industries in Europe and Japan began competing with producers in the valley and the rest of the United States. These companies had cheaper labor, accepted lower profits, and reinvested in more advanced equipment. U.S. industrial dominance began an accelerating decline. In 1985, the vice president of a Waterbury brass company told a newspaper, "The brass industry is almost completely disintegrated to foreign imports. Nine years ago, 6 percent of the brass in this country was imported; today, it's 42 percent."[17]

U.S. companies generally responded not by attempting to make their production more competitive but rather by various forms of financial restructuring. Large corporations became conglomerates and engaged in speculative buying and selling of companies: in the Naugatuck Valley, Anaconda was bought by Arco, Kennecott by Sohio, and General Time by Talley Industries. In many cases, such corporations treated their older plants in the valley as "cash cows" whose cash flow they milked rather than reinvested. As the plants ran down, many were sold off or shut down.

In the case of the Seth Thomas Clock Company, for example, ownership passed out of local hands early in the Great Depression; the company became a division of the General Time Corporation, based in Connecticut; by 1970, General Time in turn was acquired by Talley Industries. James Wilson, a lifelong Thomaston resident, observed the effect of Talley's acquisition of Seth Thomas from the vantage point of his job at the Talley Industries Computer Center, which was housed in the Seth Thomas plant:

> All Talley did was buy the company out. I didn't see them putting a dime into this building. They took the money and gave it to the stockholders but they didn't put any money back in here. They just let it deteriorate. I think they bled it. You ask anybody that worked in production. They didn't give them new tools. They didn't throw any money back in to keep this alive.
>
> You wouldn't believe what we had on our computers. They owned oil wells; they owned property. Real estate businesses. A big clothing business in New York. Big plumbing supply businesses. All Talley is—I was out there once—is an office. They buy and sell corporations. I could see them on the computer: if one wasn't making a profit, you'd lose it. They didn't even know what Seth Thomas was or even where it was. All they looked at was dollars and cents.[18]

Much of the profit made by these corporations was reinvested not in the United States but abroad. What were once American corporations became transnational corporations with decreasing identification with or commitment to any one country, let alone any community or region. As trade restrictions were lowered and new communication, transportation, and computer systems developed, markets, corporations, and economic institutions increasingly decoupled from the nation and became part of the global economy.

These processes devastated the Naugatuck Valley industrial complex. From a peak of more than fifty thousand during World Wars I and II, the number of brass workers in the Naugatuck Valley fell to fewer than five thousand by 1980. Waterbury's official unemployment in the mid-1970s at times exceeded 15 percent, and *Connecticut Magazine* described Waterbury as "a dying city." In 1992, *Money Magazine* rated the quality of life in three hundred U.S. metropolitan areas and declared Waterbury number three hundred—the worst. According to Waterbury city planner Howard Ploman, "Waterbury is a classic example of what an economic collapse will do to you. This town went through some tough times. No question about it. From the early seventies into the early eighties, a good ten-year period, unemployment was very high, people were moving out of town—they just gave up, packed their bags, and went someplace else. Investor confidence was very low. The city was—albeit prematurely—labeled as a dying city, the classic victim of the Rust Belt."[19]

Sociologist Fred Perella saw the social impacts of deindustrialization from his vantage point as codirector of the Office of Urban Affairs of the Catholic Archdiocese of Hartford, whose responsibilities included the Naugatuck Valley: "There was a growing population of new poor. There was desperation among folks that maybe were middle aged about the future of their jobs. And it was affecting the whole climate of possibility in the cities, because those are the people who normally are the backbone of your economic base for a city—your taxpayers, your property owners."[20]

Good jobs were replaced, first by no jobs, then by not-so-good jobs. Brass workers became gas pumpers and hamburger flippers. Many of the valley's large plants, after standing vacant, were turned into "industrial commons" shared by many small companies, most low wage and nonunion. The City of Waterbury and the Waterbury Hospital became larger employers than any local factory.

Deindustrialization also had a devastating effect on Waterbury's working-class institutions. Unemployed parishioners meant impoverished parishes. Young people, finding no opportunity locally, abandoned the area, leaving the valley's ethnic neighborhoods, churches, and extended family networks an aging remnant. The newest in-migrants, primarily Puerto Ricans and groups admitted as a result of legislation that reopened immigration after 1965, found few of the industrial jobs that had greeted previous waves of immigrants in abundance.

Perhaps hardest hit was the labor movement. Large, powerful locals with thousands or even tens of thousands of members shrank to organizations representing a few hundred. This was part of a national decline that saw the proportion of the workforce in unions decrease gradually from 34 percent in 1956 to 24 percent in 1980; during the 1980s, it would plummet to less than 17 percent. Union power was decimated by declining memberships, plant shutdowns, and the credible threat that if employers didn't get their way, they would simply move away.

Workers and unions were often blamed for the region's industrial decline. Many companies maintained prior to closing that excessive wages and expensive work rules made local operations unprofitable; they offered to stay open if only workers would make sufficient concessions. Many concessions were in fact made, but when workers refused to go beyond a certain point, companies closed their plants and placed the blame on workers' greed. That explanation was widely accepted, even among unionized workers themselves.

Deindustrialization liquidated not only factories and jobs; it liquidated a legacy of community building in the Naugatuck Valley and in working-class America. While family networks, unions, churches, ethnic associations, and other working-class institutions had been able to establish considerable control over daily life, they had hardly even attempted to influence the basic decisions of capital. Those decisions, it turned out, could lay waste to everything they had gained.

Stirrings of Response

Through the later 1970s, plant closings, especially in the Midwest industrial heartland, made "deindustrialization" a national issue. Coalitions developed all over the country to pass national or state legislation or both that would require prior notification of plant closings and establish some minimal requirements for corporate responsibility in the event of shutdowns.

Local coalitions developed to fight against particular plant closings in communities from New Bedford, Massachusetts, to Ontario, California. There were occasional instances of workers purchasing companies that were threatened with closing. In the Youngstown, Ohio, area, religious leaders and steelworker union locals conducted a massive and widely publicized campaign to reopen a closed steel mill under worker-community ownership. (The effort died when the Carter administration decided not to make the necessary federal financial commitment.)[21]

In Connecticut, a statewide Plant Closing Coalition of labor and community groups formed to press for a law requiring advance notice of plant closings, benefits for laid-off workers, financial aid to impacted communities, and technical assistance to save threatened companies. The Connecticut Business and Industry Association attacked the proposed legislation as the "industrial hostage act" and a "foot in the door" for socialism. Nonetheless, the bill came close to passage.[22]

In the Naugatuck Valley, there were flutters of response to the industrial crisis. A state Plant Closing Coalition was strongly supported by valley unions and by a rapidly expanding community organization called the Connecticut Citizen Action Group (CCAG). Videotapes documenting the impact of plant closings on the valley were shown in a series of public forums.[23]

In the face of shutdown threats, the labor movement also began turning to new tactics. When the Waterbury Rolling Mills brass company threatened to close unless workers granted deep concessions, the Community/Labor Support Committee of unions, the CCAG, and other community groups was formed, providing what one local labor veteran called the first major community support for a brass workers strike since the 1950s. As the conflict deepened, workers seriously considered, though ultimately rejected, the idea of occupying the factory in a sit-down strike. Instead, they accepted concessions in exchange for a profit-sharing plan and the placement of a former United Automobile Workers (UAW) international vice president on the board of directors—indicating an awareness that economic crisis required some kind of change in the relation of workers and business. The Community/Labor Support Committee continued after the strike as a vehicle to pull together a community-labor coalition around a wide variety of issues.

The state government was also drawn into efforts to keep local plants alive. In 1975, the Scovill Manufacturing Company, which had changed from a brass products company to a miniconglomerate via multiple acquisitions, decided to sell its aging brass mills to one of its suppliers. The Connecticut Development Authority, under tremendous local and state pressure to keep the plant running, agreed to guarantee a ten million–dollar loan to help finance the sale and pressured workers into accepting major concessions.

Perhaps more typical of local response, however, was the UAW's decision to open Unemployment Information Centers in Waterbury, Torrington, and other high-unemployment locations. The centers ran food banks and helped laid-off workers get government services. They were staffed by volunteers and paid for by voluntary contributions from working union members, who were asked to donate an hour's pay. By March 1983, UAW Region 9A, which covered Connecticut and adjoining industrial areas, estimated the unemployment rate among its members at more than 33 percent.[24]

Another response in the valley was a broad loss of confidence in Keynesian economic policies identified with liberals and the Democratic Party. In the pit of the recession, a once popular liberal Democratic congressman was defeated in Waterbury by a young conservative Republican, one of the biggest crowds in the city's history turned out for a Ronald Reagan rally, and Reagan's managers proclaimed their support in Waterbury as a model of the new conservative trend among formerly Democratic blue-collar workers— the so-called Reagan Democrats.

The colossal economic forces that had lifted the Naugatuck Valley from a rural backwater to a center of global industry had, with seeming indifference, thrown it on the economic scrap heap. Grass literally grew in the yards of the valley's factories. The promise that Naugatuck Valley workers felt they had been made—the "promise of American life"—seemed to have been broken. The system that once seemed to provide secure employment and a rising standard of living now appeared to provide the opposite. Many were angry at what they experienced as a betrayal of their hopes and expectations. Yet the scale of the forces that were dictating the valley's decline seemed entirely out of proportion to what the valley's people could do to affect them.

The Sources of Powerlessness

In 1955, back-to-back hurricanes struck western Connecticut. The resulting floods broke dams, washed away downtowns, and devastated the massive brass mills that dotted the banks of the Naugatuck River. Many predicted that the thriving but aging industry would be decimated. But before the waters had even receded, workers struggled back into the factories and pitched in to restore them to working order. Within a few weeks, the plants were back in production.

When the economic floods began destroying the region's industry in the 1960s and 1970s, there was no similar response. As we concluded work on *Brass Valley*, we looked for, but failed to find, a single person with a positive vision of the region's future. A common prescription was that workers should accept lower wages and worse working conditions in order to make the region "more competitive."

Why was there so little attempt to resuscitate the valley's economic life? Part of the answer lies with the political culture of the region. The valley nurtured a pervasive political and social conservatism that looked askance at anything that might reveal a hint of radicalism or socialism. The local newspaper maintained a drumbeat of hostility against anything it found too pink—from a college professor on the board of alderman to the nuclear freeze campaign to an activist Catholic bishop assigned to the city. Many valley residents mobilized to protest the visit of Jane Fonda to Waterbury.

Few in the valley argued that those affected by corporate decisions had a right to control them—or that companies should have ethical or legal responsibilities that took precedence over their obligation to maximize profits for their stockholders. The problem of plant closings was most often seen as narrowly economic—costs, especially labor costs, were too high, so businesses were going elsewhere. A claim like "Seth Thomas belongs to Thomaston" would undoubtedly risk being denounced as creeping communism.

Such attitudes were part of a more general insularity often noted in the valley. As an industrial manager who did a stint in the Naugatuck Valley town of Seymour put it, "There's a lot of valleys all over the U.S., and I've visited a few. Every what you call the Rust Belt industries, there's a lot of commonality. First of all, there's always a river; number two, there's always a railroad track on the other side of the plant. One of the problems in these valley settings is that they're somewhat—it's a little bit like Brigadoon. They're somewhat removed from what's going on in the rest of the world."[25]

But less conservative and insular regions also had great difficulty in developing an adequate response to plant closings. There are more structural patterns in the valley, and in much of American society, that pose impediments to those trying to address deindustrialization.[26]

Accountability

From the mid–nineteenth to the mid–twentieth centuries, Waterbury and the other valley towns were marked by what historian John Cumbler has called "civic capitalism," in which an elite of local industrialists not only ran the major local companies but also held major leadership on community issues.[27] In the late nineteenth century, the local elite had saved the valley from deindustrialization by investing heavily in local railroads and western copper mines. But by the 1970s, the remnant of that elite lacked the power, the resources, and the vision to play such a role.

Although issues of job loss affected almost everyone in the valley in some way, those affected were fragmented. Each particular closing directly threatened only a particular group of workers and those who depended on them. Nor were plant closings the clear responsibility of any one institution: churches, unions, community groups, and government were all affected, but none of them traditionally regarded business location decisions as any of their business.

Under federal labor law, workers had the right to bargain collectively over wages, hours, and working conditions, and corporations had a legal obligation to bargain collectively with their employees. However, the subjects on which employers had to bargain were carefully delimited. These limits were sketched in a concurring Supreme Court opinion that stated that the duty to bargain does not extend to management decisions that "lie at the core of entrepreneurial control," including decisions "concerning the commitment of investment capital and the basic scope of the enterprise."[28] The Supreme Court applied this logic specifically to plant closings when it held that a decision to close a business was among the types of employer decisions that are "peculiarly matters of management prerogative."[29]

The legal definitions of ownership meant that corporations had virtually no accountability to local communities; indeed, it was their "fiduciary responsibility" to eschew anything that would interfere with maximizing profits for their stockholders.[30] Until the Worker Adjustment and Retraining Notification—WARN—Act went into effect in 1989, employers did not even have to notify workers or local officials of a decision to close or move a workplace. As a smaller and smaller proportion of the workforce was covered by collective bargaining agreements, and as the labor movement grew weaker, even the modest accountability unions provided diminished. There was no established channel for local community members and their organizations to challenge the corporate decisions that were affecting their lives.

Ownership

The factories and other economic resources of the valley and the capital it would have taken to renew or diversify them were not owned by the people who were suffering the effects of industrial decline. The plants threatened with closing were private property, whose owners had the legal right to close them if they chose.

Typically, the valley's factories had initially been owned by partnerships of local individuals. By the 1840s, limited liability laws had allowed them to become corporations. Over the first half of the twentieth century, many local companies had become part of national corporations, but a high proportion continued to be run by local managements and to retain a strong local identity.

In the 1970s, however, plants in the Naugatuck Valley had become targets of speculative buying and selling by conglomerate corporations. By the early 1980s, more than thirty conglomerates owned factories in the Naugatuck Valley. Since these were generally viewed as short-term speculative investments, the plants were often milked and then closed or resold. The owners not only had no long-term interest in the valley but did not even have a long-term interest in their own factories. With the economic globalization of the 1980s, ownership became even more remote as conglomerates grew increasingly transnational.

Workplace

Following the lead of Frederick Winslow Taylor's "scientific management," twentieth-century corporations divided the workforce into a cadre of managers and professionals and a mass of workers. They concentrated knowledge and responsibility in the management hierarchy and subdivided the tasks of the mass of workers to make them as unskilled and repetitive as possible. The result was not only an adversarial culture in the workplace but also a general acceptance by workers of the management maxim that "we're not paying you to think." Everything in this structure discouraged collective responsibility for the fate of the enterprise.

This structure had impacts far beyond the realm of production. It shaped motivations, expectations, time horizons, personal "investment" decisions, and ways of life. For many workers in the valley, economic security based on stable employment in a major factory became a central life strategy. Responsibility beyond the family level—whether at work or in the community—was neither encouraged nor regarded as necessary. For many, this pattern generated ingrained motivations and habits that militated against responding proactively to the valley's economic decline.

Resources

Resources to support economic alternatives were limited in the valley. Most residents owned nothing except perhaps a bit of equity in a house and a car. They were among the 90 percent of Americans whose net worth at that time barely equaled that of the top one-half of 1 percent.[31] They had few resources beyond their ability to work.

The remnant of the local elite retained some personal wealth but not the kind of control of economic resources that would have allowed major investment in the local economy. The valley had few charitable foundations; it was almost devoid of a liberal middle class who might contribute funds to a social effort. Its churches were struggling financially with declining memberships. Local governments faced a declining tax base, shrinking revenues, soaring welfare costs, and a dominant laissez-faire ideology.

Markets

Corporate officials regularly explained that their decisions to close and sell Brass Valley factories were dictated by "market forces" and that any reasonable person in their position would have had to do the same. And indeed, nobody deliberately willed the destruction of the valley's economy. It appeared to result from forces beyond anyone's control.

In Adam Smith's hoary theory, markets bring together a multitude of competing buyers and sellers. Prices rise and fall with supply and demand. Individuals and firms try to maximize their wealth. Investments flow to uses that maximize profit. The "hidden hand" of the market thus coordinates production with need. Prices serve as "market signals" that guide market participants to produce the products that society needs. According to Adam Smith—not to mention contemporary advocates of "free markets"—unrestricted markets will lead to the benefit of all.

The beneficial side of this process could be seen in the rise of Naugatuck Valley industry. Local craftspeople made buttons and sold them to their neighbors. This allowed them to hire workers and make more buttons that they then sold first in the larger market of the surrounding towns, then throughout the country via "Yankee peddlers." This provided the money to invest in new machinery for making buttons more cheaply and in far greater numbers. It also gave them money to import brass technology and skilled workers from England, allowing them to produce brass for their buttons and for sale in the market. A huge expansion in employment, production, and wealth was the result.

But people in the Naugatuck Valley have frequently experienced—and fought—the less favorable effects of free markets. Naugatuck Valley button and brass manufacturers, along with other American manufacturers, supported high tariffs as a way to block competition from destroying America's "infant industries." And when the American brass industry was threatened with destruction by foreign competition in the 1880s, brass companies successfully lobbied for a 45 percent tariff on foreign imports. According to the leading historian of the brass industry, "The tariff acted at this time more effectively than at any other in the history of the industry in discouraging foreign competition."[32]

Adam Smith notwithstanding, unregulated markets permit resources to lie idle even while needs are unmet. "Market signals" have repeatedly produced periods of overproduction, glut, and deflation. In response, the brass companies, like those in other industries, formed trade agreements, fixing prices as a way to block "ruinous competition." At the turn of the twentieth century, most of them merged to form the American Brass Company, which monopolized two-thirds of all brass production. Despite antitrust laws, price-fixing remained common in the industry, leading to significant prosecutions into the 1950s.

Workers as well have found it necessary to try to limit the effects of free markets. They discovered early on that when employers faced competition, they would try to cut their labor costs in order to sell their goods more cheaply. The result could be a "race to the bottom," as each company slashed wages to survive. To block the race to the bottom, workers organized themselves into labor unions that tried to establish uniform labor conditions throughout a trade or industry, thereby eliminating labor costs as a factor in competition. They fought for legislation that would restrict competition by establishing minimum wages, standard working hours, and support for unemployed workers so that they would not be forced to work for starvation wages. Workers and their organizations often supported "countercyclical" or "Keynesian" economic policies that used interest rates and government budgets to counter recessions and depressions and stabilize economic growth.

The destructive effects of competition, races to the bottom, and depressions and recessions all illustrate how markets can produce unintended effects. These may be side effects, like the destruction of New England industry by the end of the War of 1812. Or they may be complex interaction effects, like the impact of investment decisions on economic cycles.

The destruction of the Naugatuck Valley brass industry was the unintended side effect of many decisions made around the world. For example, the development of highways and truck transportation made it feasible for brass companies to relocate away from the specialized Brass Valley industrial complex on which they had depended for skills, technology, and markets. The destruction of industry in Europe and Asia during World War II gave American manufacturers a temporary advantage, but it also meant that European and Asian producers rebuilt their factories with far more advanced technology when they revived, making them more competitive in U.S. and world markets. The willingness of workers in those countries to accept lower wages was largely the result of social policies that guaranteed them a share of the benefits as production rebounded. The rise in the price of electricity on the East Coast in response to the energy crisis of the 1970s gave some important Brass Valley mills the coup de grâce.

In addition to such side effects of particular decisions, "market forces" also included the effects of unintended interactions among the consequences of myriad decisions. For example, uncounted particular decisions resulted in the severe global economic downturn that reached its nadir in 1973. The resulting decline in profits led to a failure to reinvest in companies like those in the Naugatuck Valley. It also led corporations to seek new investment opportunities worldwide, leading to disinvestment in American industry. To pursue diversified investments, many companies restructured themselves as global conglomerates, often oriented to buying and milking companies rather than building them up for long-term profitability. These trends were part of the early stage of what we now call "globalization," but they were little recognized and less understood by those making specific corporate and governmental decisions, let alone by those affected by the results.

The interaction of these and many other decisions unintentionally contributed to the destruction of the Naugatuck Valley brass industry. People in the valley experienced them as irresistible and incomprehensible "market forces."

Individuals and firms all over the world had pursued their self-interests, but the result was not the benefit of all. Some—like the communities of the Naugatuck Valley—discovered their livelihoods and ways of life destroyed by these anonymous uncontrolled forces.

Government

The U.S. and Connecticut constitutions locate ultimate authority in the people and provide popular elections and other mechanisms to make governments accountable to them. Several factors tended to immobilize government response to deindustrialization, however.

Whereas the early Puritans who settled the Naugatuck Valley established a semicommunal form of property ownership, over the next century and a half common rights were eroded and the protection of individual property ownership became an overriding responsibility of government.[33] Nineteenth-century federal interpretations of "due process of law" extended to "corporate persons" the rights constitutionally protected for natural persons. These definitions of property rights forbade government action that might have challenged the decisions being made by the owners of the valley's factories.[34]

The day-to-day functioning of government is also strongly influenced by property interests. Campaign contributions from corporations and wealthy individuals associated with them pay for most politicians' electoral expenses. Political-party personnel are largely drawn from business. Direct corruption—often pervasive to the point of being systemic—also plays a significant role: a criminal conspiracy among Waterbury's mayor, several city council members, and a local banker blocked important NVP initiatives during the 1980s, for example.

In a larger sense, too, governments are dependent on property interests. Town, state, and even federal incomes ultimately depend on each jurisdiction's tax base. To the extent that businesses are mobile (and that extent has been rapidly growing), public officials—whatever their own views and wishes—must please business interests or face "capital flight" and loss of their tax base. Geographically mobile businesses are in effect able to make governments compete to do their bidding.

The non-property-owning population of the valley, and of the United States as a whole, is diverse. For their interests to be expressed in the political process, they need unifying political vehicles. In the past, this role had been played to a greater or lesser extent by the Democratic Party, by labor movement political action organizations, and by various coalitions. A number of factors increased the fragmentation of these groups during the 1960s, '70s, and '80s.

Evolving mechanisms of fund-raising, professional lobbying, and targeted mobilization led to a proliferation of and a growing political role for institutionalized specialized interest groups. Organizations that at one time claimed to represent broader class interests, such as the labor movement, also evolved in this direction. Such interest groups became adept at winning specific narrow objectives, but this very success entrenched a pattern of "silos" that made the formulation of broader objectives more difficult. Deindustrialization was hard to challenge in the political arena in part because there was no vehicle for addressing it as a broad community or social concern, rather than as solely the concern of the particular unions whose members were being affected.

In the same years, political parties moved from a central role in the political process to a more peripheral one. Politicians became to a considerable extent individual political entrepreneurs, dependent for support less on their parties than on a personal coterie of supporters. The accountability provided in democratic theory by the party system became an increasingly weak reed.

In this context, the government itself was able to become an increasingly self-maintaining institution. Government agencies became able to protect their own interests and budgets largely by means of "iron triangles" in which external beneficiaries, friendly legislators concentrated in oversight committees, and entrenched bureaucracies were able to establish virtually unassailable positions.[35] The consequence was not only a lack of responsiveness to public concerns but also a deep public disillusion with government, providing grist for the attack of political conservatives on the value of using government to solve social problems. Few in the valley had faith that appeals to the government would lead to constructive action to save their economy.

To effectively challenge plant closings and deindustrialization, people in the valley would have to address all these sources of powerlessness. They would have to establish some means to hold somebody accountable for what was generally regarded as just the way blind economic forces were supposed to work. They would have to reckon with the control of the valley's main enterprises by transnational conglomerate corporations that found it profitable to milk and abandon them. They would have to share responsibility for enterprises that had always excluded them from voice and control. They would have to find resources to support their efforts when most of them owned little but their ability to labor. They would have to tame the "market forces" that had led to the colossal "market failures" that had devastated their valley. They would have to wrest control of the government from dominant economic actors and self-serving and at times corrupt public officials.

It seemed a tall order. It's little wonder that people in the valley felt even more powerless than they actually were.

2. Banding Together

Hank Murray remembers feeling angry as he watched a symbolic funeral procession carry a clock across the Thomaston town green to commemorate the closing of the Seth Thomas Clock Company. Murray was one of a dozen UAW officials who had come to the funeral to urge support for a law requiring employers to give their workers advance notice of plant closings. He still felt angry as he drove home.

Murray was born and bred in the labor movement—his birth was announced on the front page of the newsletter of the CIO Political Action Committee, for which his father worked, with the headline "Labor World Heralds New Champion." He went to Yale, hired in at the Fafner Bearing Company in New Britain, then in 1977 joined the staff of UAW Region 9A, which covered Connecticut and adjoining areas, including most of the unionized plants in the Naugatuck Valley.

Murray saw the devastation that plant closings were causing and felt that something had to be done—not just legislation requiring notice of factory shutdowns, but some alternative strategy for economic development that would save the jobs. He talked it over with Miles Rapoport, head of the Connecticut Citizen Action Group, who, it turned out, was thinking along the same lines.

Fred Perella, codirector for policy and planning of the Office of Urban Affairs of the Catholic Archdiocese of Hartford, was also seeking a better way to respond to the plant closings in the valley. Trained as a sociologist, before coming to Connecticut he had published a controversial book called *Poverty in American Democracy: A Study of Social Power,* calling for a redistribution of wealth and power on the basis of Catholic social doctrine.[1] He saw the Naugatuck Valley as a place with many Catholics where the church

was currently just helping mop up the social problems created when people
lost their jobs.

Perella knew that more was needed, but he was not sure what that might
be: "I had been looking for a way to deal with this issue and didn't have any
ideas."[2] No doubt thousands of people in one way or another shared Murray,
Rapoport, and Perella's sense of the need to do something about the economic
devastation that was striking the Naugatuck Valley, but there was scant vision of what to do. There were few channels available to influence corporate
investment decisions—there was no reason to believe that companies would
even discuss plant closings with representatives of local communities. The
government accepted little responsibility for plant closings, and even advocates of a more active government role had few concrete ideas for what it
should do.[3]

The Organizer

In the summer of 1982, a few months before the closing of Seth Thomas, a
veteran community organizer and recent graduate of the Yale School of Organization and Management named Ken Galdston began contacting people
he thought might be concerned about plant closings in the Naugatuck Valley.
Fred Perella recalls:

> Ken Galdston had started doing some door knocking around, finding out which
> were likely institutions or groups to support an idea he had, which was using
> his organizing skills and business skills to create a coalition of institutions to
> stop plant closings. I guess he got my name from people who knew we were
> about funding organizing projects and economic development ventures that
> were community based.
>
> I had some money and had a kind of idealism about the issue based on the
> church's social teaching. But nobody had come in and said, "Let's look at the
> basic economic system that is causing these plants to close or to be disinvested,
> and look at the way in which we ourselves could get in control of these eco-
> nomic dynamics."
>
> And Ken walked in the door one day, introduced himself, and said, "I've got
> this idea." And I said to him that day, "You may be an angel—a Jewish angel."[4]

Ken Galdston was a college student at Brown University during the 1960s,
and like many of his generation he was filled with anger at what he saw going on in his country and the world. He helped develop a tutoring program
for university service employees and the Campus-Community Involvement
Project to bring university resources to bear on poverty issues in Providence,

Rhode Island. He wrote an honors thesis on Saul Alinsky, the godfather of modern community organizing in America, and decided he wanted to try out organizing for himself. He graduated in 1968 and immediately went to work as a VISTA volunteer in Clinton, North Carolina, organizing door-to-door in poor black neighborhoods around such issues as street paving, housing, day care, and urban renewal.

Galdston also had a strong interest in issues of worker and community control. In 1970, he took advantage of an Arnold Fellowship that provided him a year abroad to study worker-control movements in West Germany, England, and Yugoslavia and community-control efforts in Northern Ireland, England, and Sicily.

Then he came to Chicago, studied organizing at the training institute of Saul Alinsky's Industrial Areas Foundation, and went to work as staff director and lead organizer at the IAF-affiliated Midway Organization, organizing around such issues as sewers, pollution, medical care, taxes, and highway construction. He then spent two years each on similar IAF-affiliated efforts in the Twin Cities and Buffalo. Galdston's approach in the Naugatuck Valley developed out of—and in reaction against—his years with the IAF. A scrawled line on his notes for a presentation on what to do in the valley reads, "Better than IAF."

The Industrial Areas Foundation was a controversial center for community organizing founded by Saul Alinsky. Alinsky and his collaborators had started the Back of the Yards Neighborhood Council in a poor, immigrant neighborhood in Chicago in the 1930s and used it as a model for subsequent efforts around the country. Alinsky strongly criticized what he characterized as the "do-gooder" individual casework approach of social welfare agencies. He argued instead that poor communities needed to be organized to represent themselves and fight for their own interests. Self-interest, not idealism, would motivate their fight: "Political realists see the world as it is: an arena of power politics moved primarily by perceived immediate self-interests, where morality is rhetorical rationale for expedient action and self-interest." The poor, Alinsky maintained, could have their self-interests represented only by creating "stable, mass-based power organizations."[5] These organizations should be based on established community institutions that would provide legitimacy and funding. The original Back of the Yards Council was composed of unions, ethnic associations, and churches, but as time went on, the IAF organizations were increasingly parish based.

Alinsky emphasized the role of professional organizers who eschewed ideology and concentrated on building the organization and developing leaders drawn from the community. The IAF trained its organizers to interview community members, find out what the important local issues were, identify community leaders, and draw these leaders together to form "mass-based power organizations." These organizations would initiate campaigns around locally important issues, using whatever forms of pressure were available, including mass mobilizations and, if necessary, disruption. It was Alinsky doctrine to steer clear of electoral politics but to negotiate deals with political leaders once they had been sufficiently pressured.

While Alinsky characterized himself as a "radical," he somewhat paradoxically denounced efforts to articulate a vision of fundamental social change or to challenge basic social structures. His goal was to help people in poor neighborhoods to develop enough clout to win the benefits and services others took for granted. Although he sometimes criticized capitalism in his writing, he insisted that his organizations focus on neighborhood concerns and avoid linking them to wider issues.

In Buffalo, Ken Galdston worked on a typical IAF project, a church-based organization that eventually included forty-two Catholic and Protestant churches. His work stressed leadership training: he taught interviewing, researching, strategizing, and negotiating to teams of pastors and lay leaders and helped them organize around issues such as redlining, bad housing, and lack of police protection. Meanwhile, Galdston recalls, people in Buffalo were losing jobs by the thousands. "One afternoon, I literally had the experience of being in somebody's house and interviewing them about their role in the parish, and the effect on their family of some of these community issues, when the father of the family walked in to tell us he had lost his job at Bethlehem Steel. It struck me very hard that we were ignoring this central activity in people's lives."[6]

After seven years with the IAF, Galdston had developed differences with the Alinsky approach to organizing and felt that in any case it was time for him to move on. He wanted to shift his focus to plant closings and job loss and to work with unions. He took a job organizing for plant-closing legislation with the Coalition to Save Jobs in Massachusetts, an alliance of unions and the consumer organization Fair Share.

By then, Galdston had been an organizer for eleven years and felt "ready to go back to get a little bit of intellectual stimulation." Wanting a broader background in economics, he entered the masters program at the Yale School of Organization and Management, then a fledgling institution with a strong interest in worker management and nonprofit enterprise. As graduation approached, he began exploring the possibility of staying in Connecticut and trying to put together some kind of effort to address job loss and plant closings:

I began to talk with people from groups that I thought might have a similar point of view to mine, which was that people were just getting clobbered, especially in places like the Naugatuck Valley. It was the pit of the 1982 recession and unemployment in the Naugatuck Valley was skyrocketing. I didn't know much about the Valley, but I had driven through it a couple of times just out of curiosity. That led me to conversations with people like Hank Murray in the Auto Workers, Miles Rapoport in Connecticut Citizen Action Group and Fred Perella from the Office of Urban Affairs in the Catholic Archdiocese, just basically going around and saying: This is my background. This is the sort of thing I'd like to do. What does your institution see as its stake?[7]

Hank Murray told Galdston there had already been some discussions between the UAW and the CCAG; he asked if there was any strategy they could pursue to deal with the plant closings in the Naugatuck Valley and whether Galdston would be interested in it. Galdston said he would be interested in exploring it, but felt that they should also try to get the Catholic Church involved. Murray said fine.

Galdston went back to Perella, who asked him what he wanted to do. He recalls that Galdston replied, "First I need a sponsoring committee. And second some start-up funding to check the validity of this theory. I need to spend some time knocking on the doors of union presidents and civic leaders and citizen action group folk and pastors up and down the Valley to see what people's consciousness of the problem is, whether or not there are some things that are about ready to come up over the horizon, and whether or not we really have a base for making an organization."[8]

The Initiators

That October, Hank Murray from the UAW, Miles Rapoport from the CCAG, and Fred Perella from the Catholic Office of Urban Affairs met with Ken Galdston at the chancery of the Catholic Archdiocese in Hartford. Galdston presented a picture of what a Naugatuck Valley Project might look like. The purpose would be "to build an organization of church, civic, labor, ethnic, veterans, and social service organizations to deal with the transformation of the valley as a result of plant closings and new business openings." Strategies were sketchy: perhaps local legislation requiring notification of plant closings or payments to a community assistance fund; perhaps use of local financial assets to influence development policy; perhaps worker-owned firms or a fund for worker buyouts. Local leaders would be given training in the techniques of organizing and in "the economic and political realities of their situation."

Galdston would spend the first four months interviewing leaders of valley organizations, exploring possible funding sources, and researching who really owned the companies in the valley. The proposal included a budget of twelve thousand dollars and a research appendix listing churches, unions, community groups, and major employers in the valley.[9] Galdston says, "The fundamental idea was, if we could organize something with those sorts of players that was there in advance of the closing, we'd have a chance of winning *something*. I could promise that." He couldn't promise much more. "I didn't know just by looking at it whether it was going to last beyond, say, four months. It was not something that you knew for sure was going to work. That was actually part of the pleasure of doing it."[10]

The group decided to meet every three weeks and to bring in some other players. John Flynn, UAW Region 9A political director, had become convinced that the labor movement needed to focus its attention on developing a community of allies; he had recently helped launch another coalition effort, the Legislative Electoral Action Program (LEAP), to draw together unions and other "progressive organizations" in developing and supporting political candidates.[11] Perella suggested inviting a representative from the Episcopal Church as well as Catholic auxiliary bishop Peter Rosazza, who had recently moved to Waterbury. Ken Galdston recalls, "My reaction, of course, knowing nothing about him, was: Let's not get a bishop in here. He's going to screw everything up. He will have all the connections with all the big players and he will not want to see anything really develop. Having no real power, I said OK, sure."[12]

Rosazza was not the kind of bishop that Galdston expected. As a parish priest in Hartford, he had "marched before television cameras and reporters, earning an unmatched reputation as a social activist as he spoke out for the city's Hispanics and poor."[13] In Waterbury, he told high school students in a speech that young people were more interested in reading Mao Tse-tung and Che Guevara than Shakespeare and Dante because Mao and Guevara wrote about distributing the goods of the earth evenly. (When the *Waterbury American* wrote an editorial attacking Bishop Rosazza as naive and "out of touch," ten Waterbury priests replied, defending Rosazza as "a bishop who cares for all people, especially the poor and oppressed. . . . Out of touch—never.")

Rosazza had grown up in Torrington at the northern tip of the Naugatuck Valley and knew personally the impact of deindustrialization:

> I remember when I was a youngster during the Second World War, thousands of jobs, brass jobs. Then they closed the brass mill in Torrington, and people who had been there a long time had to move. My brother's father-in-law had to go to work in Waterbury. And then little by little the Torrington Company and Torin—jobs were lost there. It just bothered me tremendously to see that

happening, and especially when the retirees were threatened that they would lose their benefits. I find that unjust.

I think all of us understand how important jobs are to people, to their whole morale and their whole well-being, the whole question of self-esteem. John Paul II's encyclical on labor pointed out that it's through work that human beings become who we are. I knew the situation was bad. And this was like the answer to a prayer.[14]

Rosazza would emerge as a strong supporter and the first chairman of the NVP.

Meanwhile, Galdston began interviewing potential participants in the valley: priests, union officials, CCAG staffers. Reactions seemed positive, but Galdston was wary. "I would come out of meetings where people had been very, very positive about the idea and I'd say, 'These guys are bullshitting me. They're basically saying it to get rid of me. They'll never deliver.'"[15]

Indeed, many felt a skepticism they didn't express to Galdston. Rev. Tim Benson, pastor of the Congregational church in Seymour, recalls, "He was making his rounds and stopped in. I thought it sounded like a good idea, but it sounded pretty unrealistic. I kind of laughed after he left and said, that sounds good but it will never happen."[16] I remember having the same reaction when he called on me. A CCAG staffer who later became active in the NVP told me of her initial skepticism: "I thought to myself, he wants to do WHAT?!"

Based on these discussions, Galdston developed a plan for the Naugatuck Valley Project.[17] It would draw on the traditions of community organization developed by Saul Alinsky and his followers, building an organization composed of already existing organizations, identifying and developing leaders, and challenging power actors to force them to bargain with and address the needs of the communities they affected. The central function of the organization would be to teach community leaders organizing skills that would make it possible for their communities to act on their own behalf.

The NVP would, however, also differ significantly from traditional Alinskyite practice. Instead of focusing on consumer and neighborhood issues, it would take on the central questions of jobs and corporate power. Like Alinsky's original Back of the Yards Council, but unlike most contemporary IAF projects, it would seek to draw together not only parishes but also unions, community organizations, and small business groups.

Galdston saw the 1980s as a new political and economic environment in which community demands on the government produced few results. A new strategy was necessary. The NVP would define local control of economic resources as the critical issue. Conglomerate corporations were using leveraged buyouts to buy, milk, and close local companies. Jobs were leaving the valley because those making the key decisions were not accountable to people in the valley. The NVP would challenge them and fight for industrial retention.

The ultimate solution was described as "broad-based local ownership" of productive resources. This might involve employee ownership or assistance to locally owned businesses or both. The ideological language was one of democratization or even of a better form of capitalism, not of public ownership or socialism. Galdston, Rosazza, and some of the project's other leaders took inspiration from the network of linked cooperative factories, banks, schools, housing, stores, insurance programs, and research facilities created by the Mondragon cooperative movement in the Basque region of northern Spain.[18]

The NVP would differ from conventional economic development efforts in emphasizing that economic issues were questions of power—who made decisions and in whose interest. Its basic goal, it was repeatedly emphasized, would be *organizing*—helping those with common interests to become collective actors.

In January 1983, the UAW, the CCAG, and the Catholic Archdiocese of Hartford formed a sponsoring committee and hired Ken Galdston to launch the NVP on an experimental basis. Galdston presented a detailed four-month work plan and a twelve thousand–dollar budget; Rosazza and Flynn agreed to kick in four thousand dollars each, and the CCAG offered to provide an office in Waterbury. They agreed the project would officially begin on February 1. The committee would continue meeting with Galdston every three weeks and evaluate in June whether to go on.[19]

Galdston began a series of what would ultimately add up to hundreds of interviews. Typical were those scheduled for the first two weeks of the project: four valley pastors, the president of Waterbury's main UAW local, a local UAW leader who headed the Waterbury Community/Labor Support Committee, the former executive director of the Lower Naugatuck Valley Community Council, three leaders of the Waterbury Citizen Action Group and its steering committee, the head of the Connecticut Plant Closing Coalition, an official from the Waterbury CAP antipoverty agency, and a historian from the Brass Workers History Project.[20] Galdston's first four months were supposed to be focused on interviewing leaders and researching the ownership of local companies. But it was a time of crisis in the valley, and he was projected into action far more quickly than his work plan anticipated.

Early Warning Signs

Nothing symbolized the powerlessness of workers and communities so strongly as the sudden, unexpected announcement that a plant would be closed. As a "plant closing movement" developed in the United States during the later 1970s, activists began to realize that there were often indications visible to workers in the plant that threatening changes were being planned. If machines were allowed to run down while the plant received a new paint job, or if the sales force was slashed while production ran overtime, it was a safe bet that something was up. Plant-closing activists published descriptions of these "early warning signs" and emphasized that workers in the plant were in the best position to detect what was really going on—indeed, they could be the eyes and ears of the community inside the plant. As Galdston made his way around the valley, one of his first efforts was to brief unionists on these early warning signs.[21]

A group of UAW leaders in the northern part of the valley was having a meeting in Torrington and asked Galdston to drop by. He gave a little talk about what he was doing and briefed them on the warning signs. After the meeting Charles Lombard, president of the UAW local at General Time Controls, a Talley Industries subsidiary in Thomaston, came up to him and said, "That's what's happening where we are. We were suspicious but we didn't know what to do."[22]

A day or two later, Galdston met with Lombard and other local union leaders in Thomaston. Big changes were clearly coming, and 140 jobs were on the line. The union had asked the company what was going on but received no answers. Galdston already had a meeting scheduled with the Clergy Association of Thomaston for the next day, and he suggested that Lombard come along. Galdston recalls, "I had already met Dick Williams, the Episcopal priest who was head of the Clergy Association. The big thing was just introducing the labor people and the church people. The union people told their story. I looked at Dick Williams: What are you going to do about this? He came back with the right answer: I think we should go over and meet with the president of the company."[23]

Williams called up Robert Carroll, the president of General Time Controls, and said they were from the Naugatuck Valley Project and wanted a meeting. To their considerable surprise, he agreed to meet. The next week, Talley announced it was selling GTC.

Galdston saw the company's agreement to meet as itself a victory—comparable to a union's winning recognition from a company. "We had our little baptism, our recognition. The company had agreed to meet with the Naugatuck Valley Project, which included all these folks that didn't work there."

Now the NVP had to come up with a strategy—fast. Galdston mentioned to Lombard the possibility of the employees buying the plant. Lombard quickly surveyed his members but found little interest—most were over fifty and weren't interested in making that kind of commitment. (Galdston admits he was relieved—he didn't yet have confidence in pulling off an employee buyout.) They decided they would ask the company to give preference to a buyer who would keep the jobs in the valley.

The NVP brought local people to the GTC meeting, but they also called in their big guns—the district-level union leaders, church officials, and others who formed their sponsoring committee. Galdston saw this both as a way of increasing the effort's clout and as a chance to educate the project's sponsors. After a preliminary discussion of what they wanted to accomplish and how they would present their position, they went over to the old Seth Thomas building for the meeting.

Ken Galdston recalls that "when we walked in the room with the guys from CCAG and the UAW and the Catholic Church and the Episcopal priest, that guy from General Time Controls was blown away by seeing this." One of those who spoke was Bishop Peter Rosazza. "We confronted the executive officer. I had never been involved with things like this before. You could just see people a little more proud of themselves because they were able to do something like that. Many of them had never been in situations where they could confront people at that level and feel supported by a group. If you took them one by one, it would be intimidating, but I think this way we intimidated the opposition."[24]

Robert Carroll promised the NVP that Talley would try to find buyers who would keep the jobs in the region. The union gave public credit for this result to the NVP. Ultimately, one GTC product line employing about forty workers was indeed sold to a Waterbury firm; two other lines were sold outside the valley.

For Galdston, the GTC effort represented a victory. "Not a huge, tremendous victory. A little proof of what we had said: that by being organized, we were going to get something. The company didn't say, screw you; we don't have to meet with you; we will do whatever we want."[25]

Pieces of the Power

The NVP was rapidly drawn into other job-related issues in the valley as well. When Galdston heard that Chase Forge in Waterbury was being sold, he researched the company and discovered it was owned by Standard Oil of Ohio, which was owned in part by British Petroleum, which was owned in part by the British government. While Ken would normally have encouraged an effort to contact the company, Father Castellani, pastor of a Catholic church near the plant and head of the Catholic Deanery in Waterbury, suggested they approach the city government instead. Castellani, Rosazza, Galdston, and people from the UAW and the CCAG met with the Waterbury Economic Development Department and urged an effort to keep the jobs in Waterbury. The plant was sold to the Canadian firm Waltec, which, for whatever reason, did keep the plant in Waterbury.

A somewhat different effort developed when the branch of the University of Connecticut in Torrington was threatened with closing. Galdston encouraged NVP-associated union leaders to lobby their legislators and to help organize a large public meeting along with the Chamber of Commerce and various community groups. He saw this campaign as a way to begin connecting union people with others in the community and to define the NVP as not just about plant closings but about anything that affected the economic health of the valley.

Rev. Campbell Lovett of the Bunker Hill Congregational Church in Waterbury recalls a "Save UConn" meeting organized by the NVP and chaired by Rev. Tim Downs, onetime president of the Waterbury Area Council of Churches: "I was so impressed because he [Ken] said, 'Okay, this is not just Torrington's issue. This is a valleywide issue. So now we're going to go around the room, and we're going to spend some time [finding out] who knows what legislator or senator, and we're going to start assigning people to make phone calls and to write letters.' He had the list: 'Who knows this person? Okay, are you going to write her or call her?'" Lovett agreed to call a state representative on the Education Committee. "I said, 'I hope this can stay open.' She said, 'Look, it's not going to happen. The place is going to close.'"

But as a result of such pressure, the decision to close the Torrington branch was reversed. Campbell Lovett says of this experience, "That showed me two pieces of the power. One, of having that many people in a room and seeing who knew who or who would do the work. But also talking to a state senator and hearing them say, 'No, it's not going to happen. It's going to close down,' and have the opposite happen. I thought, gee, this is fun."[26] Lovett would become an active leader in the NVP.

The project also became involved in what would turn out to be long-running struggles at the Torin Company at the northern tip of the valley in Torrington and at the Farrell Machine Division at the southern tip in Ansonia. According to Galdston, these activities in the first few months were fledgling efforts just about meeting the requirement of making some difference in the situation.

Galdston also continued with research. He developed a questionnaire on employment issues for use in local parishes and other organizations.[27] He listed all the valley's banks and the size of their deposits. He identified all the major employers and, using the library at the Yale School of Organization and Management, determined who really owned them. He coordinated this information with the local knowledge he picked up in his interviews—how these factories had once been locally owned enterprises known as the Rubber Shop, the Pin Shop, the Button Shop, or the Needle Shop. The result was often a three-generation genealogy of local companies bought by national companies that in turn were acquired by multinational conglomerates.

Galdston began presenting this synthesis of local knowledge and library research to groups in the valley. Rev. Campbell Lovett recalls a presentation to the executive committee of his church council: "He did his great flip-chart presentation about 'Okay, name me some of the industries here in town. Okay, who was that before?' And he worked all the way back to the historical beginnings of the different companies. And people here appreciated that. That was a great presentation because it really connected them in a very personal way to what had happened, with how many of the companies were becoming more international or at least national in scope and losing that contact with the local economy."[28]

The NVP also brought in Janet Saglio of the Industrial Cooperative Association, a Boston consulting organization specializing in creating "worker-owned and controlled businesses in low-income and blue-collar communities," for a meeting with the sponsoring committee.[29] The ICA had developed an approach deeply influenced by the network of cooperative factories and other institutions created by the Mondragon cooperative movement in Spain. The ICA, itself a cooperative, had helped develop worker cooperatives throughout the United States. This briefing helped make the possibility of worker ownership real to the sponsoring committee and initiated a long-term relationship with the ICA that was to prove a critical resource for the NVP.

Research, interviewing, and actions were all going on with the idea in mind of forming an organization, and by June the sponsoring committee, augmented by representatives of the United Church of Christ and the Methodist Church, decided the effort should go ahead. Galdston made repeated visits to "those who seemed to be the real leaders—the ones who had some followers and seemed the most interested." Meanwhile, "Rosazza had been doing all the things a good organizer-sponsor should. He had individually introduced me to probably a dozen pastors by inviting them out to lunch with me or by getting us invited to their rectories."[30]

Up to this time, the NVP essentially consisted of a sponsoring committee of state-level officials and ad hoc coalitions pulled together on a town-by-town basis in the valley. The goal, however, was to create a valley-based, valleywide organization. In October 1984, in response to a call issued by top state church and union officials, a hundred people gathered for the first valleywide NVP meeting.

Bishop Rosazza explained the project as an effort by people to band together to take back the ability to control their lives. Galdston gave a presentation on the shift in ownership of the major local companies, showing that there were thirty-two multinational corporations that owned businesses in the valley. The high point of the evening came when leaders from Thomaston, Torrington, and Waterbury stood up and testified about the contribution the project had already made to their struggles. Ken Galdston recalls, "Typically they were union leaders who stood up to say, 'This is what we are faced with. And this is what happened when we tried to do it on our own. And this is what happened when we did it with this Project. I think this is a good thing. I think it's a great thing.' It was very, very powerful, I think."[31]

The meeting voted that the project should go on and passed a proposal to form an organizing committee to meet every six weeks with two people from each of the institutions in the valley that were interested. Ken Galdston recalls, "Afterwards, at the meeting after the meeting, a lot of people stayed, a lot of people were standing around talking and there were comments that it's been a long time since we've been together. A lot of good natural outflowing of some emotion. I was having a hell of a good time during all this and was just realizing how much fun it was going to be to get them together. It was just wonderful to see the old connections."[32]

Need and Pride

Galdston found that, despite his initial fears, local people were willing to make the NVP work. "It turned out that people who said positive things about the Project showed up at meetings and made commitments and delivered. That's been one of the joys of working on this project."[33]

Why, despite the obstacles, did the NVP gain such support? First, the need was apparent. This need was experienced differently by those threatened with the loss of their own jobs; members of their communities; leaders of local churches, unions, and community organizations; and officials of state and regional organizations. But the valley's crisis was palpable to all. Second, there were many people who wanted to help meet that need. Some might hope to gain directly by having their own jobs saved, but most were motivated by values that were deeply embedded in the valley—indeed, deeply rooted in the traditions of the American working class. For many, participation in the NVP was an expression of religious values, a belief that "I am my brother's keeper." For many, it was an extension of core labor movement values of solidarity among working people against oppressive and exploitative employers. For most, it was also an expression of democratic values, a belief that people should have the right to participate in the decisions that affect their lives.

Participation in the NVP reflected a commitment to local communities and the dense web of family and social relationships that had grown out of the valley's ethnic settlements. As Rev. Tim Benson noted, "In Seymour and in the Valley in general there's a real pride about this being a milltown. People are proud of that, and that's good. That makes it desirable to want to save a heavy industry. A lot of towns now are glad to see the big old mills going down the tubes because they want clean industry and stuff like this. But we're proud of being a milltown and are doing everything we can to preserve that aspect of our community."[34]

By the end of 1984, the NVP had made a modest but promising beginning. As Galdston maintained, "We had fulfilled the basic premise: We can bring people together on these issues that affect them in a way nobody else is doing and we can change the relationship between people in the Valley and the decision-makers."[35]

Some core aspects of the NVP's approach were already evident. The NVP defined a common interest and a common "valley" identity. It brought separated groups that were affected by the same problems together to act in a coordinated way. It drew in the established organizations that had constituencies in the valley and responsibilities toward them. It grounded itself in long-established communities, values, and traditions, but gave them a new twist to meet changing conditions. It combined the "local knowledge" people had about their own situations with other knowledge provided by research and experience elsewhere. It provided training and support for people to become leaders and education for understanding the forces affecting people's lives. It tried to establish direct channels of negotiation and accountability with those whose decisions were affecting people's lives. It utilized whatever forms of pressure it could mobilize to influence their decisions.

The NVP's emerging approach began to address some of the sources of valley residents' powerlessness. It began creating a vehicle through which community members could try to hold powerful individuals and institutions accountable for actions that were often regarded as simply the results of blind economic forces. It began to confront the transnational conglomerate corporations that were devastating the valley's economy. It was helping workers develop a voice in decisions about the future of their enterprises. It began drawing together resources to help sustain organizing for change. It began to challenge the idea that if the market produced an unfavorable outcome, there was nothing that could be done about it. And it began insisting that the government, at least at the local and state levels, begin responding more to the needs of valley residents and less to powerful economic and political interests.

3. Buyout

The Seymour Manufacturing Company was founded by a local entrepreneurial family in the little factory town of Seymour in 1878.[1] It was a typical Naugatuck Valley brass mill, turning out brass sheet, rod, wire, and tubing. It started with twenty-four workers; by World War I, it employed fourteen hundred.[2] When workers surreptitiously took me through the plant in 1980, machines were old, work was slow, and the workforce was down to a couple of hundred.

For most of its history, the plant's workforce was predominantly Russian and Polish. Eddie Labacz's father came from Poland and went to work at the Seymour Manufacturing Company around 1891. Eddie remembers, "When I was a kid, being of Polish descent, I talked better Polish than I could English when I went to school. One side of town was German, with the doctors, high class. On this side of the river was all tenement houses and rundown buildings. The Polish and Russians, we stayed on one side of the river. If you came over [to] this side of the river, you expected to get beat up with a baseball bat or something because you were coming into another territory."[3]

Eddie followed his father into the plant in 1941. He remembers that when workers tried to organize a union in the early 1940s, "A lot of the people were scared to meet. They had to meet in cellars or in somebody's house. They couldn't bring it out in the open; they were afraid that the company would let them go." In 1944, an NLRB election forced the company to recognize the union. In 1961, Eddie Labacz was elected president of UAW Amalgamated Local 1827, a post he held until he retired in 1984.[4]

Seymour Manufacturing typified the "industrial genealogy" of Naugatuck Valley companies. For most of its history, Seymour Manufacturing was under the control of the Matthies family, who resided in a large house next door to the plant. In 1950, the company was sold to the Bridgeport Brass Company. In 1963, Bridgeport Brass was in turn acquired by the multinational conglomerate National Distillers and Chemical Corporation. National Distillers manufactured Old Granddad Whiskey and Almaden Wines; it owned Suburban Propane and an insurance company in Indiana. Seymour Manufacturing represented three-tenths of 1 percent of National's assets. National had invested little money in the company, and its productivity was rapidly falling behind Wisconsin-based Valleycast, its leading competitor.[5]

Early in 1984, a worker at Seymour questioned a manager about something and was told not to worry about it, that the place was going to be sold.[6] Instantly, rumors began flying around the plant. Mike Kearney, then a furnace operator, recalls that while workers gathered in the union hall, "Eddie Labacz made a phone call to New York and asked the president of National Distillers if the rumors were true that something was in the works. And he told Eddie that National Distillers was going to divest of all their metals industry, and Seymour was included in that plan. They didn't really give a reason why they were divesting, they just said, look, we want out. Whether it was profitable or not."[7]

Tom Curtin, the UAW staffer who serviced the Seymour local, happened to be in town for negotiations at another plant, and he casually told workers at Seymour, "You guys should think about buying your place. I can put you in touch with someone who can give you some information."[8] He told them that there was a new organization called the Naugatuck Valley Project that was trying to help workers and communities threatened by plant closings; Curtin served on the sponsoring committee and had worked with the NVP trying to save the Torin Company in Torrington. He suggested the Seymour workers contact Ken Galdston, the initiator of the NVP. Curtin also called Galdston, who went down to Seymour to meet with the executive board of the local.

Galdston remembers that he was immediately captured by the look of the union headquarters. "It's a sort of brick building with a glass brick front; where the window would be is glass brick. The sign says UAW-CIO Local 1827 in metallic letters that look almost hand crafted but very professional—but also a little bit broken down."[9]

Galdston gave a presentation on the NVP and employee ownership. "I explained why I thought it was to their advantage to look at the buy-out regardless of almost anything. Strategically, it was going to put them in a better position even if they decided not to buy; they were going to learn a lot that would help them in dealing with some in-coming owner, for example." The new local president, Tom Klimovich, and several others seemed receptive; Galdston identified furnace operator Mike Kearney as "*the* skeptic from the start, peppering me with questions and somewhat negative—pretty much a pain in the ass."[10] Kearney recalls:

> Because of Seymour's reputation, because of their niche in the marketplace, because of the specialty alloys, we figured the plant was going to be here forever. It was here since the late eighteen hundreds. Generations of families had worked there. The place would never shut down. A white knight would come in, buy the plant, and save all the jobs.
>
> We just couldn't understand, how do you own and run your own business? And especially from a rank and file perspective. What do you need a union for? What's our role in this? There were just too many questions. It was just one dark cloud.[11]

Galdston explained that the purchase could be made through a leveraged buyout—the same technique that allowed Wall Street speculators to buy companies with bank loans while putting up virtually no money of their own. The buyout would be organized through an employee stock ownership plan (ESOP), which recent federal legislation had made practical and financially attractive. Galdston also quizzed them on the business: its products, employees, competition, profit, and potentials.

When the new local union president, Tom Klimovich, asked, "What's the next step?" Galdston suggested they let National Distillers know they were interested. The company's response to a call from the union was, "Fine, we'll have our investment bankers, Dillon, Reed, send out a copy of the prospectus." Ken suggested the union tell the press, and they called the local reporter for the local newspaper, who came notebook in hand and took down the story.

Interested Buyers

Two weeks later, Galdston made a presentation on employee ownership at the Knights of Columbus hall in Seymour. He was accompanied by Jan Saglio of the Industrial Cooperative Association, a consultant organization specializing in employee-owned companies. They described "how many worker-owned firms there are; why people are interested in worker-ownership; how you do it; what does a worker-owned firm look like; where do the finances come from." More than half the union membership showed up. After questions, they unanimously voted to explore a buyout. This was the first real buyout effort the NVP had attempted. Galdston recalls, "It was very much going by the seat of our pants. But that was very exciting. It was like the teacher reading a few pages ahead so that you can tell what's happening."[12]

Following his instincts as an organizer, Galdston began treating the buyout process as an outreach effort. At his very first meeting with local union leaders at Seymour he had said, "If you're going to go ahead, it really has to be white and blue collar and so what you should be saying is that you're acting on behalf of all the employees." When he asked if there were any managers they respected, they mentioned Carl Drescher, who had been plant manager for a number of years. Drescher came over to the union hall "sort of on the QT" and told Galdston he thought they could make a go of the company. Galdston encouraged the union people to continue reaching out to white-collar employees. Rev. Tim Benson, pastor of the Seymour Congregational Church, who would become an active supporter of the buyout, recalls that the blue-collar people "began to pull in some of their white collar friends and get them involved too. That was a long process. A lot took place on a one-to-one basis. They would talk about pulling in person x and person y and get them involved. It seemed a precarious position: Some of the white collar people were concerned they would be perceived as defectors if they threw in their lot with the blue collar people. But it all came around."[13]

The union executive board also met with retired UAW leaders Eddie Labacz and John Mankowski. For Ken Galdston it was a special occasion.

> Here we were in this old union hall—the walls with old wall paper, the photograph of Phil Murray. Just a sense of down home. This is our home and these are guys who'd worked there all these years. The younger people that I was dealing with primarily were in their thirties. They had fathers who had worked in the brass mill. There was this sense of support between the generations which was really powerful for me. It was probably the most exciting thing that had happened to me since I'd been in the Valley, that sense of connection and solidarity.[14]

The NVP also began reaching out for community support. Rev. Tim Benson, who grew up in Danbury, Connecticut, and became pastor of the Seymour Congregational Church in 1981, remembers, "My first ride into Seymour, I saw all these hulking, empty-looking, huge old factories all over. I just scratched my head and wondered what that was all about. It wasn't too long before the picture began to fill out that they were vacant factories and that there was lots of unemployment because of that situation. I didn't know what to do about it at that point. It was a little bigger than I was."[15]

Benson met Galdston early in the formation of the NVP: "He was making his rounds and stopped in." Benson got involved with some early NVP activities; his church joined the project and put up some money. He began to take on a role that he described as "the chief cheerleader" for the nascent buyout. "I went to some of the very first meetings with Mike Kearney and Tom Klimovich and some others. Everybody had to be convinced that this was even vaguely possible. Everybody says when they first hear about an employee buyout, how can a bunch of guys come up with ten million dollars or whatever it is going to cost to buy this thing. But people began to believe."[16] Several other pastors joined Benson and local union officials to form what was in effect a nascent Seymour NVP chapter.

The project also began dealing with political leaders. At the very first union meeting on the buyout, State Representative Eugene Skowronski had shown up and insisted that he be allowed to speak. Ken was wary. "My reaction from most of my organizing is that you resist this sort of thing. These guys were trying to take over the meeting. That's bullshit. It's your meeting. You sort of keep them in their rightful place."[17]

But in fact, Skowronski simply said the buyout was a great idea and that he was with them. Ken found this the first of a series of unexpectedly positive experiences with local politicians.

> I found a lot of these politicians on this issue going to bat in a pretty straight-forward way. When you are dealing with a conglomerate, there's not much opportunity for them to sell you out. You are moving so fast and so far ahead of them. You understand the business, you understand what's involved in the buyout. If you were trying to stop a highway and they wanted to come in the middle of a meeting and dominate it, you'd really put them in their place. But here, there's a natural niche for them. It gives people a sense of confidence.[18]

The local coalition began inviting Seymour's first selectman to their meetings. Then they began going to the Board of Selectmen and requesting support for the buyout. Ultimately, the town kicked in three thousand dollars for a feasibility study.

Any buyout would clearly need a supporting team of professionals. The NVP already had a contract for business consulting services with the ICA. Fred Perella suggested that Galdston call Roger Hanlon at the prestigious Connecticut firm of Day, Berry, and Howard, who was the chairman of Perella's board at the Office of Urban Affairs. Hanlon told Galdston, "This is a great coincidence, because just today Paul McAlenney, one of our attorneys, walked in with a news article about the buyout and said, is this something we should be looking into?" McAlenney began working on the buyout, initially on a pro bono basis.

Early in the buyout effort, Galdston had gotten a call from John Schuyler at the accounting firm of Deloitte, Haskins, and Sells. Schuyler was working with the state's Department of Economic Development on a task force to support buyouts. Galdston was leery. "My experience with governments, es-pecially in things like this, is that they're either not competent and/or subject to other people's pressures. It's going to get in the way more than anything. So I was not particularly inviting to him."[19]

The state, however, had established a fund of twenty-five thousand dollars for buyout feasibility studies, and the Department of Economic Development wanted Schuyler and his associates to do the study for Seymour. The NVP and the union local wanted the ICA, with whom they already had a relationship and who had extensive expertise with worker buyouts. The state, however, insisted that it wanted a Connecticut company. Catholic bishop Peter Ro-sazza, the NVP's first chairman, called state development commissioner John Carson, and ultimately a compromise was worked out: the state would pay seventy-five hundred dollars to Schuyler's firm, which would do the business projections known as "pro formas," but most of the money would be passed on to the ICA, which would do the business analysis.

With its community support and its expert team in place, the buyout coali-tion asked National Distillers for a meeting. National arranged for two young men from the Dillon, Reed investment bank to meet with them in Seymour's ornate company boardroom—a room dominated by a huge multicolored mural painted in 1943 depicting the role of brass in American history. The NVP delegation included the three top local union officers (all in suits), a UAW international representative, a Catholic priest, a Protestant minister, the town banker, an official from the town of Seymour, a representative from the Valley Citizen Action Group, and Jan Saglio from the ICA. They had carefully planned the meeting in advance to impress the sellers both with their competence and with their breadth of support; they had the capacity to pull off a buyout and also the capacity to put significant pressure on the company if it did not cooperate. They went around the table, each explaining who they were and why they were involved. One community representative said, "I'm here because I've seen enough people lose their jobs, and I'm tired of mopping up." Then Jan Saglio began an intensive questioning, based on the prospectus, of the company's past investment and profitability figures.

At the end of the meeting, the men from Dillon, Reed said, "We're really pleased you're interested in buying it. We have three or four other interested buyers, and we're asking for offers. We'll give you the same access to the books and the managers that we would any other buyers." Then they dropped the bombshell: "We want final offers within five weeks."

The coalition knew there was no way it could prepare a final buyout plan in that length of time. At this point the difference between an organizing orientation like the NVP's and a more conventional economic development approach became evident. The NVP's response was to initiate a community campaign demanding that National Distillers give them more time. According to Galdston, "Initially we were told that Drummond Bell, Chairman of the Board of National Distillers, was angry about the publicity and the managers warned us about pressing publicity. But public attention and support are your only protection and weapon here so we pressed on."[20]

The campaign focused on Drummond Bell himself. It was kicked off by a community meeting in Tim Benson's church. Hundreds of valley residents wrote letters and signed petitions asking Bell to give the NVP more time. A Catholic archbishop, an Episcopal bishop, the head of the UAW, the governor, and senators and congressmen from Connecticut all wrote letters to Bell.

It worked. Two weeks after the start of the campaign, the NVP received a letter from National Distillers saying, "We are impressed by the efforts which have been undertaken by the community and the employees." National Distillers agreed to extend the deadline, reduce the asking price from $13.5 million to $11 million, stop seeking additional purchasers, and provide staff assistance. They further pledged to match up to $25,000 of the cost of a feasibility study. From then on, National Distillers was the very model of a cooperative seller. The Reverend Benson says, "My sense is that they really didn't believe that this was a credible option until they got this kind of community response. After that they began to believe that these were real guys: if they could do this, they can really pull this deal together too. It gave them credibility."[21]

Feasibility

With cooperation from the company assured, ICA business analyst Roland Cline began intensive work on a feasibility study. As he explained:

> When you are trying to figure out a purchase price, first you have to figure out how profitable the company is likely to be; that's one indication of what kind of purchasing price, what size investment this level of return would justify. Another angle you have to look at is the liquidation value of the assets, because that's the bottom line for the seller. We had an appraiser look at the building, real estate and equipment, and give us rough and dirty walk-through numbers; the managers had a pretty good idea of what the inventory was worth.
>
> You have to analyze the market and the company's sales over the last five or ten years, try to find out what megatrends are taking place, how the company is performing within these trends, and not only to statistically understand it but to talk to the sales manager, and some of the customers, and some of the sales people in the field; try to understand the causes and the reasons behind these trends.

Cline set up a spreadsheet on historical sales and costs, then peppered the managers with questions about ways to shrink production and human resource costs.

Preparing the feasibility study was an organizing and educational as well as a technical process.

> All of this analysis comes back to the steering committee in bits and pieces. Maybe there would be a two-page summary of the market demand for the last twenty years, with a graph showing that the mechanical wire industry has been declining since 1965, which is the case, and showing Seymour's sales and market share. That's one example out of forty or fifty. When we get to the end of the study and there is a report written up, there are few if any surprises to anyone. It's just a cleaner and more comprehensive picture of the parts that were analyzed and understood and massaged and changed by the group as a whole.[22]

Ken Galdston recalls, "It was very up-and-down. You'd come in one day and Roland Cline would say, 'It looks miserable. At this selling price we'll never be able to do this. I just don't know how it's going to be profitable.' And then at another point he'd say, 'Well, if we can do this and this, maybe it's going to work.' There were a number of times when we'd leave on an afternoon with the conclusion that it was probably not going to work."[23]

Ultimately, Cline concluded, "There was no way that the employees could buy that company at a price that would be acceptable to the seller without significantly reducing costs." The union and managers developed a plan to cut the workforce by nearly 20 percent, mostly by attrition. "From a business analyst's point of view, every job is roughly twenty-five to thirty thousand dollars in costs, so if you delete twenty jobs, that's a half-a-million dollars that goes right to the bottom line."[24] Managers also debated whether the price of the product could be raised, with Carl Drescher maintaining that it could; ultimately, the study compromised on a modest increase.

The feasibility study concluded that the company could be profitable at a purchase price somewhat below the asking price. In a daylong session, employees came into the company office in groups of twenty to hear the results of the study and an explanation of how the ESOP would work. Anyone interested was asked to volunteer for a steering committee, which became the governing body for the buyout effort. On May 23, the committee gave National Distillers a bid to buy the plant for $8.7 million—above liquidation value but substantially below the asking price.[25]

A week later National Distillers unexpectedly informed the steering committee that Seymour's principal competitor, Valleycast, had submitted an $11 million bid—far above that submitted by the employees.[26] While National had agreed to let the employees match others' bids, there was no way they could match this one and still have a viable company. The buyout committee announced that they were withdrawing their offer. Local newspapers headlined the story that the buyout was dead.

Representatives of Valleycast (at that time a subsidiary of the British firm Turner Oak) came to Connecticut and met with the union, management, and the state. Then the next week, just as unexpectedly, Valleycast withdrew its offer. Why Valleycast pulled out—or even whether its initial offer was serious or just a spoiling operation—was unknowable to people in Seymour. In any event, Valleycast's withdrawal put the employee buyout back on the burner.

Who Governs?

The buyout effort had initially been guided by a committee of the union, then by a volunteer steering committee. Galdston believes, "That was the right strategy for us in this situation—to keep the door open and just keep going on slowly." But after the Valleycast episode, "The people were sort of pissed off with the steering committee. In part, they felt that they'd been kept in the dark. The steering committee wouldn't tell them what the bids were." One woman office worker recalls, "It started wrong. We heard there was a steering committee, but we didn't know how it was chosen. I didn't know that anyone could be on the steering committee."[27]

The steering committee called a meeting for all employees in Tim Benson's church. With an overwhelming turnout, the employees voted 191 to 41 to go ahead with the buyout effort.[28] They also voted to elect a new steering committee based on representation by departments. According to Mike Kearney, "The majority said, we're worried about our jobs. If the deal looks good, we'll go along with it." But that didn't mean support was universal. "We had the crew we called the bench boys. The guys used to sit out in the yard and preach how bad it was: 'This is not going to work. We're not going to give up 10 percent.' But they never left." Even many of those who voted for the buyout effort remained skeptical. An office worker said, "We thought it would never happen in a million years. Where would workers get the money? How would they run it? We thought we'd be better off having someone else buy it."[29]

Ken Galdston reported to the NVP sponsoring committee that he was spending between half and two-thirds of his time on Seymour. He was not entirely happy about the role he was playing there:

I was doing a lot of the talking. I would be a spokesperson at these meetings. I was doing a lot of teaching inside about employee ownership. I'd run all the training sessions and I was doing a lot of the mediation. I would end up chairing the steering committee meetings, sort of mediating between the groups.

I was not real comfortable doing it as an organizer, on the one hand. On the other hand, it felt, at least initially, as if there was really nobody else to do this—emphasizing both the community power and the goal.[30]

Galdston's role changed with the election of a new steering committee. Although the committee had a blue-collar majority, it elected Carl Drescher as its chair. Galdston recalls, "He said, 'OK, Ken. I'm ready to take over.' And that was it. I think the managers felt that I was this outsider sort of running the shop. They wanted to take back some of the control. I understood that. They should."[31]

The new steering committee submitted a bid of ten million dollars.[32] The reply came back from National Distillers: the answer is not no. National asked for a bit more, but the committee refused to budge. On June 16, National accepted the bid. Klimovich called the press to his house and announced that the buyout was going ahead.

Now the steering committee faced the problem of deciding just how the employee-owned company would be run. From the start, it was assumed that the basic vehicle for purchasing the company would be an ESOP. ESOPs were the brainchild of business lawyer Louis Kelso, author of *The Capitalist Manifesto: How to Turn 80 Million Workers into Capitalists on Borrowed Money*. ESOPs, according to Kelso, would make every worker "an employee by day, and an owner by night."[33]

ESOPs combine the financial mechanisms used for pension plans with those used for leveraged buyouts. The company sets up a trust fund as it might for a pension plan. The fund then borrows money to buy company stock, just as a purchaser might in a leveraged takeover. The company thereafter pays stock dividends to the ESOP. These are used initially to repay the original loans. The ESOP holds the company's stock in trust and allocates it to individual employee accounts on the basis of compensation, years of service, or some other formula. Employees receive their shares or payment for them when they leave or retire.[34]

With the support of Louisiana senator Russell Long, ESOPs were granted special advantages under the Employee Retirement Income Security Act of 1974, which regulates pension plans. Employer contributions to an ESOP, like any employee benefit plan, are exempt from corporate income tax, but unlike normal pension plans, ESOPs can invest their assets in the employer's stock. At the time of the Seymour buyout, a new tax law further sweetened ESOP deals—for example, by allowing banks that loan money to ESOPs to deduct 50 percent of the interest income earned on those loans.

In 1975, there were sixteen hundred ESOPs covering 250,000 employees. By 1987, there were eight thousand plans covering 8 million workers, some

7 percent of the nation's workforce. Most ESOPs were set up in ways that prevented workers from gaining any real control over their companies; only 10 to 15 percent of the plans owned a majority of their company's stock.[35] There were few if any models for ESOPs that were fully democratic and 100 percent employee owned.

Paul McAlenney brought the steering committee a set of standard corporation bylaws. There was considerable discussion of whether they could or should be made more democratic. Roland Cline noted, "There was a certain amount of friction and struggle between the management group and the union. I was really tired of it and was going to suggest they find someone else to assist them."[36]

Attitudes changed markedly when a carload of people from Seymour drove to New Jersey to visit the less than democratic buyouts at Hyatt-Clark and Atlas Chain. Cline recalls, "That sure scared that carload of people. They had heavy, heavy-duty problems. At Hyatt-Clark the board was controlled by outsiders. There was little sympathy or sensitivity to the rank and file employees. It was a dynamic that was destructive. It upset Carl Drescher and the other people who went down there, the management as well as the union people, and it set an example of what they wanted to avoid."[37]

With help from the ICA, the steering committee worked out highly democratic bylaws. The new company would be wholly owned by an ESOP open only to company employees. It would be run by a nine-member board of directors. Five members would be elected to rotating two-year terms at the annual ESOP meeting on a one employee–one vote basis; the board would also include the presidents of the company and the union and two outside directors chosen by the board. Employees could petition for special ESOP meetings and recall members of the board.[38]

An initial ESOP meeting was held for the 170 hourly and 50 salaried employees. Nominees for the board gave two-minute speeches. The next day elections were held in the workplace, with each employee voting for any five nominees. One hourly and four salaried employees were elected. Mike Kearney says, "We couldn't figure out what happened. I don't know if the people on the floor felt the hourly people weren't qualified to sit on the board. Or if the hourly vote was split. Or if a couple of managers got in by mistake."[39]

A management selection committee put a blind ad in the *New York Times* and received 170 responses. After reviewing them, it decided to hire Carl Drescher, the current plant manager, to be the president of the new company. Drescher had graduated from Yale in 1952 with a degree in psychology. "The personnel director of Chase Brass and Copper offered me a job in time study. I didn't even know what time study was, but I took it and stayed."[40] He came to Seymour in 1974. By the time of the buyout, he had thirty-four years of management experience in the nonferrous-metals business. Once he was selected to head the buyout effort, he began taking over many functions from the former general manager, eventually directing all functions at Seymour except for sales and administration.

Financing the buyout proved surprisingly easy. Employees agreed to an across-the-board 10 percent wage cut that would be credited to them as equity. As often happens in sales to privately held companies, National Distillers agreed to take a note for a substantial part of the selling price—in effect loaning the employees part of the money they needed to buy the company. The finalized business plan was sent to a variety of banks; after discussions with several of them, National Westminster Bank (NatWest) in New York was selected. Thanks to strong collateral and ESOP advantages, interest rates were below prime.

The Union

Most ESOPs are in nonunion firms; some are even instituted as part of an antiunion strategy. At Seymour, the ESOP had actually been initiated by the union. Yet the role of the union remained to be addressed. The UAW sent in a lawyer to make sure that the bargaining rights of the local would be protected in the new company. But the role of the union in practice would be determined by the local itself.

By this time, Mike Kearney had been elected president of Local 1827. Kearney had grown up in Seymour, graduated from Seymour High School in 1970, and served four and a half years in the U.S. Air Force. "I came back here looking for a job in the field I was in [in] the service. I couldn't find anything that paid. I got referred to the brass mill by a friend. I went down one day and got hired the next." After a couple of years he became a steward. "As the oldtimers started retiring, I ran for other offices"—grievance committee, negotiating committee, vice chairman of the bargaining unit, and finally president of the local. Local president was a very part-time job, and Kearney continued to hold down his regular job as a furnace operator as well.

It is an adage among experienced organizers that the person who is most skeptical about an effort at the beginning may become the most firmly committed in the end, and by this time Kearney had become a strong advocate of the buyout and an active leader in the NVP. As local president, he helped shape the role of the union in the Seymour buyout:

> The banks wanted to see a ratified labor contract. We went upstairs to negotiate
> and we were negotiating with ourselves. Usual negotiations we say, we want this,

this, and this. We said, we want a raise, we want this. Carl said, we'll give you a raise, but who's going to pay for it? So we stopped and took a caucus and said, we've never been in that predicament before. What are we going to do?

Finally, we took apart all the money items and went over them with a fine tooth comb to see what was necessary. Insurance, pay, vacations, all our economics. Before we had a sickness and accident insurance policy with Aetna. We paid approximately $50 thousand a year in premiums. I said let's drop that and go self-insured. First year we saved $37 thousand. That's the approach we had to take from our side of the table. We brought Blue Cross right to the table. They went over the different policies and explained the costs. So we could understand what we were buying.

When it came to the contract itself, non-economics, we had items in the contract that were obsolete, that we had to get rid of. Items that were cumbersome. They'd been in there for years, that didn't really help us—we had to change the wording so we could better react to conditions for ourselves. For example, the [job] bidding procedure was so involved it took two or three months to react to a layoff. We're in business for ourselves, we said we can't let that happen. We changed the bidding procedure so it was fair but it was quick. That's the attitude we took.

For Kearney, despite the ESOP, the managers represented an entity distinct from the workers—"the company": "The company understood where we were coming from and they tried to cooperate. They didn't pull any fast ones on us."

To maximize turnout, the union held its contract ratification meeting in the plant. "I read only the changes in the contract. There were questions. Somebody said, this is a matter of survival. The contract doesn't sound too bad. 'I make a motion the contract [be] accepted.' There were only two who stuck their hands up for no. They voted and started filing out. There wasn't that big a discussion."

Closing

Everything seemed set, but various technicalities continued to delay the closing. An officer at the bank left, and his successor had to be brought up to speed. Somebody neglected to file for an environmental permit. Roland Cline felt the delay was beneficial in that it gave the new management team time to get organized. But "people kept coming back to the same old job; everybody kept saying 'When?'"[41] Finally, more than a year after the buyout effort began, the final papers were signed, and on April 17, 1985, "Seymour Specialty Wire, an Employee-Owned Company" took over the assets.

A gala ceremony was organized inside the plant. Bishop Peter Rosazza says, "One of the proudest or happiest moments of my whole life was to be present at the ceremony when the governor came down to cut the ribbon at the opening of Seymour Specialty Wire and to see the pride reflected in the faces of those workers there, who knew that this was theirs and that they weren't working for anybody but themselves. That was a beautiful experience."[42]

Workers and community members in Seymour challenged some of their most important sources of powerlessness. Despite some false starts, they managed to pull together both a community coalition and a buyout steering committee that could bargain with local and state government, their employer, banks, and other powerful actors. Their pressure campaign led a large multinational conglomerate corporation to change its plans and help them buy their company. They created a democratic structure to share responsibility for their company. They found resources to buy the company through a small deduction from their own wages, borrowing in the credit market, and modest government assistance. They won support from local political leaders and from town and state economic development programs. One of the things their efforts left little changed, however, was the impact of market forces on their company; they might hold the title to their factory, but its survival continued to be affected by the price of copper in Chile, the rate of interest in Japan, and the investment decisions of a company in Finland.

The creation of Seymour Specialty Wire represented many aspects of the NVP's emerging strategy. It treated the issue of jobs as an issue of power. It focused on the centrality of ownership in establishing power over economic decisions. It used the techniques of community organizing to gain power. It provided workers with knowledge from which they had normally been excluded. It built a coalition of organized workers and a broader community that included white-collar workers, local religious institutions, and local and state governments. It recognized the conflicting interests of workers and local managers but also their common interests in the face of economic extinction.

Only time would tell what the long-term impact of employee ownership would be on the Seymour brass mill.[43] The impact of the highly publicized buyout on people in the valley was far more immediate. Rev. Tim Benson noted a year after the buyout:

> We have proven that people in the Valley can stand up to giant mega-corporations and get their way. And then do a whizbang job of running their company locally, too.
>
> We have also educated people in the Valley that employee ownership is a viable option for companies. Where people had never heard of it and when they had heard of it thought it was a crazy idea, now whenever a company begins to waver a little bit, the union gets together or even white collar people get together and come running to the Project saying, tell us about employee ownership, because we want to know about it. So we've made it a real option.[44]

4. Organizing

Behind dramatic actions like the Seymour buyout lay something the Naugatuck Valley Project called "organizing." The project clearly meant by that something more than simply forming an organization and recruiting members. Organizing meant taking disconnected individuals and groups and connecting them in ways that allows them to act in concert. But how could that be done?

In the Alinsky Mold

Notwithstanding its exceptional focus on plant closings, many aspects of the NVP's strategy were standard community organizing techniques worked out over the course of many decades and taught by Saul Alinsky's Industrial Areas Foundation and other organizing centers. They involved finding and developing leaders, teaching organizing skills, establishing new relationships, strengthening community institutions, as well as building the organization itself.[1]

Saul Alinsky's followers often repeat his remark that you do more organizing with your ears than with your mouth, and it was standard IAF procedure for Ken Galdston to start his work with dozens and dozens of interviews. Such interviewing familiarizes the organizer with multiple aspects of the community that are likely to prove resources or barriers, it identifies key issues and concerns around which people are likely to be mobilized, and it lets many people in the community get to know the organizer and form their own opinion of the organization's character and purpose independent of media and other third parties. Above all, it identifies people whose experience, roles, personality, and concerns mark them as potential leaders for the organization.

Once potential leaders are identified, a good deal of effort typically goes into their development and training. Some of this occurs in formal training sessions, like Janet Saglio's presentation on employee ownership and Ken Galdston's training sessions on the early warning signs of plant closings.

At least as important are the leadership training and support that go on in the course of action. As Galdston put it, "From the start, the point was not that I was going to call up the President of this corporation, but you were going to do it and if you hadn't done it before, we were going to walk through how you were going to do it. I think it's that sort of opportunity for people to grow and stretch that keeps people coming." Peter Rosazza recalls, "Ken would say, we should call this man. And he'd go through it with me. We'd role-play."[2]

As part of their strategy for leadership development, Galdston and other NVP staffers almost invariably held meetings before and after any activity. Rosazza recalls that when a group was going to meet with officials of a company, "We always would have a preparatory meeting with Ken Galdston and talk about strategies for how we were going to present things, what we wanted to accomplish at the meeting. And then we would go into the meeting, and afterwards you would have a debriefing on how things went and what we would do for follow-up."[3]

Another feature of organizing consists in building relationships. Some of these are between institutions: for example, the relationship among the original sponsoring organizations of the NVP. Some are within institutions: for example, the linking of bishops, archdiocese staff, local priests, and activist parishioners that went on within the Catholic Church. Some are relationships with the organizer: Galdston's developing personal relationships with various individuals undoubtedly contributed to their willingness to work on the project. Some are relationships among individuals and local leaders: the cooperation among local union, church, small business, and political leaders in trying to save the Torrington branch of the University of Connecticut or General Time Controls laid much of the groundwork for subsequent cooperation, including cooperation in establishing the NVP itself.

People and communities have large arrays of problems and concerns; crucial to effective organizing is selecting from them specific issues to organize around. Experience has taught organizers to seek issues that matter enough to some people that they are willing to act, that will not divide those the organization is trying to bring together, that provide visible targets on which pressure can be brought to bear, that allow something significant to be won, and that embody the goals, methods, and philosophy of the organization in a way that inspires others to join or emulate. The threatened closings of GTC, the University of Connecticut–Torrington branch, and the Seymour brass mill all met these criteria. And they emerged and were tested in community meetings and one-on-one interviews.

Many organizing efforts flounder in a sea of words. Experienced organizers aim to help leaders define specific activities that groups of people can undertake to advance their objectives. Holding a meeting with the Waterbury economic development agency, telephoning state legislators, even researching the ownership of a company—all of these were concrete "actions" that required that people cooperate, provided new information about the reality they confronted, and hopefully moved them closer to their goal. The choice of actions often involved a decision of what level of militancy and confrontation would be most effective both in winning an objective and in unifying and expanding the coalition.[4]

People organize precisely because they are excluded from the current decision-making process. Therefore, they have to find a way to become players in the arena. Sometimes there are institutional means already established for doing this: lobbying legislators or petitioning for a union representation election, for example. If not, action is often limited to what is essentially an expression of opinion: issuing a statement or holding a demonstration. Becoming a player means getting beyond just expressing an opinion to affecting the other players and the outcome.

In traditional organizing strategy, becoming a player means establishing a relationship with the other players. This is what the NVP did when it organized meetings with city governments, corporation presidents, and state legislators. It somewhat resembles the process in a drama in which antagonists and protagonists are brought together to interact. The NVP often used high religious officials to initiate such contact. Bishop Rosazza recalls, "Ken would say, 'We want you to call the chief executive officer of this company out in Phoenix or another place. If you could, say to him this and this and this.' So I would make these crazy phone calls."[5] When there were no existing institutional channels, "becoming players" meant winning recognition—creating a new form of collective bargaining between the coalition and established players.

Organizing presumes that those being organized have interests that conflict with other interests that are already represented. The result is bound to be conflict. Traditionally, organizing uses "fights" to help mobilize those who share common but underrepresented interests, to demonstrate that they are not powerless, and to change the alignment of social forces. The fight to save the Torrington UConn branch was a classic example of this mobilizing and transforming effect.

In such fights, "the issue is not the issue"—or at least, there is more to it than the issue. As Galdston put it, "Since I see my work as teaching people how to organize and finding and developing potential leaders, I knew from the start the idea for me was we were going to build something that would have as a reason for being more than just winning on issues. The reason for doing this is, we're going to develop more of our own leaders."[6]

In Galdston's view, the effort to develop leaders is one of the things that made "organizing" different from purely results-oriented electoral action or economic development. "Once you start saying, this is really what we are about, this is our prime activity, you begin to measure yourself not by leaders developed, by campaigns won, but by numbers of houses built or by numbers of legislative seats won. If that's what you want to do, fine, go do it. But I don't think there are enough people organizing people to develop their abilities to get into the sorts of fights in the street that are less housebroken as Alinsky would say than fights like that."[7]

The NVP's organizing aimed to produce not just individual but collective leadership. A Galdston explained:

> When we say developing leaders, it means in part developing as a team, not only individuals, but teams of people. If you have that as a focus, leaders hopefully see the different campaigns as opportunities for their own growth and that's what knits it together. You're not just out there trying to get results on a wide scatter shot of issues. It takes an appreciation for what you're creating and for the possibilities of what you can create in the way of relationships among people and individual abilities. If you don't have that then you are much more likely to just be thinking about, well, what's next? Where is the next hot activity?[8]

Such an approach involved an ongoing tension, one that Galdston saw as creative. "This is always the organizer's and the organization's dilemma: process and results. Getting enough results so that you're actually affecting people's lives, but doing it through processes that develop people and stretch them, getting them to really work their groups."[9]

The NVP, like traditional Alinsky-style organizations, was wary of manipulation by politicians or other organizations. As Rev. Tim Benson, first chair of the NVP steering committee, put it:

> We need to keep a distance from the political process. We can't be in anybody's pocket, because as soon as we are we lose our effectiveness as an organization. So we can't be in any political party's pocket, or any politician's pocket, just as we couldn't be in labor's pocket entirely or in management's pocket. You have to be an independent entity. A lot of our strength lies in independence. I don't believe local politicians are allowed to be representatives to the Project. That's one way we have said we have to steer clear of the politics of these towns and this valley.[10]

This didn't mean ignoring the political process. "We intend to influence the political process. We've done that with legislation for example. We make use of our legislators and we are anxious to call on them when we need some help or some clout. The legislative committee did call on a lot of local representatives. When the brass mill [buyout] here was going through we called every state and national representative we could get involved with to help us with that. Maintaining an independence from it but intending to be involved with the political process."[11]

Benson attributed some of the project's success to its independence: "If you just become a support group for the union you can make their picket lines longer, but you can never sit down at a table and pull together all the interested parties in a buyout effort and be a factor that can help bring off something like the Bridgeport Brass buyout. Independence from any of the competing factors is important, staying out of the pocket of labor, of management, of various political parties. You have to establish your own identity."[12]

A central goal of IAF-style organizing is not simply to initiate a protest or win a battle but rather to build an ongoing organization. The NVP's efforts were seen from the beginning as means to that end. Each relationship built, each training or action experience, was selected and developed as an element of and a step toward the creation of the NVP. The question "Does it help build the organization?" provided a constant criterion for selecting activities.

The NVP fitted the pattern of what is known in the trade as "institution-based organizing." Like IAF efforts, it started by forming a sponsoring committee of important local institutions. Such institutional backing also provided legitimacy and protection against charges of being "outside agitators." This institution-based strategy contrasted with most previous community organizing in the valley, which had focused either on neighborhood organizing of the previously unorganized or on addressing the political arena.

Institutions are complex creatures with multiple levels and their own internal tensions. Planning for the NVP began with staff people at the state and regional levels. They brought in higher-level officials in their own institutions and ensured at least tacit toleration if not active support from the top. At the same time, they encouraged Galdston to make direct contact with their local leaders in the valley. The initial sponsoring committee of state and regional organizations was designed to be a sort of temporary holding company that would eventually allow a redistribution of power downward to a valley-based steering committee and ultimately to a democratic organization based on local churches, unions, and community groups.

Such an institutional strategy has to reckon with institutions' common preoccupation with self-protection. Institution-based organizing sometimes requires challenging institutions and their leaders to act in accord with their justifying missions, not just their institutional interests. Galdston defined this as "getting institutions to do their job" and treated it as a necessary dimension of institution-based organizing. Fred Perella's work to win support from the Catholic archbishop of Hartford, and Bishop Rosazza's to win support of Naugatuck Valley parish priests, illustrates how organizing can challenge institutions to move beyond their established approaches.

Ken Galdston exemplified Alinsky's concept of the "professional organizer." In the IAF model, organizers are paid staff members, clearly distinguished from the organization's elected leaders, who serve as volunteers. (This contrasts with the usual trade union practice, in which the top paid positions are filled by elected officials.) Organizers are typically skilled and experienced "outsiders" who work in a community for a few months or years and then move on. They may play a major role in initiating an organization, but they are ultimately accountable to its elected leaders or, initially, to the sponsoring committee. The NVP took this role structure for granted from the start. In Tim Benson's view, "A group like this would be impossible to function without staff. There's a lot to do to make this happen."[13]

Breaking the Alinsky Mold

Although the NVP took off from the IAF model, it also deviated from that model in many ways, at times directly violating some crucial Alinsky dicta. The IAF tradition puts great emphasis on having issues and concerns percolate up from the community. Alinsky's first commandment might be expressed as "Find out what community members are concerned about and organize around that." Although Galdston's intensive interviewing helped guide the specifics of the NVP's development, the basic intention to organize around plant closings was determined before he conducted his first interview in the valley.

The IAF approach generally led its organizations to focus on very localized issues: putting up a streetlight or tearing down an abandoned house. The NVP from its inception set out to challenge basic economic relationships—the power of large corporations over the community's economy. Galdston saw that as requiring a different kind of organizing strategy:

> It was pretty clear that we had to come in at a pretty high level; we weren't going to start with stop sign fights and build up over five years to a powerful

organization that could take on National Distillers. It wasn't just that we didn't have the time. People really do tend to get stuck at some level. You may have the best little organization that you ever wanted to create, to defend its turf, its twenty or thirty or forty square blocks, but, unless that closing was going to happen right in their back yard, it was going to be tougher for them to have the imagination or the desire to stretch, take on something bigger.[14]

A central strategic decision was to base the NVP on a coalition or alliance of different kinds of organizations, rather than either the primarily parish-based organizing that marked contemporary IAF projects or the various types of co-alitions stimulated and largely controlled by organized labor. This meant that no single organization or type of organization would dominate the project. It also provided "cover" for supporters in different organizations. Fred Perella noted soon after the start of the project, for example, that "the continued support of the Archdiocese . . . is key to the social credibility and leadership of this Project, particularly with the labor unions."[15] Initial interviewing identified leaders who were willing to work within such a context. It also made the organizer aware of where potential conflicts among such groups might be. Many actions, whatever their direct purpose, had as "secondary gains" the drawing together of people across existing institutional lines.

Galdston was particularly interested in individuals who represented previous connections among different groups. An important role was played by Helen Johnson, for example, who was a retired local UAW leader and a current leader in the CCAG. Retired UAW international representative John Mankowski had worked closely with the Catholic Church's Diocesan Labor Institute in the 1940s and 1950s in opposing left-wing influence in the local labor movement. Galdston saw these preexisting relationships as a major source of the project's initial success:

One of the wonderful things about this project has been the interactions among the key players of institutions that were already there. There's a lot of this stuff that you might normally spend months on and never develop. You had UAW, CCAG who had already been working on things like [the progressive electoral coalition] LEAP for a while. CCAG and the Archdiocese had a connection because CCAG had gotten Campaign for Human Development money. So Fred Perella knew Miles Rapoport. The Catholic Church and the Episcopal Church knew each other, of course, and they worked on things together. See, you've got these sets of relations that are already in place, but nobody has ever brought them all together yet. And that's part of what is exciting about this.[16]

Such a coalition involved delicate decisions about who to include or exclude and on what basis. From the outset, the NVP was defined as a "nonpolitical" effort in which people would be welcome regardless of party affiliation. Although the CCAG was an important part of the coalition, the NVP was careful not to identify itself with the self-defined "progressive community" in the valley. (One CCAG staffer recalls Ken Galdston calmly working away in his office on NVP business as the entire Waterbury progressive community rushed around him in a massive election-eve voter-turnout effort for a key local progressive candidate.) Inclusion of both the Catholic Church and abortion rights advocates ensured that the abortion issue would have no place in the NVP.

Traditional organizing, whether of workers, neighborhoods, or tenants, generally starts with a clear constituency—the employees of a company or the residents of a community or building, for example. And it generally has clearly defined opponents—the employer, city government, or a bad landlord. Specific grievances create an obvious common interest and a clear basis for demands. The "sides" in deindustrialization were less immediately evident.

The NVP responded in part by developing a strategy that united the intense energies of those directly affected with a broad though less intense mobilization of support in the wider community. From its first efforts at the GTC, the NVP developed a policy of addressing any issue by first going to the group most directly affected—in the case of a threatened factory closing, the unions representing the workers. It next tried to create some kind of working relationship with white-collar employees and local community leaders. If necessary, it then tried to draw in support from the entire valley or beyond. This required combining an appeal to strong direct self-interest with broader appeals to community solidarity and other values. This became easier as time went on and a sense of common interests and patterns of mutual support were already in place.

Traditional community organizing was based either in particular neighborhoods or in defined political jurisdictions, usually a particular city. The NVP was conceived from the beginning as a regional organization. Historically, the Naugatuck Valley had been an integrated economic region linked by railroads and an intense interdependence among industries. But there were few valleywide political or other institutions that might serve as a focus for action, and town identification—as throughout Connecticut—was strong. This had one advantage: the region as a whole constituted social "turf" that few existing groups laid claim to. But it made a tough organizing problem. Galdston initially raised the possibility of focusing just on the upper or lower valley, but the decision was made to include the valley as a whole.

In practice, this was dealt with by focusing at the start on some of the smaller towns where the direct impact of a plant or college closing was evident to all.[17]

Indeed, the project was well established in Torrington, Thomaston, and the Derby-Ansonia area months before it was in the city of Waterbury and before the first major valleywide meeting was held. Rev. Tim Benson noted, "You need to have an area like the Valley that has some historical or geographical connectedness, and we have both. It's a difficult group to pull together because it is a large geographical area. It's difficult, but it's working."[18]

Although Alinsky spoke in general terms about the importance of democratic values, he was well known for his scorn toward anything he considered political ideology or belief that change could be made by appeals to conscience rather than self-interest. Over the decades, the IAF has somewhat changed its approach, increasingly emphasizing the important role of values in community organizing. But the NVP developed if not a full-blown ideology, then at least an explicit interpretation of the valley's history, an elaborated analysis of the forces that were causing plant closings, and an articulated alternative emphasizing broad-based democratic ownership of local economic resources. This approach grew out of a combination of localist sentiment and the realities of what had happened in the valley. The project, as Galdston put it at the first valleywide NVP meeting, is "reacting to something that other people have been doing to us, which is taking ownership of these places away. We've got to try to get some of it back. It's about organizing to bring back the ownership where it makes sense to a broad-based local ownership; by broad-based ownership, we mean, typically, employee ownership."[19]

Some such articulated viewpoint was probably essential to counter the valley's prevailing blame-the-workers mentality, which would have rendered most collective action pointless. At the same time, the emphasis placed on local versus nonlocal ownership gave this perspective a localist rather than an anticapitalist thrust, making it less vulnerable to the valley's endemic red-baiting. Indeed, according to Rev. Tim Benson, the NVP's approach "seems to be an affirmation of capitalism. The nice thing about it from my perspective is that it puts people in control of their lives. When you have remote ownership, people feel really out of control of their lives. When somebody in London or Los Angeles owns a mill in the Valley, you feel helpless and out of control. It's a source of depression and anxiety," he noted. "When you are in charge of your life by being a member of a democratically owned company like this, you're going to feel less anxiety than you would if somebody in Los Angeles is pulling the strings."[20] From Benson's point of view, the goal of local ownership was not radical change but stability:

> One of my motives for being involved in this whole thing is trying to restore stability and maintain a sense of community around here. One of the nice things about the Valley is it's a stable community. People tend to be here generations

on end. I want to do what I can to help make that possible. I see local ownership as being a very stable form of ownership because factors that are going to
influence the sale of this company are not going to be trends on Wall Street.
And if the company has a bad year and only makes a two percent profit instead
of a ten percent profit, there's not going to be a lot of motivation to liquidate
it because the owners, who are the employees, still want a job. If they're turning a two percent profit they're still making a profit, and that's good enough,
and they'll hope for better times next year. If you're owned by someone in Los
Angeles, you just want to unload it, liquidate it, you don't care as long as you
turn a profit. One of my hopes about employee ownership is that it will lend
more stability to people's lives, because that's crucial: stability and control, those
are the crucial factors.

The church ends up dealing with a lot of the refuse of economic turmoil:
unemployed people, people who are laid off. We in the churches are running
food banks, emergency shelters, and what have you to get these people by until
they get settled again. I'd rather give them a steady job than have to keep dealing
with these situations.[21]

Emerging trends in Catholic social doctrine also contributed to the NVP's
home-grown ideology. Requesting support for the NVP from Archbishop
John Whealon of Hartford, Fred Perella wrote:

In re-reading John Paul II's encyclical "On Human Work," I noted again how
important the question of ownership of the means of production is in the Pope's
vision. He notes in section 14 that all property has as its first principle a common
or social end. The use and disposal of capital cannot be chiefly for the end of
production or return on investment, but for the development of enabling work
for people. Yet the analysis of the disinvestment of the Naugatuck Valley shows
that national and trans-national corporations are buying, selling, milking and
closing mills with little local input or regard for the social fabric and human
lives around them. Production is primarily seen as a function of investment,
and employment as only a means to the end of production.

Local ownership options, and the education of labor, church and other leaders
are crucial in a practical effort to test the viability of themes in the encyclical.
Now, American models must be found which offer alternative approaches to
the current patterns of economic development.[22]

While the NVP rooted itself in the Naugatuck Valley's working-class communities and identified strongly with the interests of its workers, its localist
ideology and its strong religious orientation blunted the valley's hard edge
of class. The Reverend Benson pointed out that "the churches do help bring
people together in this coalition" because "the people who are in the union
and in management might all go to the same church. You bring both management and labor people in through the churches, so you have a lot of business

people involved in the Project one way or another. There's a common interest that brings us together also. Everybody is against having an empty building where there used to be a factory where two or three hundred people used to work. So we do have a lot of common interests and we do try to focus on those when we can."[23]

Building the Organization

Although the NVP started as a coalition of different forces and institutions, it aimed to be a permanent organization. As Galdston put it, "Most coalitions are organized ad hoc around a specific fight. They may go on to fight again, but one of the reasons that people join them is that there is a lot of energy around the issue and around bringing a diversified set of people together, but you are not necessarily committing yourself to something bigger, or something more permanent." He continued, "The trade off that people hope to get is a lot of action for a relatively little structure. They are excited about that because a lot of times, especially in institutions that are older and have been around for a while, they may be getting a small amount of action for a lot of structure." From the start, the idea was that "we would draw people together around something that was going to be for the long haul, and to have a series of fights. Not just, let's pass some legislation, say. As with the regular coalition there was the sense of some emergency; we were facing a pretty strong wave of closings and sales; there was a sense that this is important to each of us there. With a sense that it might be fun to work with these people that we don't normally work with."[24]

Initially, the NVP was a creature of statewide church and union organizations. But Ken and the sponsoring committee were laying the groundwork for making the NVP a truly valley-based organization. The first valleywide NVP meeting in October 1983 had voted to form an organizing committee with two people from each of the interested institutions that would meet every six weeks.[25] Ken's strategy was to work gradually toward "formalizing the organization." They would hold another valleywide leaders meeting in another half year, then move during the following year or two to establish an organization with formal membership, dues, bylaws, and elected officers.

At the first meeting of the organizing committee, Ken asked what issues people thought were most important and what they most wanted to learn about. A labor group wanted to study early warning signs. Some people from business backgrounds were interested in the possibility of a local ownership development corporation. Some church and community people were just interested in the broad issues of the project.

Soon committees were researching such matters as plant-closing warning signs, local ownership, and local banks. The legislative committee drafted, lobbied for, and helped pass a law to make a state buyout fund more accessible. The local ownership development committee sponsored workshops to encourage retiring small business owners to sell to their employees or other local buyers. An early-warning committee trained workers in local plants about the warning signs of impending plant closings.[26] A banking committee encouraged banks to make loans for buyouts and explored getting unions, churches, and other local institutions to invest in a loan fund.[27]

During 1984 and 1985, an epidemic of plant closings and sell-offs spread through the Naugatuck Valley. Meanwhile, word of the NVP and especially of the developing worker buyout in Seymour spread nearly as fast. The NVP became involved with dozens of threatened companies and developed serious buyout efforts in several of them. In Torrington, at the northern end of the valley, workers at the Torin Company organized with community support and made an offer to buy their spring-making company from the multinational conglomerate owner that was threatening to sell or shut it down. In Waterbury, workers tried to pressure AMF Alcort, maker of the Sunfish sailboat, to sell the company to its employees. In New Milford, to the west, the project organized a study of the feasibility of an employee buyout of the tube mill owned by Waterbury's Century Brass. In Ansonia, in the south of the valley, the project pressured Emhart to sell its Farrell factory to a company that would provide manufacturing jobs. These efforts led to the development of nascent NVP chapters, each made of organizations in six valley towns. According to the Reverend Benson, "In practice it's a group of people who you can count on to show up for something in each region. That grouping of the Project is the grass roots."[28]

By the summer of 1984, the chapters started electing members to the steering committee. The sponsoring committee began meeting less often and the steering committee more often; as Ken put it, "the steering committee is taking over." Rev. Tim Benson was elected chair; Mike Kearney of the Seymour buyout campaign was elected cochair.

With Galdston increasingly absorbed in the buyout campaigns, the project brought in another experienced organizer, Carol Burkhart, who had worked with Galdston in Buffalo. Galdston recalled that, "In the two years I was in Buffalo, she went from being a local leader to becoming an officer of the citywide organization. She sort of insisted on meeting with me every two weeks for lunch to review my work and her work and was just eager to learn about organizing." She brought experience in parish-based organizing, which

Galdston described as "the other half of what we're trying to do with this project."[29] She began following up on the contacts Ken had initiated and bringing new groups into the NVP.

Burkhart had watched plant closings in Buffalo undermine communities, churches, and her own family.

> Back in 1971, my father had worked over 25 years in the machine shop, and all of a sudden, one day, it was announced it was closing down and moving out. My parents were deaf, so I had to go to bat for him. I went to the union and they were just as helpless as my dad was. And it made me very angry to think that this man had worked all these years thinking he was protected with the union and wasn't protected at all. I ended up going to my Congressman, my Councilman, and fighting to get his pension. He ended up with about $21 a month for the rest of his life which is pretty pathetic.
>
> With that kind of history, and watching my aunts and uncles moving out of town because Westinghouse closed up, when I came to the Valley I was just very inspired by the work that Ken was doing.[30]

Burkhart saw her own contribution as deepening the organization. "When I say deepen it, I mean to get people to look at who they are, why they do what they do in their daily lives, to look at their values as far as home life, church life, union life, job life, to really take a good look at that and to wrestle with it and to be uncomfortable with it." She continued, "I get people telling me that I'm turning them into a bitch and they say that with a laugh. I think they realize that that's not what I'm doing at all. I'm waking up a lot of anger that they already have. And very justifiably so. That they should be angry and they should be awakened to fight these outside giants that have come and ravished their personal lives."[31]

Burkhart made the rounds of organization leaders in the valley, then made presentations on the NVP to their memberships and asked them to join and pay their membership dues. Then she would "sort of agitate people into thinking about what it was that they needed to do in their own church or in their own town." For example, "We got people in St. Vincent Ferrer doing homework on Peter-Paul Cadbury because it was showing signs of changing hands. They said, what can we do? I said, first you've got to find out who Peter-Paul Cadbury really is. That was something they could really take on as a group of people in the parish. They dug out some Dunn and Bradstreet reports and the early history of the company. They even started a study of the candy market."

They decided it was time to meet with the owner, so they took a small delegation to talk to the president of Peter-Paul:

They felt pretty good about the fact that they went in there to talk to these corporate heads on very much the same level, because they knew just about as much as anybody could about their business and about what was going on. They asked very intelligent questions and the president of the company and the vice-president were extremely impressed and also very, very tense. That was neat. It gave the people a sense of power, a sense of "Power is knowledge." And the fact that their church was sort of in the forefront of this, you could see a sort of pride in them. They got a statement and signed letters saying that if there was any change coming down that they would be notified as soon as possible. That's about all that they could do at that point.

Burkhart described the leaders of this effort: "The guy is a mailman, the other lady sold cosmetics. And so, these people were just plain ordinary people who just really cared about what was going on around them."[32]

By the spring of 1985, the organization felt ready to start preparing for its first convention. It formed a convention committee. The committee itself served as a vehicle for organizing and training. Burkhart recalled:

The convention committee was people from all over the Valley coming together, each one working on a fight in their own town. We [made] the convention committee a sort of social thing, as well as a working committee.

In preparing for the Convention, we started to take all their issues and bring them to a forum. This is the first time that these people have ever been organized, so there was a lot of resistance to it. There's a golden rule that Ken and I have now. It's called: Don't do anything for someone that they can do for themselves. There's going to be some day where Ken is going to leave and I'm going to leave and this is their organization and they have to own it. There was that tension there of transferring it from the organizers to their organization and getting them to own that.

As they began to hold each other accountable there was a lot of tension. "Oh, yes, I want to be nice to that guy because they're from Torrington. But, you ask them to do something and they never come through." Teach them to hold that person accountable.

We're brought up in our churches to feel very polite—that we should be very polite to each other and courteous and nice. And that's part of our ethnic background and Christian upbringing. But there is also accountability to each other. We have this tendency to say, yea, Joe is a nice guy, but don't ever ask him to do anything for you because he doesn't do it. Instead of going to Joe and say, "You said you'd do this. Why didn't you do it?"[33]

The committee set an October date for the convention so that issues raised there could impact the elections.[34] The convention would formalize the organization, recognize paid-up member organizations, elect officers, adopt bylaws, vote on issue resolutions, and allow people to "present to each other what they've done and what help they want from each other in the year ahead." It elected officers who included labor, religious, community, and some businesspeople. It endorsed rules and bylaws that "transferred the organization to an organization as opposed to something a lot less formal."[35]

The convention also set dues at a minimum of one hundred dollars, with higher amounts for organizations with more members. Galdston commented, "I think the dues were set low, but there was a choice being made. We could have tried to get an organization of ten or fifteen churches and a half dozen labor unions [with] dues up around two or three thousand dollars. If we were in a single town I might have gone for that. It produces a much deeper type of organization. The amount of dues that can be charged really is a function of how deep do they see their self-interest." The lower dues reflected the reality that, as a valleywide organization, the project was likely to be less intensely involved with the interests of each member organization.[36]

Burkhart recalled the convention: "There were some very influential people there; the head of the UAW region, the Bishop, the Archbishop. Plus hundreds of people from small institutions who were displaying themselves all over the room in what they made. We had a sailboat sail up on the wall and brass products all over the place. They had a little part of themselves literally on the tables."[37]

The convention had fifty-three organizations represented, including twenty-three Catholic churches, eight Protestant churches, a dozen or so labor unions, buyout committees, CCAG chapters, various civic groups, and one Chamber of Commerce. In all, 270 people attended, including the Catholic archbishop and sixteen politicians who were officially recognized. Valley residents testified emotionally to the impact of job loss and plant closing on individuals and the community.

Two conflicts revealed some of the tensions within the NVP coalition and the project's strategies for dealing with them. In the buildup to the convention, Waterbury bakers union head Ron Napoli, who had been involved with the project, tried to bring the Waterbury labor council in as a member. But the Health and Hospital Workers Union 1199 had had bitter experience with Waterbury's Catholic hospital, St. Mary's, which had hired a notorious strikebreaking legal firm to oppose an effort by their workers to unionize. While the statewide leadership of 1199 was generally sympathetic to the NVP, some local leaders did not want the labor council to join an organization in which the Catholic Church was involved.

Napoli organized a meeting with Bishop Rosazza and local 1199 leaders. Leaders of the local said they wanted the NVP bylaws to include support for the right to organize and a statement that the project sought jobs with dignity and fair pay, not just any jobs. A compromise statement was worked out, and the labor council voted unanimously to join.

But the deal was quickly shot down by opponents within the project. Although the NVP was generally prolabor, some people from business backgrounds were leery. More important, some project leaders with strong labor backgrounds resisted what they considered an effort at outside dictation. They argued that the unions should join the project first and then argue their position from within. The labor council thereupon suspended its decision to join. Galdston felt "in between": "It was important for the Project to take a move toward saying that we're not just about jobs, we really are about jobs with dignity and equal fair pay and that recognizing some of the union part of it was important." But "I was real excited that people felt enough ownership of the organization and that it was worth fighting over, that they were going to stick to their guns."[38]

Another conflict arose in the issues portion of the convention when the Connecticut Citizen Action Group introduced a resolution supporting their campaign on utility rates. Vance Taylor of the Torrington Chamber of Commerce opposed it. Although this was virtually the only contested issue in the entire convention, the *Waterbury Republican* headlined it as a split in the NVP. Galdston, temperamentally not averse to conflict, was not upset by the lack of consensus, noting that "normally you'd try to stimulate some fights, and that was as good a one as any." But a high local official in the Catholic Church later made it clear to Galdston that "from his point of view the project was about jobs in a fairly narrow way."[39]

Galdston reflected that as part of the project, the CCAG should be able to bring its issues in and say, "We're your allies on a lot of fights, we give a lot to the Project; we want your support on something else." But because the Project is broad based, "the number of things that people agree on gets narrower." Project activity "grows out of people's perceived self-interest at the time."[40]

Something New

The NVP was unquestionably something new. Although the Naugatuck Valley had a rich tradition of organizing, much of which reemerged within the project, nothing like the NVP itself had ever been attempted. And although many of the project's approaches had come from the traditions of community organizing and from the experience of efforts to respond to plant closings in Youngstown, Pittsburgh, and elsewhere in the Rust Belt, it was different from any of these predecessors.

When something new appears, it is always tempting to define the cause as a single individual—the so-called great-man theory of history. Alternatively, one can look for "objective historical forces" that made the result inevitable, notwithstanding what particular individuals were present. The cause in this case must be sought primarily in the close fit between the historical conditions in the valley and the organizing strategy developed for the NVP.

Superficially, it might appear that a brilliant organizer appeared with a plan that allowed people to do what they were unable to do before. Ken Galdston was and is without question a brilliant organizer. But he does not at all fit the image of a charismatic leader riding in on a white horse that people follow in a spirit of worship. Both his personality and his view of the organizer's role lead him to function more as a coach and teacher of local leaders than as one who "gives the word" to a group of followers or accumulates his own power and authority.

Galdston's philosophy of organizing the NVP emphasized the constant downward recycling of capacity and initiative: "When we say we're developing people, we see the ultimate goal and role for folks as leader/organizers, which means you've got to organize. We're not interested in just saying we're going to help you become the best speaker or the best negotiator you can become. That's nice, but the constant emphasis is, we want you to develop your own base and your own institution. So we really are pushing people to go back into their organizations or to bring in new organizations. We're as strong as our collective team of leaders' relationships with their own base."[41]

Leadership development was seen as an ongoing process. As early as 1986, a draft of long-range goals was calling for "self-renewing leadership" with a "succession of leaders throughout the Project." It proposed "working with leaders to help them move up through increasingly responsible positions in the organization." It called for "formal training" in several parishes; "self-conscious evaluation of actions, meetings, conventions, staff, etc."; and "self-conscious planning—strategic and short-term."[42]

Galdston saw his own role as defined by the needs of the community he was working in:

> I'm a gardener. We're in the Valley, we're building a Valley organization with the folks that are here, and whatever we develop needs to grow out of their experience and who they are. My role is to challenge them, and part of challenging them, part of the specific steps or strategies that I can challenge them on, grows out of my knowledge that comes in part from outside. In terms of

long-term strategy and immediate tactics that come from organizing and from what I know about what's going on in other parts of the country. I will bring ideas and resources in from outside, say through ICA. On the other hand, it really needs to be something that grows from out of here.[43]

Galdston promoted interaction between the somewhat insular world of the valley and the world outside in other ways as well:

Leaders from the Project go out and give talks elsewhere. They get responses back. They read about themselves and their work in publications. There's a *Boston Globe* article last week by [Robert] Kutner about Seymour Specialty Wire that mentioned the Project. We distribute that at executive council meetings. People can see what other people think of their work. It's important for people to have the benefit of seeing the outside world hold a mirror to them. Kutner's phrase is, projects like Seymour are important in the development of democratic institutions. He's absolutely right from my point of view, and while that's maybe a little bit high flown for some people—that's not why you initially get people into your organization—I think it's an important thing for people to reflect on.[44]

At the core of Galdston's success was his ability to identify forces in the situation that could be brought together to cooperate—and to ward off forces that might potentially disrupt their convergence. His "plan" worked because he had already adapted it to the needs and state of mind of the other potential players. Rev. Tim Benson observed, "It is incredible how the Project has grown in three years from nothing to a group with fifty member groups, two full time staff people, a budget of 90 thousand dollars." In his view, "It mostly comes about because people see that the project is actually doing something. There's a lot of conscious organization building going on, but on the other hand I think people are basically attracted to it because they have perceived the same problems that the Project has and they have seen the Project successfully doing something about it, so they are very ready to jump on board."[45]

"Organizing" created a vehicle through which people in the Naugatuck Valley could begin to challenge the sources of their powerlessness. It allowed people to identify and construct common interests. It provided them a way to develop strategies that utilized what power they had. It let them use their pooled power and capacity to demand accountability from corporations, governments, and other powerful actors. Their power was limited, but by organizing, the valley's people could make the most of it.

5. Century Brass

The Scovill Manufacturing Company was the Naugatuck Valley's first brass company, tracing its roots back to 1802. At its peak in World War I, it employed fifteen thousand workers. By 1975, it was Waterbury's last integrated brass facility, employing about two thousand workers.

Scovill workers had tried to organize since the 1890s, but unions became a permanent force only in 1952, when the Scovill UAW local, with only a few hundred paid-up members, challenged the company in a four-month strike that became a general community struggle. It resulted in the consolidation of a union whose power and militancy tapered off only gradually over the following two decades.

In the early 1950s, Scovill built one of the most modern brass production facilities in the country. Thereafter, however, it allowed its brass plants to deteriorate, with little new investment. It used its profits to buy up other companies like Hamilton Beach and NuTone, becoming a multinational miniconglomerate. In 1975, Scovill president Malcolm Baldridge decided to close or sell the company's aging brass operations, keeping only a modernistic world headquarters building on the outskirts of Waterbury as a memento of its historic ties to the area.

The Scovill brass complex was valued at eighty million dollars. But no buyer seemed eager to take on its very substantial unfunded pension liabilities. Hence, a rather peculiar deal was worked out to purchase the Scovill brass division. The principal purchaser was Charles Rubenstein, a scrap-metal dealer who was one of Scovill's suppliers. People long involved with Scovill served on the board of directors of the new company. Under considerable pressure to "save" the business, the Connecticut Development Authority agreed to guarantee a loan of ten million dollars for the purchasers of the mill. The investors in the new company acquired the Scovill brass operation for a mere two million in cash.

Scovill's decision to unload its brass operation posed the union a dilemma. The purchasers insisted that, before the deal was closed, workers would have to accept a three-year wage freeze. UAW representative Mike Vernovai recalled, "The [state] Labor Commissioner came in and sat down with us. He said, these guys are going to move; once they go, the plant's gone. The company's going to shut down." The local union committee voted that night eleven to five to reject the wage-freeze offer. But the next morning someone told Vernovai, "Hey, I see you settled the Scovill thing." He called the local union president who told him, "Yes, we had a meeting this morning in the mayor's office." At the secret meeting—attended not only by the mayor but also by Governor Ella Grasso—the local president had promised to accept the offer. After three months' delay the union had a ratification meeting and voted to approve the deal.[1] One union member recalled, "We accepted the freeze. It went that way because the thinking was: These guys are willing to give us work. Let's take a chance. Let's go along with them and see if they can turn the place around. We believed he was a knight on a white horse."[2]

The mills reopened as Century Brass. But the union remained bitterly divided. An active opposition group opposed the original settlement and continued to challenge the local leadership at every turn, once going so far as to lead a four-day wildcat strike and conduct a sit-in at union headquarters to protest union acceptance of company work rules.

The long decline continued. Between 1976 and 1981, the Century workforce was cut from two thousand to fifteen hundred. In 1981, the company announced it would close unless workers accepted cutbacks in benefits, including abandonment of the pension plan, one of the signal gains of the 1952 strike. Workers struck for four days, then accepted another wage freeze.

In 1984, opponents of further concessions won important leadership positions in the local. Then workers voted down a proposed three-year contract and struck for a week. Governor William O'Neill intervened, strikers returned to work, and a contract with a wage freeze followed by a modest wage increase was finally accepted.

In March 1985, barely a half year later, Century Brass officials announced after a meeting with one of their creditors that they would close the company unless workers accepted $4.8 million in wage and benefit concessions over the coming year. An emotional union meeting, addressed by Century president Lewis Segal, voted two-to-one to reject the concessions.

Two days after workers rejected concessions, the company started laying workers off, and its officials asserted the entire operation would be closed before the spring was out. The union continued divided: a minority within the local, spearheaded by the previous leadership, urged acceptance of the take backs and pushed for reconsideration of their rejection.

As the company started to shut down, I heard reporters assigned to the Century story and others unfamiliar with the local labor scene repeatedly expressing amazement that workers would vote to eliminate their own jobs. I saw a young man stick his head out of a car window passing the Century plant gate and holler, "Hey, you Century workers, you're a bunch of suckers: you let the union lose you your jobs."

Workers' reasons for rejecting the concessions, however, were articulated clearly. They hated working in freezing temperatures in the winter, with fumes blown around by inadequate ventilating fans in the summer, with broken toilets, and with inadequate cleaning and maintenance of the plant. The company seemed bound to fail sooner or later, so sacrificing to keep it open provided little future security. Although unemployment in the Naugatuck Valley was high, jobs were plentiful in the rest of the state; many workers figured that if they were ever to escape from Century, this was as good a time as any to make the move. Many workers felt they had been subsidizing the company for years already by working at substandard wages. They distrusted the company's claims of poverty; as one worker put it, "For a place to continue to work, big shots to continue to make $232,000 in a year and then cry poor, continue to run a place and not fund a pension is obscene."[3] Some wondered whether the concessions demanded of them were to keep the plant open or rather to pursue an unspecified "acquisition opportunity" that company president Lewis Segal had recently described as a reason for optimism about Century.

Down the Tube

As the Seymour Specialty Wire buyout moved toward completion, Ken Galdston began looking ahead to the founding NVP convention. But there was a problem: "We were working actively in Ansonia-Derby and Seymour and Torrington and Thomaston. I'm thinking if we're ever going to build this thing, we've got to get a base in Waterbury. It's almost half the people."[4] He had made individual contacts with Waterbury clergy, union leaders, and community activists, but the project had no real activities there.

Century Brass was the largest remaining brass mill in the city, and its UAW Local 1604 had just elected Attilio D'Agostino as its new president. D'Agostino had immigrated from Italy in 1966 and gone to work at Century.

Described by the *Hartford Courant* as a "fiery chief," he spoke with unrefined English and a feisty, unpolished manner that seemed to fit his given name. He compared company officials to a pack of sharks: "Once they sense blood they come back for more, just like a white shark in the ocean."[5] In October 1984, Galdston took a half-dozen NVP activists to meet with him. As they met, it was announced that Century was putting its tube mill in New Milford, a few miles to the west, up for sale. The Century union leaders asked the NVP if they would work with them on it.[6]

The professional team that had worked on setting up SSW—Ken Galdston from the NVP; Roland Cline from the ICA; Paul McAlenney from Day, Berry, and Howard; and John Schuyler from Deloitte, Touche—visited the plant. Galdston made presentations first to the union committee at the New Milford plant, then to a meeting of the union membership, and finally to the white-collar workers, which each enthusiastically approved the exploration of a buyout. Next came a joint meeting of all employees. They structured a steering committee, set up an elections committee, printed ballots, and elected delegates. Individual workers contributed money for a buyout study, joined by the town and the state. "We'd learned some from Seymour about how to do the internal stuff," Galdston believed. "Unlike Seymour we got employees on sub-committees studying production, coming up with all sorts of ideas to cut costs."[7]

The New Milford mill made huge tubes for everything from steam genera-tors to nuclear submarines to solar energy, using brass from the Century plant in Waterbury. If they became an independent company, where would they get their brass? The preliminary feasibility study indicated that even if they could get the business for nothing, they still could not make a go of it as an independent company: there was no place they could get the stock cheaply enough to compete. Unless they could buy the place as part of a buyout of the whole Century Metals Division, they might as well suspend the buyout study. Galdston recalled:

> We had this pretty painful experience of having meetings where we explained to them why it wouldn't work. They kept coming back with ways to save other costs. These folks knew better than we did what was going to happen if they lost their jobs. It was really a pretty bitter experience to go in and tell them that they should go out and start looking for jobs. I ran into one of the union leaders nine months later and he said sixty percent of the people still didn't have jobs; of the forty percent who did, a number were working, as he was, in gas stations and things like that. People in their fifties who had years of experience and skill were just going out and getting nothing.[8]

Buyout?

After closing the tube mill, Century Brass announced that it wanted new concessions from the union to keep its Metals Division in Waterbury open. Galdston recalls that the announcement presented a problem for the project: "Here we are in Waterbury with the largest manufacturing operation threatening to shut down and here's this Project: What are you going to do about that, or are you just about buy-outs? It was hard to figure out exactly what the handle was." He met with the union leadership and offered to help push the company for more time. "I said to them, Who is really the target? Perhaps it is General Electric Credit Corporation. They made a much better target: They really controlled things to a great degree, they were much more visible, much more public. I thought strategically it made a lot of sense. The union leadership wanted to continue to fight back and forth with the company."[9] The NVP began to push for more time. In one day it gathered signatures from eighty or so pastors, union presidents, and community organization presidents for a telegram asking the managers to give the workers more time—NVP leader Father Thomas Dwyer got twenty-five signatures just from Catholic priests in Waterbury.

Century president Lewis Segal addressed a union meeting to argue for the new concessions, but the workers voted them down. One worker recalled, "What was told to us by Segal was that he had to have $2.5 million cuts or he was going to close the mills. And he told us that General Products could not continue longer than two or three months because now it would be bearing all the costs of everything and we couldn't bear that cost. So we would go under. So when we said: NO MORE CUTS, we fully expected to be out of work in two or three months." Thus resigned to their fate, "we all decided that we'd had enough. Nine years was enough of cuts and enough of promises and enough of everything going into a few pockets." (Galdston was allowed to attend the meeting and was outraged both by management's attempts at manipulation and at anti-Semitic remarks about Segal and other managers—"Send these Jews back to Israel" or "Send them to Germany"—he heard in the back of the room.)[10]

A few days after announcing it would close, Century instead filed for protection from its creditors under Chapter 11 of the bankruptcy law, which held off the creditors while allowing business to continue. Officials maintained that its general products and ordinance divisions were still profitable. Waterbury mayor Edward Bergin offered to seek a deferment of $2.5 million in tax liabilities to keep Century open.

The NVP set up a meeting for all the employees and gave a presentation at the Scovill recreation hall on the possibility of an employee buyout to about 170 blue-collar workers. Carol Burkhart recalled:

> At that point we only had Attilio D'Agostino that we were dealing with. And we didn't know of any other real leaders inside the union that we wanted to develop and bring into the Project. So I was standing in the back of the hall, and I was looking around, and Ken had finished his presentation about what it's like to do a buyout. He said now we'll take a break for five minutes. All of a sudden this swarm of people got up in a pack and they moved all over to the right-hand side of the hall, and they were talking to Theresa. And she was sitting there. It was like they were standing in line, single file, waiting to talk to her, like she was some pastor. I was astounded. For ten minutes this was going on. Attilio called the meeting back to order. I ran over to Ken and said, I know who the next leader of the Naugatuck Valley Project is going to be in this union. Take a look. Sure enough, she was the leader, because everybody was going over to talk to her about whether or not she thought it was a good idea to do a buyout.[11]

"Theresa" was Theresa Francis. She later recalled that she had just gone to the meeting to see what was going on. When they set up a steering committee for the buyout exploration and no one volunteered to head it, Attilio D'Agostino proposed her. She later commented wryly, "Oh, yeah, Theresa. Get the other guy!"[12]

Theresa Francis almost immediately became a key leader in the NVP and part of the heart and soul of the organization. Ken Galdston observed:

> There's a phrase that sometimes you hear among organizers that it's very important to look at people and see them with two eyes: one is as they are, one is as they could become. What I really felt with Theresa was that the two eyes had to do with actually discovering what she already was. Which I found, especially in the first few months—I was constantly underestimating who this person was. She amazed me at every bend in the road. For one thing, she took very seriously commitments, and she was very quick to step in when a responsibility had to be taken. So within the first few weeks we started to work with her on Century, as we were getting ready for the convention, she was right in the middle of convention preparations. She sort of took it over. I remember walking into the convention and she had taken the remaining convention posters we had, had gotten somebody on a tall ladder, to plaster the wall on either side of the stage with all of these posters. It was just her taking over and making this happen.[13]

I went to interview Theresa Francis in her ramshackle house in the heart of Waterbury's predominantly Lithuanian Brooklyn section. She told me that she grew up in Brooklyn, but that her family was French Canadian and Irish.

> I went to school at St. Joseph's, at a Catholic school, got involved with the choir. I love singing. Most of my volunteer work so far has been church-related. So this is probably the first time I'm getting outside that experience and into something that is much broader that takes in everything: your work relation, your social clubs, government now. I'm one of the Georges. I was perfectly content to work, come home and take care of my husband and my three children. We both worked. We put three children through school. Our oldest is a doctor. So much of our finances went into education for our children. While they were young I was very involved in being a mother. Now they are all grown up, that leaves me a lot more time to look at the broader picture.[14]

In 1963 her children started going to school for a full day and she started working at Scovill. "I was a piece worker. For many years I was lead girl on automatic switches. I trained people doing burring work for nine or ten years or better. My drive has always been to make sure they get a fair shake and the possibility to make money on piece work because that's where I came from."[15]

More recently, she had worked as a quality control inspector. "I like being responsible for what's going on in a room. I like keeping track of quality—making sure the things are good. I've always worked well with the foremen and the foremen I've got now—the two of them are wonderful. I'm in a position where it could be a lot of trouble for them—where they'd have to come down on me. I don't think they have a question that I'll do anything I can to keep that place going, to help people that are working, and put in my day's work."[16]

Theresa went to union meetings on important decisions but otherwise was not active until she moved to a new part of the plant. "There were a lot of problems. Little deals going on. If they liked the way your hair looked, if they liked the color of your eyes. I could see that sometimes the contract wasn't being enforced. Now I don't believe that, if you're in the union, no matter what you do you're right. But I could see things that weren't being taken care of. I ran for room steward and I got in."[17]

Late in the interview I asked Theresa to reflect on things in her life that might have made her get so involved with something like the NVP. "I didn't want to be the prettiest or the richest. The story that got me was Solomon. I wanted to be like Solomon. The story about the baby—each one claimed it. He said, OK, cut the baby in half. From the time I was a little kid, I wanted to care about people and to understand." Her outlook showed itself in relation to her family:

They used to kid and say that I was like a mother bear with her cubs. Don't
go near them. They were right. You try to mess with my kids or my husband:
Look out! That's the kind of person I am. Everything won't be put away in the
bureau drawer; things are fairly in place but I didn't worry about the house.
Didn't worry about possessions as much as some people.

When I got older, I kind of enlarged my outlook to include everybody in my
church and all my friends. Then when I went to work, it was included to that
group and then, that feeling that people are more important than possessions
kind of grew to include everybody.[18]

It rapidly grew to include the NVP.

Local and state officials agonized over what to do about Century. There was
some recognition that the company was created by public funding, and
therefore had special responsibilities to the public. Edward Stockton, who
had been state economic development commissioner when Connecticut
guaranteed the loan with which Century was started, said, "I don't think
Charles Rubenstein or the president of the union have got the right to close
the doors of Century Brass."[19]

Yet most information about the company was inaccessible to the public.
The public was refused all access to Century's reports to the State Development Authority, and those reports were so incomplete that they did not even
show management salaries. When I found myself on a television interview
show with the head of the state Department of Economic Development, I
challenged him regarding government oversight of Century; he replied that
the state did not gather information on company policy or conditions beyond its regular financial reports. To address this problem, Mayor Edward
Bergin and State Representative William Scully sought public disclosure of
all Century Brass finances.

The UAW, using the NVP as an intermediary, asked to purchase the entire
company. Century officials said they were not interested at this time. Nonetheless, UAW Local 1604 established a steering committee and started to
conduct a feasibility study for an employee buyout with the ICA. The state
and city put in ten thousand dollars each. According to Theresa Francis, who
headed the steering committee, "We were to raise $10,000. By this time, a lot
of people in the shop were so turned off because they didn't get their vaca-
tion pays and their benefits had been cut and the wholesale laying off—it
was like they were whipped, beaten. 550 people—about half the workforce—
were left, and out of that 550 about 250 or a little better gave us $20 apiece
towards the study."[20]

The study ran into several difficulties, according to Francis:

The company blocked any attempt by us to look at the appraisal. They would not allow ICA to go talk to the customers to find out what kind of market was out there. There were no management people in on the steering committee and with good reason. An engineer had opened his mouth and had been fired. And all it took was them to fire one person in upper management that was liked by all for opening his mouth against some of the company's practices and everybody got the message: Management cannot open their mouths, because it means their jobs.[21]

The feasibility study tried to find ways to fix some of Century's management failures. For example, "We've got a department right now that has two production workers and two foremen. You cannot exist that way."[22]

Initially, a buyout looked feasible if the sales projections were right. But by May 1985, sales were down. At that point, according to Ken Galdston, "It was clear that the answer was not an employee buyout but a sale to someone who would make a commitment to keep the business there, to take losses of a couple of million dollars for a couple of years, and to reinvest."[23] In December, the buyout study was put on hold.

Stop Milking Century

In February 1986, union and company stopped talking with each other. Leaders of the Waterbury Progressive Coalition and the CCAG wanted to put a picket line around Century. Ken Galdston did not encourage this approach, and the NVP was criticized for being insufficiently militant.[24]

The NVP developed an alternative strategy based on two points. First, research by the project and investigating journalists had turned up considerable evidence that Century managers had been milking the company for their private benefit. Second, the state was beginning to talk about putting money into the Century complex. The assumption was that the mills were going, but the real estate was valuable. The NVP decided to raise a question: why should the state bail out owners who had used public investment to loot the company? A score of people from the NVP plus State Representative Norma Capoletti met with state economic development commissioner Carson and asked him to agree that the state would not put more public money into Century until the managers' management was reviewed by the bankruptcy court.

Further, the buyout steering committee decided to hold a public meeting in April to present the case against Century's managers. The theme was "Stop Milking Century." Rev. Campbell Lovett recalls, "Theresa Francis called me

and said, 'We are having this big community meeting at Sacred Heart High
School Gym. We're going to have Father Dwyer give the invocation; Father
Coleman is going to give the Benediction; would you be willing to chair?' I
said, 'Theresa, that would be great. I'd love to. I know how to facilitate that.
That's very easy.' We had our preparatory meetings. It was very important to
stick very tightly to the agenda; there were some of the dynamics that Attilio
might want to take over and lambaste everyone."[25]

Theresa Francis carefully drew up a fact sheet based on the available research and gave a presentation on the company. She recalled:

> There are times in your life when you have to stand up and be counted. That's
> not the way I was raised. I was raised to be a good Catholic girl and respect
> everybody, respect my elders and respect our officials and the mayor and your
> representative.
>
> Here's this company sinking, and we printed the salaries of the president,
> the vice president, who had gotten interest-free loans, and where the money
> had gone. That was not my nature, not the way I was brought up. And we did
> a power analysis: I did a power analysis, put up on the board who sold it, what
> they made out of it, and it was the scariest thing I'd ever done in my life, because
> we had the mayor there and the aldermen, and some of our top company of-
> ficials, and we were naming names.[26]

"Theresa does her power analysis, linking all—the Malcolm Baldridges, sale
of the company below rate to get out of it, using the pension fund money: It
was an eye-opener," the Reverend Lovett recalled. "You could see the politicians squirming."[27]

Francis said, "The reaction I got from some people at the shop is, 'Oh my
God, you're going to get fired!'" But others said, "That's it, kid, tell 'em. It's
about time it came out." In the broader community, reaction to the NVP's
Century initiative was mixed, Francis remembered. "I've had a gentleman
who goes to my church come up and say to me, 'why are you doing this, why
are you fighting Century management? Why are you going up to Hartford?
The Chamber of Commerce does all that.'" But Campbell Lovett noted, "There
was a lot of animosity toward Century Brass by the community at large. I
would hear people say, 'Hey, we think it's great what you're doing for those
guys. They took this place; they took all the money.' I did get a lot of support from the parish and from the community for being involved with this.
Century Brass had kind of abused a trust of being a supposedly responsible
employer, the last vestige of the last brass mill in the town where all these
folks' parents and grandparents had worked."[28]

The goal of the "Stop Milking Century" meeting was to demand that the mayor agree that no public money would go into Century until there had been a review of management. When the mayor was asked to respond, he said the answer was no. But according to Galdston, "the consequence of the meeting was we got a reaction."[29]

Starting to Talk

One immediate reaction was that Century president Lewis Segal wrote the Reverend Lovett and other clergy involved with the public meeting and asked that they meet with him because, he said, "I believe that you know little or nothing" about the company. The local paper published the letter and noted pointedly, "Segal's invitation to area clergy makes no mention of the union. Also conspicuously lacking mention in the invitation are non-clergy members of the NVP and the NVP itself, including the organization's executive director, Ken Galdston."[30]

The Reverend Lovett was called by local reporters but declined immediate comment.[31] Carol Burkhart told him, "Look, no response, yet. Don't. We still haven't received the letter yet. It was in the paper. This is a divide and conquer strategy. Don't respond . . . This is the NVP. The NVP will set the rules." Theresa Francis explained why this was critical: "Mr. Segal has split that union any place they find a split; they drive a wedge in it and get it bigger and bigger and bigger. He's not going to do that with the NVP because we know that's what the tactics are."[32]

Lovett remembered "an awful day of reading this in the morning, trying to deal with this all day long, wondering what my parishioners were thinking about this. I'd only been here a couple of years at this point, and I was very worried about the ramifications." After waiting most of the day to hear from Ken Galdston, he told a reporter that the clergy would meet with Century management. Lovett recalled that NVP leader Father James Coleman "was not pleased about this response since it was NVP that held the meeting and NVP that should meet with Century." He was relieved to get a call from Ken Galdston that night. "He said, 'Hey, how you doing? You feeling all right?' I really felt that this was a supportive call. He said, 'I realize that you talked with these folks and that's what you said. Well, we can deal with that, and we'll move on.'"[33]

The issue, according to Francis, was that Segal "wanted to determine who from our side would come to the meeting. Our response was, 'This is the Naugatuck Valley Project. We will decide who comes.' We finally got him to say all right."[34]

The NVP delegation met with Lewis Segal and other top Century officials at Mayor Joseph Santopietro's office. Campbell Lovett recalled that the company officials began handing out their cards and saying, "How're you doin'?" "Fine, Mr. Segal." "Aw, no call me Lew. Aw, this is fine." Lovett noted, "We were all best buddies. But we had all done our prepping," and they knew "there's a difference between personal relationships and public relationships." This was not a time for a first-name basis; he remained Mr. Segal. Lovett also remembered, "We started the meeting before Joe Santopietro came in. It was out of my naiveté. I remember him coming after we had set up an agenda. He came in about fifteen minutes later, sat in a corner at the end of the table, and was never a part of the meetings from then on. Ken, afterwards, said, 'Man, that was great. What a power move.' And I said, 'What happened?' I didn't even know what happened. But it cut him out completely from being a key agenda-setter."[35]

More meetings followed, first in the mayor's office, then at Century. As Lovett put it, "It was amazing, going into their boardroom. It was so elegantly furnished, beautiful pictures, and looking at the corporate offices, they were amazing. 'These people are bankrupt? They have tens of thousands of dollars of furnishings here.'"[36]

One day Lovett got a call from Lewis Segal. "He and the vice president wanted to meet with Ken and me as soon as possible. We went to a meeting that day, at which they said, 'How serious are folks about the buyout? How does a buyout work?' I think from that point on there was cooperation from management."[37]

In November 1986, it was announced that Century was up for sale. The employee buyout effort was revived, and in early 1978 elections were held for a joint labor-management steering committee. This time interest was high. There were printed campaign flyers and floor managers for the candidates. A high percentage of workers voted. Five hourly and five salaried workers were elected. Galdston said, "It was exciting to think that in a place so troubled, we might be embarking on something that was bringing people together. Some of it of course was that people were voting because the boat was rocking and they wanted to make sure that they were protecting themselves. It wasn't by any means a joyous outpouring—'we get a say!'—although there was some of that too."[38]

Co-chairs of the steering committee were Theresa Francis from the union and Ray David from management. But the depth of support for the buyout was hard to judge, according to Galdston. "No one could say for sure that the buyout would work, or was even necessarily the answer. The union felt it had to guard its position in case there were other outcomes." A major role was played by the company's director of employee relations, Frank Santaguida, who had been a power both in the union and in Waterbury politics. Santaguida "played a very constructive role in the meetings. My instinct is that he was a dead foe of this thing, or at least at a critical point he became a foe of it, and that at some point Attilio became a foe of it too."[39]

Roland Cline began working on the buyout study again. Mike Kearney from Seymour Specialty Wire worked with the committee—until SSW's company president demanded that he stop helping a potential competitor. A subcommittee on employee equity worked with the NVP banking committee and Connecticut National Bank to come up with an innovative approach to employee equity under which even the poorest employee could become an owner: Roland Cline's figures indicated a worker could become an owner for as little as fifteen dollars a month. Another group analyzed sales. A production and workforce group addressed the necessary but difficult question of reducing employment and came up with about twenty-four jobs that could be cut, mostly salaried people. Conflict arose because the local union president was not on the committee that talked about job cuts; the union maintained that it was really a collective bargaining issue.[40] Meanwhile, Century's labor-management conflict also continued; while money was being raised in the plant for the buyout study, managers would not let D'Agostino into the plant to solicit funds. D'Agostino in turn attacked the managers and, at times, Theresa Francis and other members of the steering committee.[41]

Endgame

By April 1997, the buyout feasibility study looked positive, but not yet conclusive. The steering committee wanted some kind of indication that people wanted the exploration of a buyout to continue. A meeting of union and management employees was called for May 30, 1987. According to Galdston, "Everybody said we need a vote of confidence, we need to know whether they want to go ahead or not."[42]

In all, 172 union people came to the meeting. "There was a big turnout but it certainly wasn't grabbing everybody"—Galdston felt the number should have been 300. The subterranean opposition to the buyout effort became apparent when Galdston saw the ballot question that had been drafted:

> The ballot question should have been, 'based on the progress report I heard at today's meeting, I want the feasibility study to continue and the steering committee to proceed,' yes or no. Instead, it was framed as 'I would be willing to put up x amount of dollars for this company.' Totally wrong, we're not at that

point—nobody can really say what you should be putting up. When I heard, just before the meeting, this is the way it was being developed, I said to Roy David, who was the co-chair with Theresa, I don't believe this, who wrote this? Frank Santaguida wrote it. I said, I think you should get him on the phone and you should put out another ballot. This is going to kill us.[43]

At the meeting, Frank Santaguida spoke. Roland Cline gave a report saying the company could be profitable, if workers invested a certain amount each week out of their paychecks. Attilio D'Agostino said the union could not recommend the buyout. "I explained that the company refused to give the right information. Second, it costs the employees too much—you would have to give up another couple of million dollars in wages or benefits. We already have a low wage. Therefore it was not feasible for us to buy. For example, if I make ten dollars an hour, if I have to give up half of that to buy the company, it's not worth it."[44]

The resolution lost 103 to 121. "So with that," Galdston recalled, "we just said okay, and everybody shook hands and said goodbye."[45] Union and management had cooperated, at least tacitly, to kill the buyout.

Ultimately, the last running remnants of Century Brass were sold to a company called Rostra. The NVP claimed credit for helping save the few remaining jobs. Galdston maintained, "The people who bought it bought it with the help, the knowledge and the perspective on the business gained by two of the key managers, Ray Ford and Joe Formica, who were very active with the buyout effort. I think we justifiably can lay claim to having helped save those jobs." According to Rev. Campbell Lovett, "People said, 'Well, what's the victory that we did get out of that?' The victory was that we helped find a buyer, and got a pledge that they would not move the jobs out of a five or ten mile radius of Waterbury, and that they would not sell the product lines off piece by piece." However, "They have sold one of the product lines off. We went to a meeting to see Ray Ford, the new president. They were selling a product line off to a group in Ohio."[46] Today, what was once the Naugatuck Valley's first brass mill is the site of the Brass Mill Mall.

In a television interview, Theresa Frances was asked if she was bitter. "Bitter? I was really bitter. Terribly bitter. The thing that upset me the most was that people I had known, worked there for forty years, the minute Century went into bankruptcy they lost their life insurance policies and they lost their health premium payments. This was something that had been guaranteed to us through negotiations. They had it in writing on paper. And these very people working right next to me were burnt at the time of the bankruptcy."[47]

Why Century Closed

Century Brass was only one of dozens of plant closings the NVP tried in one way or another to address. More than a dozen of them involved serious investigation of the feasibility of worker buyouts. But it turned out that successful worker buyouts were possible only under unusual conditions. Exploration of a buyout often provided workers and community members a way to be players, but rarely a way to take over the company. Of all the explorations, only Seymour Specialty Wire was consummated.

The closing of Century Brass was a monument to a public policy that subsidizes entrepreneurs ostensibly to save jobs but regards public oversight of those so subsidized as an interference with the free market system. It is possible that Century was part of a "sunset industry" that was bound to go out of business sooner or later. But even then it could have served as an "industrial hospice"; public policy could have ensured that subsidies to the company went to preserving jobs where possible and easing the transition for workers whose jobs could not be saved. Instead, it provided incentives for the owners and managers to milk the company for private gain.

The Century story reflects the difficulty of integrating a narrow definition of class struggle—workers versus their employer—with a broader orientation of local community versus capital. This was reflected in the union leadership's focus on fighting management while the NVP was focused on trying to save the jobs. This was a difference not just of policy but of identity, mentality, and culture.

Indeed, a legacy of conflict, and a no-holds-barred style of conducting it, left little room for mediation. As Rev. Campbell Lovett reflected, "The inner battles of the union, and so many years of mistrust between union and management, just derailed that whole process. A union president who was not endorsed by a lot of the people, who was not trusted, and who seemed to have a separate agenda that was more self-serving than for the promotion and the welfare of that company, and an almost universal mistrust of management."[48]

Galdston tried to put the conflicts into perspective. Part was personal. "Attilio is definitely a hard charging guy. It was virtually impossible for him to imagine, especially with those particular managers, being in a position where he was not free to be very adversarial. I think he is right—at least somebody had to be free to do that. Then the intra-union stuff caused some problems." Part was institutional. "The union would like to seize the opportunity to buy the place if it's feasible. It has a more fundamental obligation to protect its situation in the face of sale to someone else or collapse."[49]

Characteristically, Galdston accepted the inevitability of the conflict, but tried to draw lessons about how it could have been utilized constructively. "One of the things I learned had to do with how much do you mediate, versus what I now think in retrospect is a more appropriate position, which is to say, look you guys, it's your problem. I'm not going to make this buyout work, you want it or you don't, you guys figure it out."[50]

Despite its outcome, the Century struggle was empowering for the NVPers who participated. Campbell Lovett said, "I learned a lot about how much power a group could have to call these five whom I should have considered untouchable executives before, into an office, and watch them squirm. It was a lot of fun. And for them, after awhile, to take us seriously, and say, 'Maybe a collaborative effort, or some sort of buyout, can be a possibility.'" Galdston agreed: "I think the Project came out of it feeling that we had done something, that we were a force in it."[51]

Perhaps the biggest impact of the Century campaign on the NVP was the discovery of Theresa Francis. For many people, she became the embodiment of the spirit of the NVP. As Ken Galdston said at her memorial service years later, "I'm always astounded at the way she could put into words these truths about what we were doing. She lifted it up way above our everyday sights."[52]

When I first went to interview her early in the Century buyout effort, she had prepared for the interview by jotting down some thoughts about what the struggle at Century and the NVP meant (perhaps something the NVP had taught her to do before speaking at a meeting), and she asked me if she could begin by telling them to me:

> When I questioned what happened in Century, people said "There's no corporate conscience." And I say if there's no corporate conscience, it's because we allowed it to be that way. We should not leave our morality captured to one hour in church on Sunday. Morality has to be in our homes and follow us into the workplace or the corporation. When you question something that happened with a company—like how come people are denied the things that they earned—they act like, "Why are you questioning this? You're asking somebody in the government! You're asking somebody in the company! This is a private corporation!" All workers have to realize that we're responsible for our own condition. And if we don't devote some time to our unions or our political party or our church organization, our social groups, the laws being enacted, we'll wake up and find ourselves with empty pension funds, bankrupt companies, disproportionate sacrifices, and a run-down community.
>
> And that's where the Naugatuck Valley Project comes in. They've decided that we shouldn't have a run-down community. If we care what happens in our city, we've got to be banded together for the good of everyone. And the motto

of "Let George do it" has to go. If all the people in the city are banded together to make it a better place to live, then it will be a better place to live. That's what Naugatuck Valley Project is all about. It's a family—it's like a larger family of churches, unions, small businesses, chambers of commerce, all working together to make their community the best place to live and work and to have fun.[53]

She added, "Because I'm chairman of the steering committee for Century, I've been very involved in that. But that could end tomorrow. But I would still have the larger sense of whatever goes on in this community. As the Chapter representative I'm there to help."[54]

The failure of the Century buyout effort illustrated some of the hard realities faced by such efforts to save companies already on the downward plunge. An early manager at Century once told me that he had found records for its predecessor, the Scovill Manufacturing Corporation, showing that every preventive maintenance operation had been performed on schedule like clockwork. For more than a century, the company had reinvested in state-of-the-art technology.

Not so with Century. Its management milked it, undoubtedly drawing far more in salaries, benefits, and purchases from other companies they owned than the pittance with which they had bought the company in the first place. The State of Connecticut poured millions into Century but declined to take any responsibility for nonfeasance or malfeasance on the part of its managers. Workers, civic leaders, and community members wanted Century to survive, but few saw saving it as their responsibility. Neither management nor union saw cooperation to save the company as more salient than the conflict for advantage between them. Behind it all was an industry and a global economy in turmoil that might have doomed even a flawless buyout effort.

6. The Life and Death of Seymour Specialty Wire

Seymour Specialty Wire was widely celebrated as the largest and most democratically structured 100 percent employee-owned industrial buyout in the United States. But from its inception, problems were apparent. For seven years, the company continued to produce and sell specialty brass products, but business difficulties and internal conflicts loomed ever larger. After several years in the red, the company went into bankruptcy. In 1993, its assets were auctioned off for the benefit of its creditors. Its problems were rooted both in the historical legacy of the old company and in the global economic context into which the new company was launched.

Upstairs, Downstairs

The Seymour Manufacturing Company was founded in 1878 by the Matthies family and their associates. Although it was formally a corporation, like most Naugatuck Valley brass companies it remained dominated by individual families well into the twentieth century. Members of the Matthies family served in top management, as well as retaining large blocks of stock, until the company was sold to Bridgeport Brass in 1950.

Initially at the Seymour Manufacturing Company, as throughout American industry, skilled manual workers possessed the crucial knowledge necessary for production and directed much of the production process. In the early 1980s, I was given a vivid picture of earlier days in an interview with three retired workers who collectively had worked at Seymour for more than a hundred years and some of whose fathers had started working there before World War I. Frank Pochron, a retired manager who started at Seymour in

1936, recalled that "years ago they didn't have all this equipment to check out what you were doing. They relied upon the people to do it. Years ago it seemed the operators had the technicalities, were proud of their work and able to do their jobs, what the customer demanded and the shop wanted." But all that began to change as American industrialists tried to redesign the work process to concentrate knowledge and authority in a management cadre whose job was to tell manual workers how to do their work. Pochron described the impact at Seymour: "Now you are directed what to do. It seems the operators wait for management to tell them what to do and if it doesn't come out right, so what?"[1]

To ensure that the deskilled workers would actually work, production standards were set for each job. Sam Kwochka, who started working at Seymour in 1935 and retired in 1979, still recalled that if you met the standards, "you were entitled to stay on till layoff. But if you faltered below a hundred percent, out the door you went."[2]

Workers responded to the restructured work process with a twofold strategy. First, they developed informal shop-floor tactics for controlling the pace of work and resisting management pressure. Retired Seymour worker John Chubat recalled, "They would time me; I would work normal, just like I've always been doing. But when they're not there, instead of shearing it in one or two pieces, I can shear four or five. It's my own ingenuity." This and the many other techniques workers developed to control the pace of work were backed up by norms set by informal work groups. As Sam Kwochka recalled, "They would tell them man-to-man what to expect and what not to exceed."[3]

Along with these informal methods, Seymour workers developed unionism. Seymour Manufacturing was the first company to go out during the great Naugatuck Valley general strike of 1919, probably because Russians and Poles, who were early promoters of the strike, predominated in the Seymour workforce. Union organization was thereafter effectively suppressed from 1920 until World War II. Establishment of the union marked a major shift in power at Seymour. Eddie Labacz, former president of the union at Seymour, recalled, "Once the union won the election, they told the company, 'If you fire anybody, we're all going to walk out.' So the company figured there was no use firing anybody for being active in the union."

Following a pattern typical in the brass industry well into the twentieth century, Seymour's top managers hired foremen who ruled their sections of the mill more or less as personal fiefdoms, with more or less arbitrary power to hire, fire, and command their own workers.[4] The foremen's authority only gradually yielded to a more modern managerial concept in which foremen, at least in theory, implemented policies established by top management and a growing stratum of middle managers. In reality, the authority of this hierarchical chain of command was limited by the extent to which managers at all levels hoarded their knowledge. I remember a young business consultant early in the SSW buyout being astonished and puzzled at the unwillingness of managers to share knowledge and information. Mike Kearney explained their motivation: "A lot of the old timers had everything up in their heads. They don't like that sharing of information because that was their power base. That was their security, too. 'How can they give it to me? I know too much.' Their resistance to [new management systems] was that they would be eliminated on the job. 'Why should I tell this guy that I can do twice as much. If I do that I might not be here next week.'" Managers as well as workers were "looking out for power and security."[5]

If the foremen's baronial authority was eroded from above, it was also undermined from below. The workers' strategy of combining informal resistance and union protection was so effective that management was forced to accommodate. I toured the Seymour plant in the early 1980s and was struck by the easy pace of work and the relaxed atmosphere. A worker who started at Seymour in 1983 noted: "There was always that laid-back attitude on the part of the foremen. One reason was the union. The foremen never could exercise their authority. Maybe because in the past they had gone to the extreme with it. The foremen had to have a very soft-spoken, step-lightly kind of attitude. Sometimes that was not good. It opened the door for too many problems. Guys getting away with things, people not being corrected, people not doing their job right, communications not being what they should be, gripes not being settled. That went on year after year."[6]

The sharp division between a managerial cadre concentrating knowledge and authority and a unionized manual workforce paid to obey orders and not paid to think became a deeply rooted feature of the company, as of most other U.S. manufacturers. It was built into labor law, the union contract, the employees' jobs and lifestyles, and even the physical layout of the workplace and the language used to describe it. Manual workers were called "hourly" and "bargaining unit"; all others, whether typists or top managers, were "salaried." Even after they became the owners of the company, workers at Seymour would refer to management as "upstairs" and to those on the shop floor as "downstairs."

Ownership and management finally became fully separated when the Matthies family and other owners sold the Seymour Manufacturing Company to a larger company, Bridgeport Brass, which in turn was purchased by the conglomerate National Distillers. This caused little change in the relations among workers and managers within the plant. But key management decisions were thenceforth made at corporate headquarters in Bridgeport or New York. Local managers lost the authority to develop business strategies, make investments, or address major problems. Conflict developed between local managers and corporate headquarters and between managers who came from the Seymour plant and "outsiders" sent in by corporate officials. Production systems remained in the precomputer era; little new investment was made; foremen and supervisors received little training; the facilities were permitted to run down; productivity fell below that of competitors.

To understand what happened at Seymour Specialty Wire, it helps to analyze the somewhat autonomous bases of power that existed before the buyout. Individual employees possessed a degree of power that resulted from their knowledge of how to do the work, their ability to keep that knowledge from others, and their freedom to grant or withhold their efficient cooperation. These powers were multiplied by cooperation in workgroups that imposed group norms and utilized control over production for informal bargaining. The union possessed power based on collective bargaining rights defined in labor law, the ability to strike or otherwise collectively affect production, the support of other workers organized locally and nationally, the contract negotiated with management, and the union's own organizational structure of roles and responsibilities.

Supervisors and middle managers possessed power based on their knowledge of the organization and scheduling of production, which remained quite informal and rather inaccessible to higher levels of management. The local plant manager had the power to buy and sell raw materials and products; to hire, fire, and promote; and to make day-to-day decisions about the operation of the company—limited by corporate authority, on the one hand, and the informal power of lower-level managers and the workforce, on the other. National Distillers' corporate management appointed the top manager and determined investment and product lines, but had little capacity to direct the day-to-day operation of the Seymour plant. National Distillers' stock owners elected the corporation's board of directors, who had a fiduciary responsibility to the owners, but the stockholders had no vehicle for involvement with a subsidiary like Seymour Manufacturing, which represented a fraction of 1 percent of National Distillers' holdings.

SSW was launched into an industry in turmoil. An article in *Purchasing* magazine noted that in the late 1970s, many brass firms were "unwanted stepchildren" that were bought up by big oil companies. Then many became "abandoned stepchildren" when "Big Oil unloaded Big Copper." Brass mills were subjected to "a pattern of mergers, acquisitions, leveraged buyouts, plant shutdowns, and product mix changes." In 1980, *Purchasing* noted, major players in the brass industry had included Anaconda, Bridgeport Brass, Century Brass, Chase Brass and Copper, the Hussey Metals unit of Copper Range, and Olin Brass. By 1990, "part of Anaconda was Outokumpu American Brass, part had become Ansonia Copper & Brass; part of Bridgeport Brass was absorbed by Olin and part was employee-owned Seymour Specialty Wire; Revere Brass is an LBO [leveraged buyout] called Revere Copper Products; Century is out of business; Hussey Copper Ltd is an independent LBO; and Chase Brass' sheet operation opened, and then crashed, as an LBO called North Coast Brass & Copper." "Will the turmoil ever end?" asked *Purchasing*'s markets and metals editor.[7]

Purchasing also noted that "global factors" play a "key role" in all "coppermetal" market activities. Expansion and contraction in the "global copper economy" was as likely to be shaped by consumption in Germany or Japan or the expansion of capacity in Asian, European, and South American brass mills as it was by events in the United States.[8]

Faced with growing imports, U.S. copper and brass companies in 1986 won antidumping duties against foreign producers. To gain access to the U.S. market, foreign companies then built "transplants." Poonsang Corporation, South Korea's largest copper and copper-alloys manufacturer, spent $80 million to build a copper products plant in Cedar Rapids, Iowa.[9] By the early 1990s, the Finnish-owned Outokumpu Copper Group owned the former American Brass of Buffalo, New York; Nippert Company of Delaware, Ohio; Outokumpu Copper USA of Chicago; and SSW's direct competitor in the wire business, Valleycast of Appleton, Wisconsin.[10]

The requirements for survival and success in the brass business were also changing radically. David A. Gardiner, president of Cerro Metal Products Company in Bellefonte, Pennsylvania, described the industry as going through "a painful adjustment to such fundamental changes in the metals market as end-product downsizing, just-in-time manufacturing, materials substitution, and foreign competition."[11]

Customers' demands for quality escalated rapidly. Burton G. Tremaine III, president of the Miller Company in Meriden, Connecticut, said, "The metal we sold just three years ago wouldn't be acceptable today," and "the metal we produce today won't be good enough to satisfy our customers three years from now."[12] Along with pressure for improved quality came pressure for on-time delivery as purchasers cut inventories and moved toward "just-in-time" production.

Meeting new requirements took capital. *Purchasing* noted that "capital spending is being put on quality improvements, not capacity expansions."[13] Revere Copper Products, Inc., in Rome, New York, for example, finding its foreign competitors' products had far less variability, spent $3.5 million to reduce the gauge variation on its sheet coils from five-thousandths of an inch to one-half-thousandth of an inch.[14] A Revere manager observed, "The survivors in the '90s are those who have been investing to improve production, quality, delivery, and after-sale service."[15]

These factors led end users of mill products to move toward "business partnerships" with their suppliers. Donald M. Commerford Jr., vice president of sales and marketing at Revere, noted, "I don't think there's any major OEM [original equipment manufacturer] with whom we do business that doesn't have a vendor-performance rating system and a vendor-reduction program. We're being measured to an extent greater than ever before." The overall result was that purchasers aimed to select a few or even a single supplier. Executives interviewed by *Purchasing* advised, "Buyers should carefully evaluate supplier bases to see who has reduced debt, invested in new equipment and facilities, is willing to give the service required, and has the 'staying power' to outlast this recession."[16]

Within the wider brass industry, SSW produced a specialty product, mechanical wire. At the time of the buyout, mechanical wire represented a mature industry with a declining market. SSW was one of five important domestic producers, and in some ways it was in a strong business position. The addition of an in-house sales force in 1982 and the failure of competitors had raised Seymour's share of the market to 25 percent at the time of the buyout. The company controlled a larger share of the highly profitable fine-wire and specialty-alloy market segments. SSW's market was also diversified: the top ten customers accounted for less than 25 percent of total shipments.[17] Many companies were eager to get SSW's wire. GM and Chrysler sourced welding wire exclusively from SSW, and its customer list included many other Fortune 500 companies.

As a seller to manufacturers, the mechanical wire industry tended to exaggerate the ups and downs of the business cycle. Downturns in auto, housing, and other markets led to a two-week shutdown at Seymour in 1986 and contributed to major company crises in 1989 and 1991. Such declines were normal features of the industry, however, which the company had previously weathered. Cyclical market declines aggravated but did not cause SSW's basic difficulties; as late as 1991, the company retained a backlog of unfilled orders and an extensive list of customers eager to get wire if they could get it on time and with adequate quality.

In its original business plan, SSW proposed to shift production toward its higher-margin specialty lines. Lower-margin products were important, however, in that they provided employment and helped pay for fixed overhead. Increasingly, global competition meant that in some lines SSW could buy brass abroad for less than it could produce it itself. Although conventionally a sound business policy, the closing out of lower-margin product lines added stress to labor-management relations. The original business plan also included the development and marketing of new products, but undercapitalization and lack of management initiative limited efforts in this direction.

The feasibility studies and business plans for Seymour Specialty Wire expressed limited awareness of the traditional social patterns of the company and the new economic world into which it was launched. But both would play a decisive role in its fate.

After the Honeymoon

As dignitaries and reporters departed, Seymour Specialty Wire reopened under employee ownership. All employees took a 10 percent pay cut. Top company officials began setting up the accounting and other systems necessary for an independent company. But little else seemed to change. According to one employee, "On paper it was different, but in actuality it wasn't much different. What he could actually see and hear, the guy in the shop, it was no different, except he knew the company belonged to him and he had X number of shares being built up on paper. There wasn't the vehicle there yet to help him realize this really was his company."[18]

Financially, the company started out well. Twelve employees laid off in the original buyout were rehired during the course of 1985. At the end of 1985, employees received a profit-sharing bonus of $425 each.

But late in 1985, problems also began to emerge. The company's legacy of roles, privileges, and power bases led inexorably to a series of conflicts. Vocal criticism erupted on the shop floor, for example, when managers went unreprimanded after ignoring posted company rules about attendance and engaging in such common management practices as combining vacations with travel on company business.

Soon after the buyout, several managers were given substantial raises to compensate for their added duties. Union president Mike Kearney recalled the reaction: "I was approached by I don't know how many of the people down in the shop. What action could they take? I said, you could petition under the by-laws for a special meeting [of the ESOP]. Over 125 people petitioned. They had a full-house meeting. They demanded to know how the company could give managers a raise when everyone else had taken a 10 percent cut."[19]

Company bylaws did not authorize the ESOP to overrule the board of directors, and despite the protest the board voted seven to two to confirm the raises. Kearney recalled that he told company president Carl Drescher after this incident, "You lost everybody's trust, and everybody is kind of leery now. Anything that happens upstairs, 'They're only thinking about themselves.'"[20]

Workers also continued to use their customary weapons. In the casting department, traditionally a stronghold of informal workgroups in brass mills, a dispute broke out between workers and a new foreman. Workers conducted a slowdown and were accused of sabotage when large amounts of unusable metal began coming out of the casting shop. The dispute continued until the foreman was withdrawn.

Workers Solving Problems

The evidence of sabotage in the casting shop alerted all parties to how dangerous the company's labor-management situation really was and made them ready to consider alternatives. The board decided to bring the ICA back in to organize a "goal-setting process" to draw the rank and file into a discussion of the company's future. The ICA held a series of twenty-minute meetings with approximately twenty employees in each to list and prioritize company goals. A lot of anger was vented in the process; one lower white-collar employee commented, "The first goal I would suggest is that we figure out some way to kick top management's ass."[21]

Delegates were selected to an "ad hoc committee" that refined the various goals to five, dealing with productivity, maintenance, safety, finance, and, above all, a system to promote labor-management communication and cooperation. The ad hoc committee developed a detailed design for such a system that they dubbed Workers Solving Problems. Under WSP, work groups would meet with their foremen for twenty minutes every two weeks to identify and solve problems; those they couldn't solve themselves would be carried by the foreman and a worker representative to meetings at a higher level.

WSP bore a resemblance to "quality circles" and also to the stages of a union grievance procedure. To its architects, however, it was intended not just to draw workers into improving production but also to make management at every level accountable to rank-and-file employees and work groups. They had high hopes for its success. But WSP met severe resistance to both worker participation and management accountability. It was revealing—and perhaps ominous—when one manager asked, "Will we allow them to wash up on their time or our time?"[22]

Work groups met and chose representatives. Those representatives and the foremen were trained in group-process and problem-solving techniques and proceeded to run WSP meetings. Many workers were already so skeptical about the whole situation that they announced they would attend meetings, since attendance was compulsory, but would refuse to say anything. Typically, after a WSP group identified a problem, the foreman and representative were told to discuss it at the next higher level and bring back an answer. If the work group did not like the answer they brought back, they had little recourse—they usually just went on to another problem, or, ultimately, withdrew from the whole procedure. WSP turned out to be unable to hold any level of management accountable; problems were passed upstairs, but if the answers were not satisfactory, there was not much workers could do about it. Workers had little interest in participating in a mechanism that gave them no real power.

WSP was defeated by two interacting forces. Supervisors and middle managers, according to many accounts, saw WSP as a threat to both their formal authority and their informal power to manage their own activities as they saw fit. While obeying the orders from top management to participate, they in practice sabotaged it by not actively using the channels WSP created to solve problems brought up at the base. The result was talk without results: problems that required action beyond the unit were simply not addressed. Seeing that WSP did not in fact provide accountability, rank-and-file workers in turn grew alienated, increasingly regarded it as a farce, and refused to participate actively. Many ultimately petitioned for its abolition.[23]

Blue-Collar Board

For the first half of 1986, business was good. In May, only a year after the buyout, the 10 percent wage cut was restored. But at the end of 1986, the auto and housing markets slumped. Although SSW turned a profit for the year, at the end of the year it had to shut down production for two weeks.

Meanwhile, internal conflict continued to plague the company. A review of salary policy had revealed that some foremen were paid less than the workers they supervised and that some lower white-collar workers were paid below the bottom of their salary range, violating the board's salary policies. Yet proposals to give raises to these groups enraged rank-and-file workers, who felt everyone was benefiting from employee ownership but them.

This conflict brought in the union in its traditional role as representative of the economic interests of the hourly workforce. But the union itself was divided over the issue of an increased differential for the skilled-trades workers in the maintenance department, who were receiving considerably less than similar workers in other plants in the area. Unskilled workers resented the idea that everybody but them seemed to be getting raises. The union proposed a wage reopener with something for everybody; management responded that it would cost the company too much. After nearly a year of discussion, the board agreed to a modest increase.

Meanwhile, frustration about WSP, wages, and many other issues led to growing shop-floor sentiment for electing hourly workers to the board. The second annual election chose one hourly and one salaried representative. Before the third election, the bargaining unit was split over the issue of differentials for skilled tradesmen, but a union caucus endorsed two bargaining-unit members who were overwhelmingly elected, giving the board for the first time a blue-collar majority.

This began to bring to a head a series of issues about the board and the role of union representatives on it that had only been hinted at when a majority of the board was drawn from management. From the beginning, company president Carl Drescher had been concerned that the hourly waged members of the board keep apart their two hats as company directors and union leaders. In his view, the company had an obligation to its stockholders to maximize profit and equity. Pursuing other goals—whether expanding employment, increasing hourly pay, or helping other buyouts—presented a potential conflict of interest with the board members' fiduciary responsibilities to the owners.[24]

Such potential conflict arose several times. When the union pushed to reopen the wage package, for example, union members on the board felt obliged to consult the company lawyer to see if they might be sued for violation of their fiduciary responsibilities. (The lawyer advised that the cost of the final proposal was too small to affect the company's viability significantly.) Hourly workers on the board voted raises for foremen over the objection of many workers because they believed it was a valid and necessary business decision. Particularly painful for union representatives on the board was Carl Drescher's insistence that they had to stop helping workers at Century Brass in Waterbury develop a buyout plan, on the grounds that Seymour's interests might be hurt by the potential competition.

When only two people from the bargaining unit were on the board, Mike Kearney encouraged management board members to spend time on the shop floor talking with workers and urged workers to bring their concerns to the board members when they came through the shop. As more blue-collar people were elected to the board, this approach atrophied, and many workers defined the blue-collar representatives as their spokespeople on the board, through whom they channeled their communications with management. Many workers objected to the idea that union representatives must act on a business basis while on the board. According to Kearney:

> There was a lot of heated debate and argument up there because we're on the shop floor and Carl and them are up in the office. But when it came time to make decisions, I'm not going to do anything to jeopardize my job. If I'm going to make a decision that's going to shut the company down, I shouldn't be up there. People couldn't understand that. "Hey, you should be representing hourly people!" "Yeah, I know I'm representing hourly people. But remember, I don't have my union hat on when I'm up there. I've got my director's cap on."[25]

Carl Drescher was well aware of this situation: "Union directors make decisions as directors. That's appropriate. But it's not always popular on the floor." One worker described the situation more bluntly: "Because of the way the voting has gone on the board, the people in the shop perceive the board members, especially those who are supposed to be representing them, as just oblivious to their concerns. They think they've been betrayed."[26] There was discussion of organizing hourly worker opposition against the existing hourly worker representatives at the next election.

With the election of an hourly worker majority on the board, questions of the accountability of management to the board and the board to its electorate were posed in a new context. The members of the board who worked for the company, including the union president, began meeting weekly with Carl Drescher, creating a sort of cabinet with undefined authority. The board created a committee on governance and brought the ICA back in to help redefine roles.

After a visit to Weirton Steel, an ESOP-owned company in West Virginia, the WSP coordinators decided to modify the program by making participation voluntary and by providing training to all participants, not just leaders. While the new plan no longer pretended to be a means to establish accountability to the shop floor, it was designed to provide a way that those who wanted to could begin to take managerial initiative. Groups started working on such problems as late customer deliveries, training, and dissemination of financial data to employee owners.

Eventually, these groups combined into two groups working on two problems that merged into one group working on the dissemination of financial information to the employees. Their proposed format was well received by management and incorporated into the employee newsletter. In April 1989, the WSP group took a "spring break" after which it never reconvened.[27]

Universal Scheduling

The company's financial difficulties in 1987 led to a sense of a compelling need for a "turnaround." In response, late in 1987 management made a highly controversial decision to bring in a new consulting firm, Universal Scheduling, for an intensive six-month intervention.[28] Universal established a database for making production and productivity goal-setting decisions.[29] It conducted management training designed to change the work culture and encourage foremen to set goals and define and solve problems. It established "ideal work centers" with optimum equipment and conditions to set productivity standards; if production fell substantially below the established standards, managers were to take corrective action. According to Carl Drescher, "The purpose of bringing in Universal Scheduling is to install better management systems. The company needs their help in production scheduling. The managers can't run the business on a day-to-day basis and put in the time necessary to install these systems. The board voted nine to zero to hire them."[30]

The decision to bring in Universal Scheduling caused an uproar on the shop floor. The blue-collar members of the board "took an awful beating down on the floor as far as verbal abuse." Foremen spoke against the plan, at least when they were in the mill. "We agree with you guys; we're on your side on this."[31] More than a hundred employees petitioned for a special ESOP meeting at which management was vigorously attacked for spending money on consultants to do a job it should do itself. Some employees attacked president Carl Drescher as incompetent to run the company. The meeting itself had no authority, and the board did not reverse its decision to bring in Universal Scheduling. At the time, several people told me they were watching to see what happened at the upcoming ESOP meeting when new board members were to be elected; there were also rumors of a possible wildcat strike or a refusal to ratify the next union contract.

Part of Universal's program involved setting new production standards— reinvigorating a conflict over control of production that went back generations at the Seymour plant. Mike Kearney explained:

> There is some resistance because we've been doing the same thing for so many years. Pacing. After a while, from generation to generation it got ingrained in the different people, no matter who came in. They start like a bat out of hell, [but] after a while they just get into a pattern. Universal is telling us, look, you

guys have a lot of idle, unproductive time in the shop you should fill. We said, we don't want to lay any people off. We came to agreement with Carl and the top managers that nobody would be laid off because of this.[32]

Workers generally gave the team from Universal the time-honored treatment workers have provided time-study men for generations: they refused to talk with them. At other times, they engaged them in shouting matches.[33]

Another aspect of Universal's program had to do with inventory levels. "Under National Distillers and at the beginning of the buyout we had tons and tons of inventory work. We kept the inventory levels high. Our philosophy was, you make a couple of thousand pounds of this, three hundred thousand pounds of this," whether there were orders for that much or not. Universal's philosophy was, "If you don't need it, don't make it. If you only need fifty thousand pounds of number 1, you make sixty or seventy thousand pounds and that's it. If you have to shut that unit down, shut it down and utilize the guys some place else. You don't make two hundred thousand pounds just because you want them stocked on the wall."[34] The new system was designed to save cash and utilize labor more efficiently, but it conflicted with the established ways of getting the work done.

The computerized production-control tracking system introduced by Universal would also remain a bone of contention through the rest of SSW's history. The first head of production control "went head to head with upper management" over "a difference of philosophy and how this was going to work" and quit. The plant manager criticized introduction of the system as untimely at best. According to Mike Kearney, "I don't think there was a foreman that wanted this system. Down on the floor it was active resistance."[35]

Early in 1988, management offered union president Mike Kearney a management job in scheduling. Despite reservations about leaving the union, Kearney "decided after talking with my wife I didn't want to be a furnace operator the rest of my life. . . . So I jumped at it." Tom Klimovich replaced him as president of the union and union representative on the SSW board. Kearney's move was criticized by officials from UAW Region 9A and some rank-and-file workers. Kearney nonetheless was elected to rejoin the board at the next election.[36]

Six months later, when the head of production control quit, Kearney was put in charge of production control. "I didn't have any background in production control except for what I'd learned from Universal. I found out real quick that there are three or four different philosophies on how this Universal Scheduling should work."[37]

Conflict in philosophy led to debilitating conflict on the shop floor. Universal's philosophy was "to update all the tickets to show a correct sequence, to computerize it, make a master schedule where you know what has to go through what machine centers at what time." But the established practice relied much more on the experience and judgment of the supervisors. When he received orders for a particular alloy, a supervisor might say, "OK, Charlie take 24 of them over here. We'll do this one next. Take ten over here and line up the work." According to Kearney, "We were trying to incorporate the system from a production control standpoint, and they were trying to keep the mill going under the old philosophy. There was a clash." As a result, production problems grew worse not better. "We started missing more and more delivery dates. I would get a call from sales: 'Mike, is this order tracking on time?' 'Let me check.' 'Hey, Tom, this order here, we'll get this out by next Friday?' 'Yeah, don't worry about it, Mike.' I'd call back sales and they'd tell the customer 'We're tracking next Friday.' Next Wednesday would come. 'Tom did you ship it?' 'No, it's not ready. Next Friday.' That hurt us because that's where the rumors started going that Seymour is closing down. That's when the customers got scared and panicked."[38]

Firing the Boss

In 1989, U.S. use of brass-mill products began a substantial three-year slide, and turmoil returned to the industry. A 1990 article in *Purchasing* noted that "ArrowHead Metals just closed, Eastern Rolling Mills is in Chapter 11 bankruptcy reorganization, the strip mill and tube mill at Chase Brass has been shut, the rod mill is for sale, and the sheet mill that was sold to employees and became North Coast Copper & Brass has been absorbed by American Brass."[39]

By 1989, SSW was again losing money. In the summer, the union accepted further wage concessions. Workers threatened to strike in response to the cut.[40]

With the cut came an offer that if the company produced a certain number of thousands of pounds, part or all of the cut would be restored. In Mike Kearney's view, "It was supposed to be an incentive to get their money back. I think sometimes it worked just the opposite. The guys said, 'Hey, they can fix the numbers and work the numbers any way they want. We can work our butts off. In the past we did this, we did that, and we lost money. What is the incentive? They keep telling us there's an incentive to get our money back. Show us where's the incentive! I'll work for $1.80 an hour less, and I'll make it up in overtime.' They know the old games down there."[41]

Production problems continued to plague SSW. "No matter what we did to try to improve the system or provide on-time delivery, when we felt we had one problem licked another problem would pop up. We never denied we had problems getting metal out the door; the numbers spoke for themselves. We identified the problems but nothing was being done to rectify them." According to Kearney, "Carl never followed through on the tracking system. After I took over production control in 1988 I was more or less floundering, because there was nobody in the company with production control background."[42]

Meanwhile, customer-quality requirements grew more demanding. "Something that in the past you could get away with shipping we couldn't do now; some of the defects and flaws that passed through the system previously we couldn't do now. So now we have to tighten our specs and our production methods to meet the specs of the customers. And we weren't prepared to do some of that."[43]

The production problems contributed to a financial pinch. "We were putting money out and we weren't getting money in, we couldn't buy raw materials or vender stock. When you can't buy raw material and vender stock, you can't make it. If you can't make anything, you're not going to ship anything." As rumors started to fly that SSW might go under or be bought out by Ansonia Brass, new orders dropped off sharply.[44]

By late 1989, SSW was in serious crisis. It had lost approximately $6.5 million in the previous three years. Raw materials suppliers were owed $2.2 million and had ceased all shipments. Pension-plan contributions from 1988 had not been funded, and no waiver had been granted. The Town of Seymour had filed a property lien for unpaid taxes. Company lawyers were preparing the board of directors for a bankruptcy filing.[45]

The board acknowledged the need to consider partial or complete sale of the company and, on the insistence of NatWest, had engaged a New York consulting firm to seek purchasers.[46] But the board still looked to Carl Drescher to decide what to do. Finally in October, on the initiative of the two union directors and Mike Kearney, the board decided that Drescher had to go.[47] Outside director and board chairman Joe Lombardo was asked to take expanded responsibility while the company sought new leadership.

New Leader

Meanwhile, a former worldwide manufacturing controller for Polaroid named Jerry Harrington, who had helped install an ESOP at Polaroid to ward off a hostile takeover, met Roland Cline of the ICA at the Center for Employee Ownership in New York City. A few weeks later, Cline called and invited him to attend an already scheduled meeting at the Seymour union hall with employee representatives from the SSW board, the UAW local and

Region 9A, and the NVP. When they made clear the company's desperate situation, his reaction was, "Boy, what a challenge!"[48] After a brief check of his credentials, the board hired him late in 1989 to become president and CEO of the company. His employment agreement specified as objectives that he should turn the company around, refinance it, and sell it.[49]

Harrington moved rapidly to initiate a turnaround. With the help of a $1 million bridge loan from the Connecticut Development Authority, he persuaded banks and creditors to give the company some more time. He raised prices on some products.[50] With the agreement of the union, he reduced the workforce by twenty-five hourly and ten salaried employees.[51] He focused on solving immediate production problems to start getting more metal out the door. The Red Date Zones indicating when the company would run out of cash were gradually pushed back from barely a week to more than a month.[52]

Harrington generated an immediate change in atmosphere at SSW. Mike Kearney, later to be one of Harrington's fiercest critics, told me in June 1990:

> He was more people oriented. He was on the floor morning, noon, and night. He wasn't afraid to get his hands dirty to learn. He went to the casting shop on the second shift. He grabbed a pair of gloves and he said, "We're going in the pit. And I'm going down there with you. I don't know anything about making wire but I'm going to learn." And he watched those guys go in the pit and hook up the starting rods to start casting wire. He showed up at one o'clock in the morning and talked to the guys on the third shift. The guys said, "This guy is paying attention to us. He's concerned."[53]

Harrington also made a point of meeting with the salaried employees and assuring them he was accessible to them and prepared to address their concerns.[54]

The change in atmosphere was palpable: I remember overhearing union president Larry Motel, exhausted but happy, telling Harrington with pride and satisfaction how many pounds over their production target they had gotten out in the previous few days. Blue-collar suspicion of management proposals became less automatic. Mike Kearney reported, "He had the guys in the palm of his hand."[55]

Board structure and function also began to change. The board chairmanship was separated from the presidency and taken on by outside director Joe Lombardo. Board meetings focused less on production and other management issues, and more on such matters as business forecasts and financial planning.[56] Harrington proposed adding more outside directors, but the proposal was challenged by some as a dilution of the employees' control and was not pursued.

Harrington's assignment had from the beginning included the search for an outside investor. Carl Drescher, who remained with the company for a transition period, dealt with potential buyers who had expressed interest in SSW. The annual ESOP meeting in February 1990 voted to authorize the president of the corporation to negotiate a sale of up to 49 percent of the company, the terms to be subject to approval of the board of directors and the ESOP trustees.[57]

Meanwhile, NatWest, SSW's principal bank lender, announced it was eliminating all its "small" loans and wanted out of the deal. The bank started reducing SSW's short-term line of credit. The SSW board even considered bringing a lender liability suit on the grounds that NatWest was forcing the company out of business. Encouraged by lobbying by the NVP and community leaders, the State of Connecticut provided a loan of one million dollars that allowed SSW to pay off NatWest. Foothill Capital Corporation of Los Angeles provided new financing. Quantum (formerly National Distillers) forgave two million dollars it was owed from the original purchase.[58]

Turnaround?

An article in *Purchasing* (prompted in part by a public relations expert hired by Harrington) stated that a year after a management shakeup, SSW is "a different, and once-again profitable, brass mill." Instead of selling low-price "commodity grades" into an "overcrowded market," the firm "now focuses on a limited range of exotic, special-purpose, and higher margin" alloys. Jerry Harrington told *Purchasing* that lateness on orders had been reduced from 80 percent a year before to 80 percent on-time, lead times had been halved to an average of four weeks, and a "Seymour Customer Service System" order-entry tracking system had been instituted. Harrington said, "The firm did incur a downturn in 1989 because it had lost its market focus as a specialty copper and brass mill, but that has changed since."[59]

After two and a half years in the red, for the first six months of 1990 the company was in the black.[60] Problems began to increase, however, as Harrington began moving from short-term turnaround to longer-range planning for the company.

The core business decision was what to make. Mike Kearney recalled:

There was always the history at Seymour that some of the big buying customers were called "the light bill companies"—the companies that paid the light bill. It kept the guys working. It was Jerry's attitude to phase them out. We shocked a lot of people by saying, "Hey! We've got to get out of the zipper business, the ordinance business, because they are not a profitable line. You are just keeping people working." He said, "Look, the name of your company is Seymour Specialty Wire. Let's concentrate on the specialties that we have the niche in the market."[61]

Harrington's second strategic focus was on building a management structure. "Right now there's no organization. I want to build a structure of this company that's going to be comparable to any other company its size." He began bringing in new levels of management, including a director of operations, a director of personnel, and a director of marketing and sales.[62]

According to Kearney, "That's when the wall started going up a little bit. All the guys think on the floor is, 'Director of Human Resources'—that's sixty-five thousand dollars a year; 'Director of Operations'—that's sixty thousand dollars a year. They're giving away our money." Kearney, who as head of production control previously reported to the president, eventually reported to the materials manager, who reported to the director of operations, who reported to the president.[63]

The new managers began addressing some of the company's problems and initiating some of the planning it needed. They began to activate the computerized tracking system initiated by Universal Scheduling but never fully implemented.[64]

The effort to establish accountability in manufacturing continued to generate conflict, however. In Kearney's view, it became apparent that the front-line supervisors "didn't want a structured system. They wanted business as usual. They wanted to be able to do what they wanted to do, when they wanted to do it, without having any kind of structure." Kearney said the effort to change scheduling practices met stiff opposition. "'This computer system doesn't work; it takes too long to train'—every excuse in the book." The new director of operations was dismissed over what he described to Kearney as "a difference of philosophy on how the mill should be run."[65] From that point forward, the selection of managers became an increasing focus of conflict both within the board and on the shop floor.

Jerry Harrington later told me that inadequate leadership, high turnover, and factionalism were significant problems on the part of management when he became president of the company:

I found a great many people that were hardworking, honest people, that needed leadership. Not just by the president, but leadership throughout the company, middle management and what have you. When I arrived the company had been without a plant manager for six months. They had a significant turnover. From 1985 to 1989 they had gone through approximately six plant managers, six or seven directors of operations, four or five production control managers, and three metallurgists. Those were people who had been there for a long time, even before the buyout. So it was all the more personality driven. There were different factions and some people were on the board—let's just say there was a lot of blame being placed.[66]

Nosedive

At the end of 1990, Warner Brothers shot a film, ironically entitled *Other People's Money,* at the Seymour plant. During the restart of the casting shop, the town's electricity went out, leading to a freeze-up of the major furnace and a two-month halt to production. Then a furnace melt-through shut down most of the foundry for two weeks. Harrington estimated the two shutdowns cost more than $250,000 in addition to loss of business.[67]

Production was eventually restored, but the failure to get a quality product out the door on schedule grew even more intense. Meanwhile, the country had entered a steep recession that particularly affected such SSW customers as the auto industry. The company was in the red for 1990 as a whole. By early 1991, it was again in crisis.[68]

Harrington had continued to seek an outside investor and thought he had found one, a Connecticut manufacturing firm with potential synergies that was willing to invest two million dollars in new money, take a minority position in SSW, and redeem the stock of retiring employees.[69] But in an atmosphere of escalating mistrust, some employees began to fear that Harrington was "selling our company out from under our feet and behind our back" for his own benefit. There were even charges that Harrington "purposely ran the company into the ground."[70]

In January 1991, the employee-directors proposed to rescind the authorization to sell up to 49 percent of the company. Harrington, outside board member and president John Harlor, and Lombardo strongly opposed the proposal. The board unanimously adopted a compromise resolution that put the president's authorization to negotiate for the sale of up to 49 percent of the company in abeyance.[71] The intent of this decision has received differing interpretations in retrospect. Harrington has stated that "the events at the Board Meeting were to determine the fate of Seymour Specialty Wire" and that "further discussions with investors ceased and were held in abeyance per the vote of the Board." Kearney's position is that the board's agreement was such that "no one person could wheel and deal and sell the company. It had to be a full board action. The employee directors never intended to stop looking for new owners or investors. We were specifically trying to stop Mr. Harrington."[72]

Whatever its intent, the decision met serious opposition. The ESOP trustees met and issued a statement reading in part, "In our opinion, the CEO and Board of Directors should be actively seeking and negotiating with any potential investor interested in S.S.W. Co as a minority investor." In the wake of the decision, Foothill wrote Harrington that "the present composition of your Board of Directors gives us concern, and we would urge you to increase and/or change its present composition to include more 'professional' individuals in order to guide the company through these difficult times."[73]

An intense two-day board meeting in March 1991 put together a survival plan.[74] As a result, 30 of the remaining 180 employees were laid off.[75] After an extended period of confused signals, in April Harrington and the outside directors reached an agreement with the union for a $0.29 hourly wage increase.[76] In May, Harrington initiated a major realignment in production roles. Although pounds of metal produced seemed to be meeting production targets, this appearance was somewhat illusory: easy orders were being filled while harder-to-produce ones were delayed, and product was being shipped despite severe quality problems.[77]

Despite apparent progress, the plunge continued. In September, 86 of the remaining 148 employees were laid off, leaving only 62 at work.[78] Shutdown was regarded as imminent. Harrington announced the formation of a military-style "Delta Team" to try to save the company. He proposed union concessions that would disregard all seniority provisions, base job assignments solely on skill and ability, allow nonstandard workweeks to eliminate overtime pay, suspend vacations, and delay holidays to the end of year.[79] When the union turned the proposals down, Harrington implemented them anyway. Many people were surprised when the union did not strike.

Amid the gloom, there was one bright spot. SSW was developing an aluminum-based spray welding wire for the auto industry. Major companies were interested and offered to give SSW lucrative contracts if it worked out. But even this resulted in conflict and suspicion, with accusations that Harrington was maneuvering either to destroy or to take over the company in order to get control of the spray welding process.[80]

On October 11, 1991, SSW announced plans to cut its staff in half and seek a major investor or buyer by the end of the month. With the assistance of the state and the NVP, at least a dozen interested investors were identified. Jerry Harrington, John Harlor, and a group with ties to Polaroid declared themselves potential purchasers. After questions were raised regarding conflict of interest, Harrington and Harlor removed themselves from purchase negotiations. The UAW regional director made it clear that any successor company must recognize the union and abide by the contract. Amid charges that top SSW officials were withholding information from the board of directors, local union president Larry Motel demanded copies of documents pertaining to the sale of the company and brought National Labor Relations Board charges on the grounds that the information was denied.[81]

On December 20, 1991, Harrington announced that the plant was shutting down. In February 1992, the company received a loan from Foothill, guaranteed by the state, and reopened on a limited basis with thirty to forty workers. It had severe quality problems, however. Although U.S. copper- and brass-mill shipments unexpectedly increased 10 percent in 1992,[82] SSW was in no position to take advantage of the rebound.

Meanwhile, in early 1992, a subcommittee of the board reviewed investor proposals. One deal, proposed by Premier Commercial Services, appeared far sweeter for the employees than any of the others and was recommended by vote of all board members except Mike Kearney. In April, the shareholders voted in favor of the Premier deal. However, checks from Premier to SSW creditors bounced, and utilities began to hound and threaten the company. Ultimately, Premier was unable to fulfill its commitments, and the deal fell apart.

On June 29, 1992, SSW closed for the last time. The state was owed more than one million dollars in loans; SSW owed an additional four hundred thousand dollars in property taxes, utilities, and other debts. SSW had no way to meet its payroll payments, and the board called in Foothill to finance the final payroll. Foothill thereupon took possession of the property. There were liens on inventory, machinery, and equipment. Various possible "saviors" appeared, but none panned out. Harrington resigned and again began trying to put together a deal to purchase the company. Some saw this as a confirmation of previous suspicions. Mike Kearney said, "We firmly believe that once [Harrington] saw that that plant could make a profit, like it did in the first six months of 1990, that he purposely ran that plant to the ground with the express goal of him and a couple of his cronies buying the plant."[83] In August, SSW's creditors battled in bankruptcy court, and the judge ruled in favor of Foothill.

SSW's last board meeting before liquidation was held Friday, November 13.[84] Board members resigned and attempted to secure company records.[85] In December, Thomas Industries, a liquidator hired by Foothill, held an auction and stripped the mill.

"The Kind of Stuff That Hurts"

Many different factors contributed to the ultimate demise of SSW. Market conditions, recession, undercapitalization, organizational structure, management style, inherited work cultures, and many other circumstances all had a greater or lesser impact. Small businesses have a notoriously high rate of failure, and the American brass industry as a whole was on the skids. Even with perfect planning and decision making, it is hard to see how SSW could have been more than an industrial hospice.

But the SSW experience has much to teach about the dynamics of any situation where groups acquire new powers in the context of an established institution. Although some of the problems that eventually destroyed SSW were hidden within market forces that few recognized, many were clearly identified by employees, managers, consultants, and other observers. Attempts to address these problems ranged from new systems for employee participation and production control to shifts in product markets and the search for outside investors. But few were implemented effectively. To carry out each of these solutions required agreement and commitment among an array of forces and the ability to win over or at least neutralize those who might be opposed. Instead, these forces became deadlocked over each attempted solution.

Legally, the employee buyout made only one change in the structure of power at SSW. Stock ownership passed from National Distillers to an ESOP that held stock in trust for employees. The members of the ESOP—the current employees of the company—elected a majority of the board of directors on a one person–one vote basis, joined by the company and union presidents and outside directors elected by the board. Far from eliminating the preexisting power bases within the company, this system created an additional arena in which individual employees, work groups, the union, supervisors, middle managers, and top managers could pursue their interests.

In practice, several other bases of power emerged in relation to the new company. Corporate functions, such as payroll, finance, and the like, were taken over by the new independent company and exercised under the control of top management. Outside board members—invariably businessmen—played a role. The state became a player by virtue of its loan guarantee and the expectation that it might play a role in future funding. Lenders became important and ultimately critical players. Finally, a series of organizations involved in the buyout, including the NVP, the ICA, local community leaders and politicians, and the company's legal and accounting firms, became players to a greater or lesser extent.

These different bases were able to exercise power for different reasons. The power of some groups—the banks, for example—was rooted in money. The power of others—such as the union and the board of directors—was rooted in legally defined authority. Other sources of power included organization, knowledge, prestige, persuasion, contacts, and the capacity to provide or withdraw cooperation.

Each kind of power had a specific and limited sphere of action. Supervisors could withhold information but could not make production happen. Worker-owners could fire a company president but could not force one to implement a board decision. Some power was positive, making it possible to act; other power was negative, making it possible only to block the action of others. An informal work group was ill-equipped to purchase a new machine, but it could easily lower production by misusing or abusing that machine.

The different sources and types of power at SSW were dynamic, interacting over time. Power in one sphere could be parlayed—utilized to compel action in another sphere: a slowdown in the casting shop was used to force management to withdraw an unpopular foreman, for example. Different power groups could form coalitions: machine operators, line supervisors, and some higher-level managers joined to resist Universal Scheduling. Power could be used to repress disagreement by means of threat or exercise of sanctions against opponents: although union rules and the presumption that employee-owners were entitled to freedom of speech made it harder to fire employees for disagreeing with management, toward the end management recovered much of its power to get rid of those it did not want. Finally, in a process that can be described variously as hegemony, leadership, or co-optation, one individual or group could use a combination of carrots, sticks, and persuasion to win the consent of others to their proposals or their general authority: the union leadership's initiation of the buyout and subsequent winning of support from the rank and file and from management represented such a process. At SSW, the negative power of coalitions that opposed particular problem-solving efforts was usually sufficient to undermine those efforts. The result was repeated deadlock.

One approach to resolving such deadlocks might have been to recognize multiple power bases, acknowledge both common and differing interests, and establish a process of negotiation among them. Coalitions trying to initiate problem-solving efforts could have recognized the interests and negative power of their opponents and created some kind of bargaining forum in which mutually acceptable agreements could be reached. For example, the process establishing WSP might have included a bargaining procedure in which foremen's job security and authority concerns were addressed or incentives were offered for effective implementation or both. Similarly, the attempt to introduce a new production-control system could have been preceded by a bargaining process leading to a "productivity deal" that would ensure individual workers and work groups part of the gains that resulted from their sharing their knowledge of and control over production. The goal of such a process would be to establish a coalition or power configuration strong enough—and an opposition sufficiently neutralized or won over—to allow solutions to be implemented.

Alternatively, an effort could have been made to end deadlock by changing the underlying bases of power. Several strategies for changing SSW's power configuration were advocated or considered. Not surprisingly, the *content* of these suggestions differed radically, since each involved strengthening some constituencies at the expense of others. But virtually all involved in one way or another changing the structure of knowledge and roles within the company.

Soon after the buyout, one consultant suggested the firm consider a major restructuring of work roles. The proposal was to have individual workers and work groups manage their own work. In a company where work roles were so deeply entrenched, such a change would undoubtedly have met significant resistance. It would have validated the fear of foremen and supervisors that employee ownership would make them superfluous; it might also have threatened higher levels of management by giving rank-and-file employees more power over the work process. On the other hand, it would have reduced the enormous gap that remained between blue-collar and white-collar employees and drastically reduced the power of foremen and supervisors to impede changes in production practices.

Some participants and observers saw SSW's problem as an inability to put limits on group conflicts and proposed as a solution a larger number of outside board members. This proposal came primarily from management-oriented quarters and was seen as a way to reduce employee influence or "meddling" and strengthen the business experience and orientation of the company. Some labor- and community-oriented people were also open to the idea and saw the addition of more labor- or socially oriented board members as a way to strengthen employees or increase the community role. In either case, it would dilute the power of employees relative to outsiders and provide a buffer to reduce the impact of internal conflict within the company.

Some employees and observers saw the problem at SSW as primarily one of excess or abused management authority and inadequate worker assertion. They urged employees to become much more involved in lobbying board members and challenging management inadequacies. Other avenues discussed for changing the balance of power included increasing the involvement of the regional or national union or both and organizing the white-collar labor force into the local union. Some envisioned increased employee intervention as a way to realize established solidaristic worker values, others as a move toward a more entrepreneurial orientation.

A number of observers identified inappropriate worker expectations and power as central to the problems at SSW and proposed various remedies. One was a clear education of the workforce—starting before the buyout—that their ownership of company stock should not lessen management's authority over work and the workplace. As one close observer put it, those who set up the buyout should have made it clear to employees that as owners their role was to vote for a board of directors to choose the best people to run the company, and that as employees their role was to implement management's decisions about how the company should be run.

Another proposal was to reduce or eliminate the power of the union as an independent force—for example, by decertifying it on the grounds that it was unnecessary in an employee-owned company. All such proposals would have met significant opposition from the union and much of the workforce. All would have tended to eliminate some of the aspects of employee-owned companies that make them different from conventional companies, restoring a more traditional form of management authority with both the benefits and the problems that entails.

One aspect of the difficulties at SSW was the weakness of management's ability to manage. Whereas management systems for an independent company were instituted, research, planning, and product development functions were never significantly developed. Nor was a computerized production-control system ever fully implemented. The result was that top management had formal authority but limited de facto control over the life of the company. Jerry Harrington approached this problem by trying to build up a larger and more effective managerial team. Such a team would gain functional authority by knowing what was actually going on in the plant and in the wider business context and by being more effectively able to make and implement plans and solve problems. It would also provide management a larger power base in the overall politics of the company. The development of such a team met opposition in the workforce on the grounds of its expense and to some extent because of its power effects as well.

One consultant who worked with SSW in retrospect compared its workers to Southern slaves who were freed by the Civil War and thereupon found themselves without the skills, knowledge, and resources to make it on their own. He suggested that the union and the rank-and-file workforce needed independent access to education, training, legal support, and a wide range of consulting services. This would have allowed them to make and implement appropriate decisions without being so dependent on management for information and judgment. Proposals were made early in SSW's history to provide training to union officials and blue-collar board representatives at company expense. Management was reluctant to support this idea, explicitly because of the cost and perhaps also because of the empowerment it would have entailed. An independent knowledge base for the workforce would probably have reduced management's independent power and turned managers into something more like civil servants than conventional company executives. It would have also reduced the gap, though not necessarily the conflict, between "upstairs" and "downstairs."

If there has been one broad conclusion from the general experience of employee buyouts, it is that trouble is bound to arise if new democratic structures are simply grafted onto the existing structures of a conventional corporation. The result of pouring the new wine of employee ownership into the old corporate bottle is likely to be explosive. The experience of SSW surely bears that conclusion out.

Seymour Specialty Wire: An Employee-Owned Company had radically changed one of the sources of powerlessness of Naugatuck Valley workers by making a group of them the owners of their own company. But many other sources remained intact. Owning the company turned out to give them only limited power to actually run the company and hold management accountable. It still left them powerless in the face of banks and potential investors. Workers faced uncontrolled market forces that rendered all their hard work, devotion, and value to the community worthless. They were forced to compete in a struggle to the death with global corporations many times their size whose deep pockets virtually guaranteed the outcome. Their heritage of sharp social, cultural, and job-content divisions between themselves and managers continued despite the change in ownership—making for irrepressible labor-management conflict despite the change in company ownership. Seymour showed that simply owning their own company was not enough to give workers power over their own lives.

David Duke, a vice president of the local union, a SSW board member, and a lab worker who became a quality-control manager, summed up his feelings about the SSW experience in a way that reflects the basic values that motivated the buyout from the beginning:

> I'm glad we did it. I wish that we could have made it work. I don't have any regrets about it, because we kept the place going for seven years. So we did serve a purpose for a while.

There's a lot of things we should have done differently. What they were and whether we have all the answers now—I really don't know. There are things that you could see where they went bad, and had we reacted differently or a little sooner things might have turned out differently. There's really no way of knowing.

We got a lot of people to retirement with their pensions before we went under. That was one of the things to make you feel good when you sit back and reflect on it. And then you think about the ones that had already lost a job in the other plants that had closed and now were in their midforties, early fifties, and it's just going to be real, real hard for them to find something now. That—that's the kind of stuff that hurts.[86]

7. Founding ValleyCare Cooperative

In early planning for the NVP, Ken Galdston had discussed with Waterbury leaders the possibility of starting an employee-owned business to serve the community and to provide jobs, including "homemaker service for the elderly."[1] But the NVP had rapidly been projected into struggles over the factory shutdowns that were devastating the Naugatuck Valley. The project was largely known for its work around Seymour Specialty Wire, Century Brass, and dozens of other plant closings. But over the next few years, while still engaged in ongoing struggles over plant closings, the NVP began responding to other local needs, such as improving community services and creating new jobs.[2]

One of the side effects of deindustrialization was the destruction of local businesses and the "demarketing" of local communities by retail chains. When Waterbury's last major downtown supermarket closed, residents had no way to shop. The NVP initiated a campaign to get large food stores in surrounding areas to establish a van-pool system to serve elderly residents in Waterbury high-rises. It was led by two retirees, retired nurse and NVP leader Ethel Spellman and her husband, Ed.

Doreen Filipiak, a home-care worker who was active in the NVP, recalled, "In the process of Ed and Ethel working on that they got into the elderly housing complexes in Waterbury and discovered that there was a lot of elderly people out there who were not getting good care. Many of them were getting no care at all." Some had aides, "but it would be different people every day, and sometimes it was frightening for them because they never knew who was coming. Sometimes no one would come at all." Filipiak added that Ethel Spellman "being a retired nurse said something has to be done. So already being involved in the NVP, she brought the idea to the board, and they discussed it, and they decided to start a home-care committee. And Ed and Ethel were on that committee, and there were several other people. I was asked to join it because at that time I was working for a home-care agency."

Over the next two years, the committee grew to a dozen members, including retirees who had personal concerns regarding care for the elderly and health care professionals ranging from home health aides to case managers to supervisors, disability activists, and social workers. Several of its white, black, and Hispanic members had strong church or synagogue affiliations, and virtually all had prior experience in NVP projects. Doreen Filipiak remembered: "You had Ethel, who was a nurse, [and] Mike Valuckas, who had the handicapped people, so he knew another whole range of people who were in need. So everyone that came into the committee basically had a reason to be there—like I was in home care, so I worked with the elderly, the same as Ethel did."[3]

Almost from the beginning, the NVP and the Health Care Committee envisioned a new venture whose intertwined goals would be home-care services and job creation. Their initial idea was to provide cooking, homemaking, bathing, chores, and possibly feeding to the elderly, acutely ill, long-term ill, and terminally ill.[4] A worker-owned business would provide stable, good-quality jobs that would not leave the area, develop leadership among the low-income valley residents who would work for the enterprise, and add to the hoped-for fleet of local companies allied with the NVP.

The committee conducted an informal needs survey among elderly people in Waterbury high-rises. Through contacts in local parishes, they found and interviewed owners and managers of the buildings. With help from the ICA, they began prefeasibility research of the market for services, the available workforce, management and governance, and financing for an employee-owned company.[5] The ICA had already helped set up a cooperative home health care company, Cooperative Home Care Associates, with impoverished minority employees in the South Bronx. The CHCA seemed to be flourishing, which made the NVP project seem a realizable goal rather than a pipe dream.

In the fall of 1989, the ICA's Seth Evans was joined by Connecticut home-care nurse consultant Carolyn Humphrey and Rick Surpin, CEO of the CHCA, to develop a feasibility study and business plan. Meanwhile, NVP staff began writing grant proposals to support the work. The Lilly Foundation came through with an initial planning grant of twenty-seven thousand dollars, and the project was on its way.

Designing the Company

Research soon made clear that the market for home health care was intertwined with some important trends in the United States during the 1970s and '80s. The number of elderly people was growing rapidly, while geographical mobility and the loosening of extended family ties meant that fewer and fewer seniors were likely to be cared for by relatives. As hospital costs escalated, hospitals tended to discharge patients "quicker and sicker." Private and public insurance programs became increasingly willing to pay for home care as a cheaper alternative to long-term hospitalization.

As a result, homemaker and home health aide service had become a three to four billion–dollar national market that was growing at more than 7 percent per year. An estimated three hundred thousand workers, mostly women and disproportionately black and Hispanic, worked as home health aides, with many more working as homemakers. The U.S. Department of Labor projected that nursing and personal care would be one of the five major job-creating industries between 1986 and 2000. Like other states, Connecticut faced a rapidly growing elderly population, and Waterbury had the second-highest elderly population in the state.[6]

Meanwhile, there was a serious shortage of trained paraprofessionals to perform this work. Not only was the pay relatively low, but the work was highly casualized, with irregular working hours, few benefits, insecure employment, and no ladders for career advancement. Home health workers in fact typified what was being called the "new workforce" of workers stuck in the low-quality poverty-level jobs that burgeoned during the 1980s. As a consequence, turnover in agencies was high and continuity of care low.

In March 1989, when Seth Evans of the ICA began to examine the potential market for a home health care agency in Waterbury in detail, he discovered a "dizzying array of overlapping agencies and mechanisms that are involved in Connecticut's home care industry." One state agency even charged just to explain how the system worked! Home-care services fell into three categories: professional services like skilled nursing by RNs, physical therapy, and occupational therapy; home health aide services provided by people trained and certified as home health aides; and homemaker and companion services. The CHCA in the Bronx had started as a homemaker and home health aide agency, providing the lower two of these three categories. But Evans discovered that "the model of CHCA does not translate well to the Connecticut environment."

Unlike any other state, Connecticut required such agencies to be licensed, with costly requirements for nursing and administrative support; only four companies in the entire state had qualified for such licenses. The new company could restrict itself to providing homemaker services—but would then be ineligible for the more profitable Medicaid and Medicare payments and would be limited to the housecleaning and homemaking industry, which, Evans noted, "has become very competitive over the last several years, spurred on by the growth of dual-income families." It could be organized as a registry, serving essentially as an employment agency connecting employees with potential employers—but that would do little to upgrade skills or build a company that employees could feel was their own.[7]

Ultimately, the NVP's Health Care Committee opted for a far more ambitious goal: to establish a certified agency providing a full range of services, including skilled nursing by RNs, physical therapy, and occupational therapy, while specializing in home health aide and homemaker services. This strategy targeted a market niche that was underserved, owing in part to the peculiarities of Connecticut's home-care regulations. Because of the licensing requirements for homemaker and home health aide services, existing service providers concentrated at either the high or the low end of the continuum, focusing either on skilled nursing and therapy services or on homemaking. While providing a full range of services, the proposed company would concentrate on the lower and middle ranges.

Initially, some administrators of Connecticut's then numerous Visiting Nurse Associations perceived the new company as a threat. But the company would not attempt to compete head-to-head with the VNAs for acute-care cases; rather, it would focus on chronic-care cases that depended more on homemakers and home health aides. This definition of its niche—implying a concentration on chronically ill elders and people with disabilities instead of acute-care patients just released from the hospital—might make it possible to collaborate rather than compete with the VNAs.

A series of "marketing outreach meetings" identified a number of agencies that were interested in contracting for such services. Almost half of the cooperative's business during the first two years was expected to come from Connecticut Community Care, Inc., a state agency formed in 1987 that administered a large portion of the homemaker and home health aide dollars spent in the state for the care of lower-income frail, elderly persons under Medicaid, Older Americans Act grants, and state funds.[8] (The CCCI was particularly attracted to the proposed company's willingness to bill separately for homemaker and home health aide services so CCCI could charge the more remunerative home health aide hours to Medicaid.) The marketing plan also called for some direct referrals from hospitals, private physicians, and the state; subcontracting from VNAs and other agencies; and some private-pay clients provided through the NVP network.

Putting these elements together, the Health Care Committee decided to establish an employee-controlled company, which they named ValleyCare Cooperative (VCC). Their objective was the creation of "a model worker controlled and owned home care company that employs mostly low-income women and men that provides the highest quality homemaker and home health aide services to its elderly and home-bound clients, while paying the highest possible wages and benefits to its workers. Another related goal of the project is to bring new workers into the industry and providing them with training so as to ease the paraprofessional worker shortage in the Naugatuck Valley area and improve service availability."[9] These elements were intimately related. NVP and VCC organizers saw employee ownership as a means to upgrade the workforce, increase motivation and commitment to the work, and reduce the turnover that plagued the industry. If employees had a stake in the company, it would improve their reliability as well as the quality and continuity of care. The competition provided by VCC as a model home health care agency would also, they hoped, create upward pressure on wages and other benefits and set new standards for the quality of working life in the industry as a whole.

Meanwhile, the committee had to establish a structure for VCC that would address its rather diverse goals of providing a service, creating jobs, and serving as a model of worker empowerment through employee ownership. Ultimately, they opted for a for-profit corporation that would serve as a "shell" for a community- and employee-owned cooperative. The company's business plan explained:

> The rationale behind the for-profit model is that profit is a motivating factor for workers—that when workers share equitably in the company's profits, they are motivated to put forth their best effort. Furthermore, when workers invest in the company in which they work and have a say in how the company is governed, their commitment to remain with the company is strengthened. There is also a tendency for for-profit organizations to manage with more attention to revenues and expenses—that is, to the bottom line. The bottom line orientation gives members and managers a clear measure of company performance and fosters an orientation toward the marketplace which is more aggressive and entrepreneurial than a typical non-profit.[10]

While the business plan was under development, the Health Care Committee began looking for staff. A recent recruit to the committee, Margie Rosati, became the obvious candidate for staff director. A bilingual Puerto

Rican woman, Rosati had been involved with the health care industry for many years, starting as a home health aide and ending as a supervisor of aides at the VNA of Naugatuck Valley. After months of searching, in October Pat Diorio was selected as CEO of the company. Diorio was also a veteran in the health care world, a public health nurse who became a top administrator of home heath care agencies in the valley. The proposed staff shared experiences that shaped their visions of what the company should be like. Pat Diorio, Margie Rosati, and consultant Carolyn Humphrey had come from agencies that had been humane oases within an often impersonal industry. Then larger companies swallowed up their small agencies. As Rosati said:

> VNA of the Valley was like a little family store, where everybody was really close and we really helped each other, and nobody was in cubicles. And then we merged with big New Haven VNA, and it wasn't the same. We lost that.
>   Carolyn Humphrey was a wonderful wonderful director. [She] ran VNA of the Valley like what a cooperative is. Carolyn never stifled anyone, anyone who wanted to learn anything about anybody else's job or the functioning, she encouraged that, and she was able to create an atmosphere where we all felt that VNA of the Valley was our place. And where the nurses and everybody was committed, not only to providing the health care to the patients but also concerned about financials and everything about the company. And Carolyn had that kind of open door policy, unlike many of the other health care companies.[11]

When working to create ValleyCare, they strove to recapture and improve upon these "lost paradises" and to institutionalize some of the lessons learned from their experiences. Margie, who was recruited to the NVP's Home Health Care Committee by Carolyn Humphrey, was attracted to the idea of ValleyCare because "it was a cooperative. So when Carolyn mentioned going back to something similar or maybe even better than VNA of the Valley, [I felt] oh my God, this is like a dream come true."[12]

Start-up

ValleyCare Cooperative incorporated on December 4, 1990, with a start-up board of directors that included two leaders from the NVP, two staff members of the ICA, and Pat Diorio, president and CEO of VCC. The new agency rented and renovated a building near downtown Waterbury. Pat Diorio and Margie Rosati developed care manuals, computer systems, and policies for personnel. "When I came to ValleyCare I brought with me a binder of VNA of the Valley, which helped when at the beginning Pat was putting together all the policies and everything. She had some stuff from her place and I had some stuff, and we were able to put forms together, and we had policies that were already written, so it made it a lot easier."[13]

VCC signed an agreement for the CCCI to be its primary source of referrals. That enabled the new company to provide homemaker and companion services while it was waiting for state licensure as a home health care agency.

ValleyCare opened its doors for business on February 25, 1991. Doreen Filipiak remembered, "When they actually got the building and set up the office and had a name on it, that was pretty exciting. I haven't seen too many things like that happen in my life."[14]

An open house on April 25, 1991, for which the NVP had called upon many of its church and community contacts, was attended by some three hundred people. Five of VCC's homemakers and companions began the two-week home health aide training course at Mattatuck Community College. Jo Knight, the consultant from the Connecticut Health Department, visited VCC to ascertain its compliance with state licensure requirements. She announced that VCC could immediately provide skilled nursing and home health aide services in addition to homemaker and companion services.

The next day, VCC applied for Medicare certification. But the fledgling company found itself in an unexpected bureaucratic catch-22. In order to be certified for Medicare payments, VCC had to demonstrate a record of providing skilled nursing and home health aide services. But the primary source of payment for such services was Medicare itself.[15] VCC learned that it would not be able to service Medicaid (Title XIX) patients until it was also Medicare certified. The news came as a surprise to staff, ICA consultants, and even state agency allies. As Rosati commented sourly, "You can have the agency and in order to treat patients you need to have licensure and Medicare certification, but you cannot have that unless you have a track record. But you cannot have a track record because you don't have licenses. So that's the way the government does things."[16]

VCC's business plan had assumed that certification would allow it to begin serving Medicaid patients, adding higher-skill offerings to its homemaker and companion services. But the thicket of Connecticut regulations, linking Medicare to Medicaid, made that impossible. With no Medicare and Medicaid patients, VCC began falling further and further behind its projected client load and income and going deeper and deeper into the red.

In this crisis, the NVP's contacts and credibility in the community proved critical. Patients recruited by the NVP helped build a record that would allow Medicare certification. Rosati recalled that "one of the members of the Naugatuck Valley Project volunteered to be our patient for no charge. And we took care of her so that we started building a little track record, and then we were able to obtain our licensure."[17]

The NVP also worked closely with Diorio and Rosati on a marketing plan. NVP and VCC staff made presentations at churches, senior apartment buildings, and senior centers. NVP leader Bishop Peter Rosazza mediated between VCC and top staff at St. Mary's Hospital to establish a good working relationship that would encourage St. Mary's to provide referrals to the new agency. VCC also worked closely with receptive agencies such as the Naugatuck VNA to subcontract home health aide work.

Making ValleyCare Work

Despite struggles and setbacks, the company's achievements in its first few months were impressive. By April 1991, when it held its open house for the community, VCC had eleven employees performing 200 hours of work a week for nine clients.[18] From the time of its February opening through June 30, 1991, VCC had provided 1,392 hours of paraprofessional service. This was 57 percent of the projected total, a notable figure given the fact that the company did not receive the anticipated Medicare certification until September.

VCC also seemed to be reaching its goals of hiring a diverse staff needing job opportunities. Its home health care, homemaker, and companion services were provided by seven home health aides and three homemaker companions, including three African Americans, four Hispanics, and three whites. Of these, one was a college student, two had been working in casual part-time positions, and all others were unemployed at the time they were hired by VCC.

In addition to planning and implementation funding from the Lilly Foundation, VCC had start-up debt financing from four loan sources: the Adrian Dominican Sisters, the Sisters of Charity, the Leviticus Fund, and the ICA Revolving Loan Fund. Through the NVP, the company had also received planning and start-up grants from the Episcopal Diocese of Connecticut, Holy Cross Fathers, Marianist Sharing Fund, and Ms. Collaborative.[19]

VCC established an advisory committee of medical professionals who would meet quarterly to set medical policy and advise on technical medical matters. Although such a committee was required by state and Medicare regulations for all home health care organizations, VCC's had a distinct flavor, according to Diorio:

> We needed to have a public health nurse, a physical therapist, a speech therapist, an occupational therapist, a social worker. All of the disciplines needed to be

represented on the committee. And we were able to recruit people locally for that, people I knew in other agencies.

In some agencies the clinical record review component is so overwhelming that it's almost like a rubber stamp. Nobody looks at anything, nobody questions anything, the process of some of the agencies is they don't even show you the charts. Our group was very involved, very interested. We had a pharmacist, and he was wonderful. He helped us understand that there were problems with some of the medications patients were taking, interactions, and he was available on a consulting basis.

The professional advisory committee also had a dedicated physician who would review charts and made herself available beyond the scope of the meetings. Other agencies might have several doctors on their list but "if you got one at a meeting you were lucky."[20]

At the beginning of October 1991, an evaluator visited VCC at the request of the Lilly Endowment and reported:

VCC is providing several hundred hours per month of home health aide, homemaker and companion service (although service hours through August were only 60%–70% of the grant milestone target). It's providing employment for about a dozen paraprofessional workers (mostly part-time), plus four administrative staff—again, somewhat less than the milestone target but still a significant accomplishment.

All of the paraprofessional staff I spoke to had been unemployed at the time they were hired. Clearly VCC is creating jobs in a region where they are needed.

VCC deserves a special commendation for the racially diverse staff it has put together. I saw and heard that Waterbury is a segregated community for the most part, yet VCC has a very even mix of Hispanic, African American and European American paraprofessionals.[21]

VCC finally received state approval for Medicare, thus becoming eligible for Medicaid-reimbursed services as well. Diorio remembered: "In September of '91 we really were starting to be able to take our own referrals and have a decent caseload, as well as doing some contracting. I would say over the next six months we really started to see the aides who really wanted full time, to get 30, 35 hours, and probably into the next year we saw those numbers growing. You're talking '92 and '93." She continued, "We really were doing very well in that period with giving people hours. Because we did have CCCI patients, and what we also started doing as we had more and more CCCI patients, is we were able to put together longer cases for the aides."[22]

As a new agency, VCC still had a higher proportion of evening and weekend hours and short-hour, short-term cases than its leaders might have wished. Diorio and Rosati worked to cobble together substantial schedules that utilized their aides' different skills, gave them a steady income, and provided continuity of care for patients:

> Because some of these very complicated, difficult patients had only a few hours of home health aide service, but they also needed homemaker and companion service, and we started putting together care plans where we had for—probably since 1991 until we closed the certified agency—we had one patient, and she was getting like 8 to 10 in the morning home health aide and then she'd get 10 to 11:30 companion, then she'd get 11:30 to 12:30 home health aide, then she'd get 12:30 to 2 homemaker. . . . And she was like an 8:00 in the morning to 2:00 patient every day, five days a week, and maybe four hours on Saturday and Sunday. And that was one aide.[23]

During its first few years, ValleyCare Cooperative grew steadily. By the end of 1991, the staff had increased to five full-time and seventeen part-time homemaker and home health aide and companion staff. At the end of fiscal year 1991–92 (ending June 30, 1992), the company had twenty-seven parapro-fessionals, the following year forty-one. By mid-1995, VCC was employing fifty-six paraprofessional staff members. It had steadily expanded its profes-sional staff as well, from a primary care nurse, a staff nurse, and three per diems to five staff nurses.

Accompanying this growth, the company's service hours and income increased faster than staff or consultants expected. VCC reached the break-even point by the second quarter of 1992, three months ahead of schedule.[24] By March 1993, the company was billing 2,582 paraprofessional hours per month, including 1,951 home health aide, 400 homemaker, and 231 compan-ion hours, exceeding its best previous monthly total by 28 percent.[25] Indeed, as Lilly's evaluator noted at the beginning of that year, "growth over the past year has been so steady that marketing efforts have been tabled; the greater challenge has been to enlarge your internal capacity to keep up with demand for your services."[26]

In its start-up year of 1991, the company earned just $18,253 in service revenues. By 1992, earnings had multiplied to $322,680. By early 1993, the company had been in the black for three quarters and had started to offer health insurance. By the end of that fiscal year, VCC's service revenues were $599,178. In the following year, VCC proudly announced that it had earned $780,503 in service hours.

The company began looking toward expansion in a number of different directions. At the beginning of 1995, VCC started to provide physical therapy, speech therapy, occupational therapy, and medical social work services to its clients.[27] By the end of that year, ValleyCare was bursting at the seams in its small office and began to make plans for a move. By the end of 1996, VCC had relocated to two floors of office space in the old convent of St. Margaret's Church, a staunch NVP member organization. It had also begun to explore other possibilities, such as developing an adult day care center for non-English-speaking patients, opening a Hartford office, and buying or hiring transportation for the use of aides without cars.

Ownership, Governance, and Participation

From its inception, a core part of ValleyCare's mission was both to create a worker-owned company and to ensure a high level of worker participation in it. Its mission statement asserted, "ValleyCare Cooperative, Inc. seeks to empower its workers through training, education, participation in decision-making, worker ownership, and by creating a caring work environment which fosters dignity and teamwork."[28]

Yet unlike the Seymour Specialty Wire buyout, ValleyCare was not established by a group of workers, and its first employees were recruited as workers, not worker-owners. Adviser Rick Surpin from the CHCA argued strongly that there was no point in establishing worker ownership of a new company, especially for low-income workers, until there was something worth owning.

VCC's founders decided that the company would be run for a transitional start-up period without employee control. Worker ownership would be introduced gradually. In the meantime, worker participation in the company would be built into the company in other ways.

VCC's design differentiated the elements of ownership into a number of rights distributed among different individuals and groups. Following a scheme developed elsewhere by the ICA, ownership was based on two classes of stock. Employees would become worker-owners by purchasing a share of Class A stock; only current employees could buy the stock, and they had to sell it back when they left the company. The stock entitled employees to vote for the Board of Directors. This system made VCC in effect a co-op inscribed within the legal structure of a profit-making corporation.

Class B or Preferred Stock was owned by the NVP as sponsoring organization. It carried a blocking vote over any bylaw or strategic change that affected the public-purpose goals of the organization. This was designed to ensure that community service remained a primary goal of the organization and to tie it in with the developing network of NVP-related institutions and enterprises. Ultimately, the co-op had the option to pay off the NVP for its stock, thus establishing full control by the workers and freeing NVP funds for reinvestment in other ventures.

How would the company be governed in the meantime? A report to funders noted: "A difficult hurdle for the committee has been trying to understand what the initial corporate board for ValleyCare Cooperative would look like. We have CHCA's model, and we have the model of Seymour Specialty Wire Company, our other employee-owned company in the Valley. . . . The two main questions are . . . how many people should sit on the board? . . . Who should be on the board in the start-up years?"[29]

Ultimately, an initial board of directors was selected with two representatives each from the ICA and the NVP, plus the president of the company, to serve in effect as trustees, governing on behalf of future worker-members until they could govern the organization themselves. Worker ownership would be initiated only toward the end of the company's second year, when financial projections suggested that the company would make a profit. At that point, an election committee would design and conduct Board of Director elections, and two workers would be elected to the board, which would be expanded to seven members. The number of worker-elected seats would grow by one seat per year until the third year following the issuance of Class A shares, at which time the workers would elect five out of seven board members, with the other two filled by an NVP representative and the president of the company.

From the start-up of the company the VCC board and staff were educated and trained about the differences between cooperative and traditional businesses, but, as VCC staff wrote at the end of 1991, "EO [employee ownership] is mentioned and described briefly, but it is spoken about as a goal, rather than a current opportunity . . . because of concern about raising expectations about ownership at a time when it was still almost 2 years off. Also, we saw little sense in investing heavily in orientation and EO training when turnover was still high as a consequence of our inability to provide full time work."[30]

VCC tried nonetheless to nourish a culture of worker participation. Tight community networks and word-of-mouth recruiting by current aides helped. A number of VCC employees had come to the agency through prior connections to NVP projects and networks and understood the principles of team-based decision making for collective benefit. Some had firsthand experience of cooperative ownership as residents of the NVP's Brookside Cooperative Housing.

VCC administrators had been chosen in part because they were committed to creating a participatory environment. Rosati observed:

> Agencies like VNA of the Valley and the one that [Pat] was from: We were small, and we had directors who were special people. And it all came from the top. It

all came from their judgment on hiring staff, on dealing with problems, from good will, from having the presence of mind that if something is happening, you take into consideration what people have to say, like for instance, a staff member is having problems, it is not an automatic written warning, but it is, let's get together and let's talk about this and what can we do to help you, and what are you going to do. So I think that that kind of system allows people to participate and to feel comfortable and to feel welcome. And it's easier to build a team when you have leaders that have that kind of philosophy. And it absolutely permeates.[31]

VCC made the creation of a participatory environment an explicit goal long before employee ownership began. At a retreat in March 1991, the staff and board developed a formal plan for introducing worker education, participation, and ownership. The first two years would emphasize the development of a participatory and caring culture through mechanisms other than employee ownership, such as:

Quality: including close yet supportive supervision; commitment to joint problem solving; clear standards and policies, especially regarding no-shows, and punctuality, reinforced by progressive discipline; and a careful selection process (based on values listed below).

Values: friendliness; caring for people; quality-commitment; reliability; fairness; teamwork; human development.

Communication: open door policy; overlapping verbal and written communication about company developments; no surprises—all important information is shared on a timely basis; and facilitating of intra-staff communication and socializing.

Participation: increasingly formal input into personnel policies; input into management evaluations; increasingly formal participation on operations committee; participation in evaluating program quality and effectiveness; and participation in social event planning.[32]

Opportunities for participation would be created through ad hoc committees that would review personnel policies, monitor quality and effectiveness of work, and plan social events. In-service training and regular memos from the president would reinforce the developing culture. In orientation sessions and written materials, employee ownership would be mentioned and described but spoken about as a goal rather than a current opportunity.[33]

In the second year, personnel, operations, employee recruitment, and social committees would be formalized. The president's memos would become a newsletter focusing on financial information and ownership, and a series of meetings would be held to discuss employee ownership and how it would function. Employees would begin purchasing shares, with a goal of 50 percent of eligible paraprofessionals becoming members of the co-op by the end of the year. The new owners would receive in-service training on such cooperative basics as governance, division of responsibility, division of profits, and the importance of participation and teamwork.[34] At this point, worker-owners would begin to be elected to the board.

During the early days of the company, VCC management and board members went to the Bronx to observe training activities and gather materials and methods from the CHCA. The ICA helped train VCC staff in participatory problem-solving techniques.[35]

In the beginning, training, conscientious office communication, good relations in the field, and a robust social life were the main means for inspiring a participatory atmosphere and a sense of ownership. Rosati remembered: "There was always a part of that in-service education that dealt with team building. Pat is absolutely wonderful at including people and getting consensus. So she always made it a point to attend the meetings and talk about what was happening, and talk about plans, and try to get them to participate and to be involved. Pat always wrote a memo; on every Friday they would get a memo about what is going on, what's coming up in the future, who wants to participate in this." Rosati stressed that "having an open door policy is imperative." In addition to trying to accommodate workers' needs for convenient scheduling and sufficient hours, Diorio, Rosati, and other office staff kept themselves accessible. Home health aide Lillian González affirmed, "Pat Diorio was always willing to listen to us." Another aide observed, "The people care, that is the most important thing. It is like an extended family to me. My bosses are great. It is the first company that really cares about the employee and what they want. To me that is very important."[36]

The family-like atmosphere of the office encouraged camaraderie among aides and office staff. Lillian González observed, "When I had free time I would go to the office, because you could go to the office at any time. If they needed your help with paperwork or something, you could do it and if not, you could go and pass the time with the nurses." Rosati remembered this atmosphere being especially comfortable for the Latina aides: "Because the type of people that they are, they walk into the office and they have food in their hands and they kiss everybody, and they really felt comfortable to behave at the company like they would behave in their homes." In creating participation, VCC tried to mix business with pleasure:

> We started a small committee, it was like a support committee. It was a group of staff, maybe four. If any staff member, any home health aide had a problem with something, they could always call this person, or they could call that

person, and talk about issues and problems, and then bring them to us, and we would meet on a monthly basis. That committee would get together and plan the picnic, and plan the Christmas party, but also talk about transportation issues or complaints that they had heard from staff or concerns. Also, that was a committee that Pat utilized for sounding off things that were coming up.[37]

The annual picnic and Christmas parties, planned by this committee, were attended by many aides and even by patients. They became a means for aides to get to know each other and to better understand each others' cultures. Lillian González remembered the picnics fondly: "We had food from different cultures. Everybody who came from a different country would bring the food of that country." When asked how staff broke down cultural barriers in their multiethnic environment, Margie said simply: "Rice and beans. Food and at the Christmas parties, playing some Latin music and everybody getting up and dancing."[38]

While VCC administrators and their advisers had been careful to inculcate an ethic of sharing and mutual support, they had been just as careful not to offer worker-ownership options prematurely. Rosati remarked:

> Think about it. Would you want to talk to people that are coming out of welfare, they're not financially stable or anything like that, would you want to sell them a piece of a company that is losing money, that is not established, that is not a viable business? We could have done it, take a chance, people should be responsible for their decisions. But no, we had to wait until we broke even and started making a little profit to be able to stand in front of them and say, this is what we are, this is what we have to offer. And do it ethically and morally correctly. And then when we were ready, oh God we were so excited. This is it, we broke even. We're making a profit. Now we can join the cooperative train.[39]

VCC had expected to start offering worker-ownership options at the end of the second year. A foundation evaluator noted, "You're on schedule for this—your timetable called for stabilizing the business first. . . . And you've established the social preconditions: an environment where workers feel respected and valued."[40] The company broke even in the second quarter of 1992, several months earlier than expected. VCC held four two-hour leadership training sessions sponsored by a grant from the Catholic Campaign for Human Development. Staff who completed the leadership sessions were offered worker-ownership training starting in September 1993 in preparation for the first offering of shares.[41]

VCC's leaders were gratified by the response to the initial training sessions, which became another way for aides who were normally out in the field to connect:

Particularly in a company where the employees are out visiting clients most of the time, with little opportunity to interact and get to know one another, it has been important for them to come together and begin the process of relationship and trust building. This is crucial for the staff to truly take ownership as a worker-owned company. During the course of the three sessions, the staff have become increasingly at ease with one another and individually more outspoken. It is apparent from the various participatory exercises that they are committed to the company and excited by the prospect of becoming owners. There is an amazing spirit of cooperation that is exhibited.[42]

VCC had done a great deal right: created a participatory culture, gradually promoted the idea of worker ownership to its workers, broken even and started making a profit, and provided training to prepare employees for purchasing company stock. Once again, however, the peculiarities of Connecticut regulations almost foiled the agency's plans, as Rosati recalled:

We were ready to print the shares and the state of Connecticut says, "You can't do that." Unlike New York, you cannot sell a share by having the person put down $25 as a membership fee and paying you the remaining price of the share of $475 in payroll deductions. They had to have all the money in. What are the chances? Never. So the issue was that they could not hold the share in their hands, so therefore they were not fully vested members of the cooperative. And you could not take payroll deductions for shares in Connecticut. In New York you could. So Pat and I, I remember that day, we're going, "Oh my God, what are we going to do? Everybody's coming in to buy the shares, and we can't give it to them. This is the whole purpose of this thing!" So we're going crazy, so phone calls are made, and the lawyer, and then recommendations for these other lawyers that have more expertise in this type of thing.

Fortunately, someone came up with a solution to the problem that was "so simple that Pat and I could have killed ourselves for not thinking of it. Make the price of the share the $25 and the $475 the membership fee!"[43]

By November 1993, ValleyCare offered staff members their first opportunity to buy shares in the company. The company had hoped to recruit five people for this first worker-ownership opportunity, but fifteen out of twenty-two eligible workers immediately took up the offer.[44] The next month, two worker-owners were elected to the newly expanded board.[45]

By the end of 1994, the company had nearly fifty paraprofessional employees, including twenty-two worker-owners, nearly half the workforce.[46] Worker-owners elected to sit on the board increased to three. The company was doing so well that the worker-owners' patronage dividends were paid for the first time that December.[47]

Pat Diorio remembered that employees had a range of attitudes toward worker ownership:

> Initially there was a lot of enthusiasm about the worker ownership. It was presented in a way that made it affordable for an individual. I think they were attracted to the idea of being involved in decision-making, to the open communication, always knowing what's going on, which doesn't happen in a lot of other agencies.
>
> It always surprised me, there were workers here who were eligible for ownership that did not even want to think about it. Five hundred dollars is a lot of money, but the way we did it was that they could pay $25 up front and then $3 a week out of their paycheck deducted so it was affordable. But there were people who said, I've never owned anything, I don't want to, I'm not interested. Others who said, well it means a commitment, and they weren't ready to do that.[48]

Margie Rosati, however, was more surprised by the enthusiasm with which many joined up. Lillian González, who joined the company in early 1993, reminisced, "As soon as I completed the six months [needed to become eligible for worker ownership] I said to Pat Diorio, 'I want to be a worker-owner.' She gave me the appointment, and I became a worker-owner at once." When asked what made her so eager, González said, "Seeing that my coworkers were worker-owners, I also wanted a little piece of the company." Home health aide Henrietta Norman, who started work at VCC in 1991 and was one of the first to take up the offer, said: "I thought the idea was good. The concept behind it, that if you owned something you would take more pride in it. Not that you wouldn't do the best if you were just working, but you had more of an incentive to push a little harder. The more patients that we had the more service that we were able to give, so it was more money that was coming in."[49]

Office and supervisory staff also signed on. Nurse Maria Gerard remembered:

> I really didn't do it because of any financial reasons, I just felt that if I was going to work for a company and I felt like I was dedicated and I was going to be there for a while, that I wanted to have as much input on the company as I could. It was really, I thought, kind of unusual. I'd never heard of a company that you could actually buy stock in or be a worker-owner, and I thought that was interesting.
>
> I think once you became a worker-owner you really did feel that part of you was investing in that company and you wanted it to succeed. And so I think the benefit was that once you became a worker-owner the company took on a different meaning for you. This wasn't just some place where you made a pit stop and you moved on to the next place.[50]

Although Rosati was surprised and delighted with the response, she sometimes worried about the assumptions that the home health aides might be making and tried to ground them in reality. "Sometimes I didn't know if they really understood what it meant. They were just so excited. I know that people hear what they want to hear. And the other parts that they don't want to hear, they forget about them. For instance, in housing, Brookside, was very exciting. My God, the idea that you could put some sweat equity and then that translates into money, that then you can have a down payment. And everybody loves concepts like that." But, she cautioned, "the part that usually people don't hear is what is it that I have to do, what is my responsibility. When something breaks, they want to know where is the man that's going to take care of this problem. So one of the most important things was to convey the concept that there are responsibilities in being a worker-owner."[51]

The responsibilities and rewards were summed up by Diorio, who explained that worker-owners had to be "involved in the decision making." As she put it, "The worker-owners approved the agency budget, they approved wages and benefits for all the staff, they approved new programs, so there was a feeling of a lot of involvement. There was a fee to become a worker-owner, but if the company had a profit, they would be paid a patronage dividend. And we did pay a couple of patronage dividends. They weren't big amounts of money, but when you think about it, the total share in ValleyCare cost $500. And if in one year you get 300, that's a pretty good return."[52]

When ValleyCare broke even unexpectedly, started turning a profit, and gave out dividends, there was excitement and high morale within the company. Doreen Filipiak remembered "how excited everybody was when girls were actually becoming worker-owners and then a while after that when they actually started seeing the monies coming back to them from that worker ownership. It actually made it more of a reality, the company was actually running and making money and giving people jobs."[53]

As the worker-owners began to hold their quarterly meetings, Rosati wondered if the aides were aware of the difficult decisions that might lie ahead. "When they realized that they have input into evaluating me, that was like a lightbulb went on in their heads, and they wanted to be a part of it. I think some of them wanted *really* to evaluate me! And that's part of their responsibility. To follow the rules, to do what they're supposed to do, to follow a policy, and to make sure that you help management in achieving the goals. Sitting down and planning the goals, doing strategic planning together. They needed to understand that; they needed to participate in that." Rosati was skeptical about how successful the cooperative could be once it hit its first crisis: "And of course I told myself, 'This is never going to work.' I used to sit with Pat and go, 'Yeah, I'd like to see this! The moment that we have the first issue that means that they are not going to get a raise, or instead of getting this much, they have to cut back, or that they have to give up something, I want to see this cooperative work.' This is what I used to say in private."[54]

ValleyCare Cooperative embodied a strategy that allowed Naugatuck Valley residents to counter their economic disempowerment by creating jobs and services without having to depend on the wealth or the decisions of distant corporations. It did involve working with larger organizations like the Visiting Nurses Association, but it did so by developing partnerships based on common interests and mutual give-and-take. It involved both working with the government and affecting government policies. It mobilized the resources needed to start a company that eventually provided scores of jobs for people who were unemployed or on welfare. The strategy involved sharing responsibilities, both within the VCC workforce and throughout the entire NVP network. It mobilized entrepreneurial energy and capacity not just to do what the markets signaled but also to link community resources and needs in ways that market-driven entrepreneurs would hardly have considered. Indeed, it hoped to reshape markets by creating a model with which conventional firms would have to compete.

8. Taking Care of Business

Starting a business was one thing; making it work—especially making it work as a participatory, employee-owned company—was quite another. ValleyCare had to recruit its workers and train them. It had to support them to perform effectively in a wide range of home settings, often with difficult clients. It had to handle all the complexities of managing a firm in the modern service economy. Like any business, it had to stay in the black. But it also had to realize the ambitious social goals for which it had been established.

ValleyCare's approach was a response to conditions in the industry it was entering. Home care was notorious for irregular work and an unstable work-force. Doreen Filipiak, a home-care worker and single mother who helped to found ValleyCare, observed that home care is a business with high labor turnover: "When I was in it, there just weren't enough hours to go around, and if you need a full time job, you can't live on maybes. I can't tell you how many times I would show up at work in the morning and not have a patient, because they'd been taken to the hospital the night before, or they'd passed away in the night."[1]

ValleyCare aimed to succeed in this environment by pursuing two linked goals: to provide high-quality jobs and to provide high-quality home health care. Its founders believed that these goals were synergistic. In a field marked by low pay, irregular hours, and disrespect for workers' needs, high-quality jobs would attract high-quality workers and merit their commitment. That in turn would make for far better care than was usually provided by the casualized home-care industry.

As a for-profit company, ValleyCare aimed to perform in the market in competition with other companies. At the same time, it had other goals fundamentally different from simple maximization of profit. Its goals could be synergistic or conflicting—or both. How their relationship played out shaped every aspect of daily life in the employee-owned company.

I got to see how all this worked out in practice when the ICA and VCC asked me to do interviews and produce a slide show about the newly opened company.[2] From hanging out in the office, I got a strong sense of camaraderie among the employees. From visiting the homes where aides gave care, I saw how demanding the work could be for aides and how important it could be for patients. I also got a strong sense of the aides' commitment to their patients and the reciprocal appreciation their patients often had for them. From observing and talking with both workers and managers, I observed the respect with which workers seemed to be treated in the day-to-day operation of the company and how much effort managers made to run the company in a way that correlated to their needs. The slide show ended with ValleyCare staff members doing a rousing impromptu rendition of the then current pop hit "Taking Care of Business."

"These Are the Nurturers . . ."

Home health care is a people-based business. It depends first of all on recruiting, selecting, and training the workers who provide its services.[3] Theresa Francis, a veteran of the buyout effort at Century Brass who became an active member of the committee that founded ValleyCare, stated that, from its beginnings, VCC's mission was not only to "serve the community that doesn't generally get the care" but also to "provide jobs with the same community that didn't have the jobs." VCC's founders selected several of Waterbury's poorest neighborhoods as target areas for employment: "We hope to provide employment opportunities to low-income people especially those living in Berkeley Heights, a public housing project with 350 families, 98% of whom are Black; in the North End of Waterbury, a predominantly Black neighborhood where the 1980 census estimated that 25% of the residents live below the poverty line; St. Cecilia's Parish [and] the South End, a predominantly Hispanic area plagued by poverty and unemployment."[4]

The NVP had been involved in organizing projects in all of these areas. The project worked hard to recruit employees as well as clients through member parishes. Its years of connection to the surrounding community and layers of prior organizing were critical to the recruitment effort's success, a fact not lost on VCC's outside evaluators: "This home care project does not constitute a new linkage of churches in community-based development. It is a new project by an existing partnership of churches and other community institutions. . . .

NVP has successfully reached deep into congregations—beyond the clergy. We were impressed by the close church ties of most Health Care Committee members. . . . It's fascinating how personal growth and community gain spiral together in NVP activities."[5]

In fact, several members of the Health Care Committee, itself drawn from diverse community sectors, became VCC home-care workers themselves or worked hard to recruit people through their own connections. Margie Rosati recalled many people arriving at VCC's doors, including "people that were involved with the Naugatuck Valley Project in their housing or other issues, and people who were friends of theirs. We never really had to concentrate on advertising. Because as soon as we started hiring people, people came. And they came not one, but three, four at the same time."[6]

Indeed, when an article about VCC appeared in the local paper, more than a hundred people contacted the NVP looking for jobs, even though the article said nothing about jobs being available. As Rosati remembered, "These were people who had lost their jobs in factories that had moved out of the area, some of them had worked in health care, were not happy with how things were, or they were not able to get the hours, some of them were on welfare. The majority of them single mothers."

Beyond serving the residents of Waterbury's most impoverished areas, VCC had made other commitments to itself, the NVP, and its funders regarding its hiring strategies. The agency planned to gather a workforce that reflected the racial and ethnic diversity of the Waterbury area. Pat Diorio noted, "The business plan called for a mix of a third, a third, and a third white, Hispanic, and black. And in the early days, in the first probably three or four years, we were pretty close to a third, a third, and a third." At the end of 1991, for example, VCC had eight African Americans, six Hispanics, and eight European Americans on its paraprofessional staff.[7]

Some Home Care Committee members were passionate about minority hiring. Elida Santana, a Puerto Rican social worker who was active in the committee, recalled: "A lot of people came to my office and asked for jobs. I lost a lot of sleep thinking in my bed at night, 'What can I do for all those people?' One of the things that I always make sure of, that they hire some of my people. Because when we started ValleyCare, one of the things that we talked about was to hire people that were minorities."[8]

The personal qualities of the workforce, as well as the social and economic ones, were critical for ValleyCare's success. As one company document stated: "Our goal is to screen applicants so that we select those who are most likely to provide high quality care, become active, involved worker owners, and remain with the agency. We specifically look for people who are friendly, caring, reliable, fair, and interested in working in a team."[9]

According to Rosati, "Before we moved into our first office, we had our little office at the Naugatuck Valley Project and we started our interviewing there." Rosati interviewed applicants and then checked references and police and motor vehicle records. VCC utilized the approach developed at CHCA in the Bronx, which was "to assume that the person didn't know anything about the business. And the questions would bring out that kind of thing, what is your interest in this field, and invariably I would hear, I took care of my grandfather because my mother was working, or my brother is in a wheelchair and has cerebral palsy and I'm the one that took care of him since I was 13 or 12." She continued, "One of our home health aides, her father was injured, fell off a ladder when she was very young, and she was the one that provided the care for her father. Because the mother had to go out and work. One thing about the people that come is that these are the people that are the nurturers."

Using her own skills and imaginative and effective techniques worked out by CHCA,[10] Rosati explored both the general personalities of the applicants and their specific responses to hypothetical work situations:

> You present a problem. This patient needs to increase nutrition. Lost a lot of weight, she's been in the hospital, the most important thing is nutrition. And the nurse leaves and you make their scrambled eggs and their juice, and the toast, and the tea, and the patient says to you, the patient is forgetful, "I already had breakfast." And you know that they didn't. What would you do? Well one person would say, "Oh, I would play with them like they're a little kid and I would say, here comes a train, or I would really talk to them and tell them how important it is, but I wouldn't force them." And then there's another person that says, "I would ask the person, what would you like for breakfast? What is your favorite thing that you want? And I would make that. And if the patient didn't eat, just had a couple of spoonfuls, I would put that dish away and five minutes later say, 'I made you breakfast,' because forgetful people don't remember that they didn't eat or ate." You get some nutrition but you leave something for supper, the patient doesn't eat it, what would you do the next day? "I would call the nurse and ask the nurse if it's okay to give them Ensure, if there's any supplement. I would think of other things that I can give her, liquids that contain the kind of nutrition." That's the person that I want. I looked for the people that show that kind of caring, that would elaborate not only on what they would do but their feelings about what they were doing.

Rosati also used the staff's wide network in the local community: "If I was going to hire somebody from a certain community, I would have the applications and I would call my staff that we already had and I would say, does anybody know this person and this person and this person. And they would say to me, she is really nice, she is a church person, she's really good with the kids, and this one is on the corner of Willow every evening. So I would utilize the staff themselves to screen some of the people."[11]

Training

Connecticut regulations made it almost impossible for agencies like VCC to do their own initial training. VCC had to send its aides to a special state-certified two-week training course at the local community college. After 160 hours in the field and 4 hours of in-service training, home health aides could be certified by the state.[12] Aides had to have additional in-service training each year to refresh and expand their skills.

The state required 10 hours of orientation to the company; ValleyCare doubled that amount. While VCC had to comply with content-based state educational requirements for its health care paraprofessionals, one of the agency's own goals was "to assure that there is growth, stimulation, motivation, and continued competence of all employees . . . to provide education in a way that develops a participative culture." VCC strove to make training comfortable, meaningful, and fun from the start. Margie Rosati realized that "the home health aides very seldom see each other, they really don't get to know each other, so what I would do is that I would always hire in groups. So that if right off the bat they didn't feel like they were a part of the whole agency, at least they were a part of this team that worked together and solved problems during orientation." Rosati tried to convey the sense that working at VCC was more than a job: "You have an introduction, you have everybody meet each other, and you start from the beginning, and you talk about the company. A very important part of the orientation was the history of the Naugatuck Valley Project and the Dominican Sisters, and the Lilly Foundation, and Ms. Collaborative. It was in addition to all the things that the government says you have to do. This was more about developing teamwork, about trust." Trainees met the office staff and played team-building games Rosati had learned at CHCA. Sometimes people outside the training room "wondered what we were doing because we would be hysterical laughing but we were going through the paces."[13]

Rosati pointed out that the games and training activities had multiple purposes: to learn content areas, to encourage cooperation, and to have aides reflect upon life-management issues.

> In one of the training sessions we talked about yourself as a stick figure and what are your priorities, what motivates you, and what is your self-interest. You could put them in order, like "the most important thing in my life today is my children, and my husband and my parents and my dogs and my job." And then

learning how these things can change when something happens. And dealing with your home life as opposed to your work life. And how when these things change your job some days is the most important thing, and then your child gets sick and it's the least important thing. And how to manage all that. And how to set up systems in place that will allow you to have an enjoyable employment. Because if your child gets sick, you don't have a babysitter, you're going to miss out on working, you're going to miss money, you're certainly not going to be empowered if you cannot work.

Trainees were encouraged to pool their skills so that each could feel like an expert and help each other out. Rosati observed: "I would identify people in the group—in fact, I would have them identify people in the group that were really good, that had expertise. Because everybody had a little something special that the other people could utilize. So that if [home health aide] Sandra Calderón was wonderful at paperwork and another of the girls was not, she would feel comfortable calling Sandra instead of handing in paperwork that was incorrect." She reflected, "It was good to give them the feeling that they could count on each other and that they were all special in some way that could be utilized by the group." Mutual support was similarly encouraged in the probationary period in the field. "Home health aides that had just received their training, instead of putting them out in the field immediately, as part of the orientation I would send them out with another home health aide. So that they became the teachers out there."

Even though many of the trainees were Spanish speaking, orientations were never conducted bilingually. In fact, Rosati regarded the use of English as an important part of the training process as well as of the personal growth of aides on the job. "I have to say that on a couple of occasions it was really borderline, they really had difficulty with English. But they were the best people, they were so wonderful with the patients." Rosati saw the use of a common language as a means of community building:

> You live in the community, you speak the language of the community, you do not associate with people that are outside of your community. This was part of understanding that we were all together, that we were all the same, so that it was important that they speak English. And it was really nice to see some of the staff, when they came in, the English that they spoke, and how shy they were, and how afraid they were of making mistakes, and it's wonderful to see [home health aide] Lillian González now standing up and talking up a storm in English. And now she's working with the VNA. That's a tough bunch over there, and she is doing wonderful, she's standing her ground.

One of the main tasks of worker orientation was to establish not only the technical and language skills but also the social skills necessary to do the job.

Rosati believed it was part of VCC's mission to help aides who might not have come in with exemplary personal styles. These included more abrasive as well as less assertive people: "I had a home health aide who was so rough. Very good, never missed a day in all the years that she worked. But she could not talk to people. So I made a commitment to that girl, and so many times I wrote down phrases to use instead of, 'Are you crazy?' when the patient asked something, because that patient really thought that she was saying that she was crazy. And that girl was wonderful for ValleyCare. She gave me a lot of headaches, but she had five, six, seven years of good income, and she was very happy with the agency." Rosati figured that "the thing was that you needed to find a patient that would click with her. And the patients that clicked with her were patients that talked the same way she did. So you do make a commitment to people [who] may not be at the top of the list. But there's something about them that is worthwhile."

Rosati's ideal aide would have been a combination between the softer and the rougher styles. Softer styles were usually the trainees' greatest asset—but often their downfall as well. "Home health aides are the most nurturing people. They are the people that want to be loved." She would tell them in orientation, "'You know why you're a home health aide? Because you need to know that people love you and you need to express your love for people and all these wonderful things. And all those qualities that make you so good at your job are the same things that crucify you.' Because people who have those feelings, it's very difficult for them to be assertive. And when they cannot be assertive, after a while of pounding, they get aggressive."

A major issue for home health aides was setting limits—being able to say no to the client when appropriate, without being too aggressive. Although Rosati expected the aides to be courteous and perform their work according to the care plan, "an agency needs to do a lot of teaching and a lot of developing these people so that they can be assertive, so that they don't feel that they have to be adored by these patients all the time. Respected, yes. And they need to set limits, and it's hard." She explained how she trained the aides in assertiveness through creative role play:

> I would do a little bit of theater. We would talk about how do you tell someone no, because you're going to have to say no to a patient at some point, because they're going to ask you to do things that are not in your job description and that are against the rules. So in the interview I would ask some of those questions. What would you do if a patient said, "I want my oven cleaned"? And if the response is, "I'd say that's not my job," I would be looking out for the attitude. It wouldn't totally eliminate [them], because I think that part of our job was to develop people. Not only to bring what we perceived as the best possible staff,

but to help some of the people that through no fault of their own maybe did not know how to communicate. And just needed to learn.

I would ask one of the girls to pretend that she was the patient and to ask me to do her oven. And I would say, "I'm going to show you right now what the correct way of doing it is. And I am going to demonstrate that this can be done about any request that is made of you that is not in your job description, that is not in your best benefit or the benefit of the company or even the benefit of the patient."

"Okay, you, you're the patient." And we would come up with a funny name, Marilyn Monroe or something like that, and then she would say to me, "I want you to do my oven. It's filthy." So I would go over to the make believe oven and I would go [gasp], "oh my God, it is, it's filthy, oh it's terrible. I'm sure smoke comes out of it and everything. I wish I could do it. But I can't do it. However, if you want me to, I can call the agency and find out if there's a chore group that would do things like this. It may be that you have to pay for the service but I'm sure that the agency can help us find somebody that can do it."

And I would say, "What does that say? First thing it says that you were paying attention, you validated [them] by going over there and looking at it and agreeing, it's a filthy oven. You are excusing yourself, and you're offering a solution. The patient may not like the solution, the part of paying for a service, but nevertheless it's a solution. And it's four things that you're doing, right? You're listening, you're validating, you're excusing yourself, and you're offering a solution, an alternative."

You don't ever go, that's not my job, and you don't cop an attitude, and you don't say, you crazy? And you don't say, no, I'm not doing that. This is the way you do it.[14]

Working in the Field

VCC's planners had deliberately chosen a challenging market niche not well served by existing companies. While the acute-care patient market was dominated by well-established agencies such as the VNA, others who needed home care—the elderly, disabled, and chronically ill—were not adequately served. "Services were being provided," Diorio explained, "but not consistently, not what I would call well. The chronic patients were getting a lot of different home health aides, they weren't able to get the hours they need. And it's a big market, we figured we could get a piece of it."[15]

Though difficult, working with longer-term patients had its advantages for VCC's employees: "I think that was a good decision because it tied in with our goal of having decent hours and enough hours for the home health aides. When you deal with mostly an acute care population, they're patients who come and go very quickly." But chronically ill patients often required care that went far beyond physical ailments. As VCC nurse Maria Gerard put it:

> [For] most of our clients, it wasn't so much the diagnosis, it was their living arrangements or not being able to comply that seemed to really keep us in the home. For example, you would get somebody and they had gone into the hospital for congestive heart failure, so you thought that you're going to go into the home and you're going to teach them everything you need to know about congestive heart failure, all the symptoms they need to look for.
>
> But that was just the beginning. Then you found out that there was just so much more. There were problems with food and transportation and getting to the doctors. Sometimes they were non-compliant because of their circumstances. You ended up actually being in there longer because of other problems they would run into, not taking their medication or not having the money or not having someone to get it for you. A lot of our work was making all these phone calls and getting all these arrangements so that they could remain stable.

Although Gerard recognized the larger context of need surrounding many chronically ill patients, she also clearly perceived the tensions between providing such holistic care and attending to the agency's bottom line. "I really don't know how other home care agencies function, although I do think that maybe it was because ValleyCare was small, maybe it was because we had that need to see the company do well that we at times took on more than we really should. I think a lot of the bigger agencies would say, you need to make transportation arrangements, or you need to do this and that and they might give the client a number. We would make the phone call or we would get the aide to make the phone call."[16]

Providing good-quality home care involved far more than mechanically going through a care plan. "You know what I think makes [the aides] good is focusing on the patients' needs. [Some] had been in a home taking care of a patient for a month and you could walk in and ask them, how's their skin and how's their feet, is there any problem breathing, and some of them just weren't focused, they were there to give this lady a bath. And then there were other nurses' aides who—you could just walk in through the door and they would say, 'check her feet, I think she has a little sore, and she's not breathing right today.' Those were the ones that you knew were focused on the patient. They picked up on everything." That kind of attentiveness was good for both nurse and patient: "When you're seeing eight or nine clients a day it's nice to be able to walk into a home and the nurses' aide gives you an idea of what's been going on, because then it helps you focus too on the problem." One aide put it this way: "I think a lot of it is psychological. [One patient says] I am not doing well today. I don't care if I live or die. I want you to live and she says why would you want me to live. I say because I care about you. I don't know you but I still care about you. Every day we sit and play cards and I let her beat me. We both laugh, you know, it gives her a different outlook on life."[17]

Being an effective home health aide—and enjoying the work into the bargain—was not easy. It demanded the flexibility to be able to deal with an erratic schedule and a changing roster of clients. It required the patience to perform the many tasks required by the clients' care plan, ranging from bathing and other personal care, taking vital signs, and feeding the client to light housekeeping, cooking, and shopping. It meant dealing with sometimes difficult patients and family members, having the courage to go into unfamiliar or dangerous neighborhoods, and possessing high levels of perceptiveness and sensitivity.

Henrietta Norman became one of VCC's first aides after she got laid off from the phone company. Norman was an African American single mother who had originally connected with the NVP through tenant organizing in Waterbury's Berkeley Heights public housing project, served as president of the NVP, and lived in the NVP-created Brookside Cooperative. She was one of numerous people who came into the company through the NVP's extensive network. At first she was skeptical about her ability to do the job. "I have no patience," she said, but "once I got involved," she liked working with the clients. "And the personal care involved, I didn't think I could do that," but, "you know, you're working with people, you get to care about them and you want to see them doing the best they can and you try to work a little harder."[18]

Lillian González was a Puerto Rican–born migrant who had moved to Waterbury from New York City in order to raise her four children in a safer environment. She was one of the many aides who came to the company by word of mouth. Through a program offered by Waterbury's Hispanic social service agency, she had trained as a nurse's aide at a local technical school. A friend at VCC mentioned her name to Rosati, and in 1993 she became a ValleyCare aide.

González's first case was a Hispanic patient, bedridden with terminal cancer. She had "to bathe him, transfer him to the wheelchair, help him eat. I went in the morning and also in the afternoon to get him ready for bed. His wife was there; she helped me a lot. After a few months he died. His family continues to be my friends, they never forgot me. He has two sons who are twins who are friends of my husband, they began to work together, and we visit each other."[19]

Norman, González, and VCC's other aides experienced both gratifications and challenges on the job. They struggled with clients who refused to be touched and with patients who called company management to complain about the services they were receiving. Often, they experienced the very boundary issues that Rosati had warned them about. Henrietta Norman said: "They want you to clean the refrigerator, they want you to mop the floors, and they want you to wash the clothes. You do light cleaning or if you have time, you would do the floor but the most important thing you're going in for is the personal care. Some of them think that you're there for the whole family, can you wash my son's clothes or can you fix my son something to eat when he comes home from work." When the aides refused, patients called the office, and "we have to explain to them, that's not why the aide is there, the aide is there for you, not your family."

At times, clients called forth the greatest reserves of compassion that the aides could muster. Norman recalled her most difficult case:

> She was paralyzed from the neck down. She was 32 years old and she had gotten shot [by] a jealous boyfriend. She had two sets of twins, but [her] daughter got killed in the same incident.
>
> No matter what you did it wasn't right. But I kind of understood because I wouldn't know how I would react in a situation like that. Sometimes I try to put myself in a situation. If all of a sudden I was handicapped to that extent and knowing that a child died and she couldn't go to the funeral, and it was always a threat that if she couldn't get the proper care she would end up back in a home—so you try to be kind of patient. I stayed there for over a year, and that was the only way I was able to stay.

Racial and cultural differences presented another challenge for aides. White patients were sometimes suspicious of their aides, typically inner-city women of color. One time during Norman's tenure as office staff, "one lady called and she said that we had sent her a black aide, 'I don't like black people in my house, you get the black girl out of my house.' And I had to sit there and listen to that without saying anything, and so then I said, 'Why didn't you want her there?' She said, 'Well you know black people steal things.'"[20]

ValleyCare was committed to successful cross-cultural mediation and found that, with time, both patients and aides had gratifying experiences with each other. Rosati reflected:

> There are certain communities that do not understand minorities as well as other communities. They have not been exposed to minorities. There's towns that are like that. And it was wonderful to see our home health aides that were Hispanic being able to take care of people in those communities, people who were clearly prejudiced, who gained an understanding, and developed a relationship and even got to love some of our staff, and I kid around and I say that there's a lot of Polish and Russian people in Naugatuck eating rice and beans

and *pastelillos,* and they love it, and the girls then have to go shopping at C-Town to make them the meals.[21] Like Friday would be the day for cooking a Spanish meal. And these home health aides would bring food from home, so that [the patients] would try it. We had a home health aide, Lillian González, and she took care of a patient in Naugatuck. From Monday through Thursday they followed the care plan to a tee. Personal care, breakfast, straightening up, doing a little shopping. On Friday the care plan changed, and it was their care plan. The bath took place, the breakfast took place, the Spanish lesson took place, and the English lesson took place. So the patients became part of the development of staff that for the longest time felt that they didn't belong with those groups of people. It was great to see it.[22]

Aides and patients got to exchange information about their different worlds. For Henrietta Norman, being an aide was often an educational experience: "This one lady, she was the first woman on the police department. I've met a lot of different people and I'd talk to them and I learned their backgrounds."[23]

ValleyCare staff tried when possible to match Spanish-speaking aides and clients. Such aides "knew the circumstances of the house, they knew why this lady got so depressed that she wouldn't take her medication because she had problems with her son or whatever." With aides and clients from the same background, "you weren't as likely to label somebody and say, well she's not doing this because it's her culture. We had great families, but we had a lot of elderly with limited resources and the extended family wasn't always willing to help. It's very easy to tell a client, well, tell your granddaughter to call. But if you knew why the granddaughter wouldn't call then you were more likely to say, all right, let's try to find another way, not just say, well, this lady, she doesn't care."

Nurse home visits aimed at increasing knowledge, ability, and independence, both for aides and for clients. "It was problem solving and teaching. We did a lot of diabetic teaching on short acting and long acting insulin, how meals would affect their blood sugars, what symptoms to look for and what to do if you find these symptoms." As Maria Gerard put it, "A lot of times it was simple things like, this bathtub bench isn't safe any more, why don't we get something a little bit different, and maybe changing the way the bathroom was set up so there were no scatter rugs to make sure that no one slipped. Does the home health aide understand that the client is a diabetic and so what kinds of foods are you preparing. Looking at the patient's diagnosis and the way the care plan was set up and making sure that they understood it and they were following it and that there were no safety hazards in the home."[24]

Home care's emphasis on caring could have its drawbacks—notably over-involvement. Rosati observed that the home health aides are "such wonderful people, and they're so caring, and they're so sentimental that they share their problems with everybody, they get so close to these patients and they become family." The aides themselves "establish this kind of system: 'I'm going to take care of you, I'm going to do everything for you.' And then they start giving more and giving more and becoming more familiar, becoming more over-involved, sharing more of their problems. So that is one of the inherent problems of being a home health aide and being the kind of people that they are."

Confidentiality was another important concern, particularly in a densely networked community:

> We had a couple of situations where a home health aide said things that they shouldn't have said at another patient's house. And in the orientation I go, "Okay, I'm going to tell you something that is very important. I'm going to tell you something that you are never to do. And I'm going to guarantee you that within one week or two weeks of employment, one of you is going to do it. And look at me in the face, straight, because within two weeks, no more than a month, one of you and I are going to be sitting looking at each other like this. I guarantee it." And it happens. And it's stupid things. They're not thinking. They make a comment about another patient. They don't realize that the day before they said the name of the patient. Now they're making a general comment that can be put together with the name that they said before.
>
> But it's hard for them to develop the habit of referring to their patients as "my first patient, my second patient," without saying sex, nothing. And I try to tell them, "There's things that you can say. It is to your advantage to say all the positive things and keep the negatives to yourself, because if you're taking care of a patient and you say to that patient, my first patient is such a pain in the neck, God forbid you should say, 'Mr. Smith is a pain in the neck.' Because that patient is going to say, 'Geez, she's talking like that about that other patient, what is she saying to the next one, to patient number three about patient number two?'" But they don't think the full picture so you have to always reinforce this. And I've had to bring staff in and talk to them and confront them about things that they've said, things that they've shared that they shouldn't have, comments that they've made about patients.

The expectation of appropriate behavior by aides sometimes led to discipline, a difficult challenge for employee-owned companies. Rosati sometimes had to fire aides: "Because they were not good workers. Because they called out, because they were not responsible, because they didn't show up at the patient's house when they were supposed to. God only knows we gave enough counseling and support and opportunities. Because we did go through progressive discipline. But especially in a cooperative, you have to look at the good of the company. At the survival of the company." She also emphasized,

"Your reputation is the most important thing. And you have to safeguard the people that are really doing a good job, and are taking care of business, and eliminate anything that is contrary to the cooperative." On one occasion she fired an aide believed to be stealing:

> And so I brought her in the office and I presented the picture to her. I told her that I was concerned that this and this person had said that something was missing from their home. I told her that I had no reason to mistrust her. Neither do I have the power to investigate because I'm not an expert at investigations. But that it was happening enough so that I looked back and I presented the picture to her. "Look, there've been at least thirteen patients and these ten say that something is missing from their house. What would you think?" She said, "I would think that person is stealing." I said, "This picture doesn't look good at all. What do you want to do about it? I don't think this is the type of situation where I could give you a warning, because there's no way that I could do the other part of it, the constant supervision and all that." And she looked at me and she said, "I'll resign." And I said to her, "If you didn't, I would have to ask you to leave. In spite of the fact that I have no reason to say that you did anything wrong."[25]

In the Office

Behind the scenes in ValleyCare's office was a support staff trying to run an agency that would provide both good working conditions for its paraprofessionals and quality care for its patients. Faith Muller, the agency's first bookkeeper and receptionist, described the demanding character of work in a home health care company office: "Home care is a strange type of business, even from the bookkeeping standpoint. And that is, it's fast paced. There's always something to do and it needs to be done right away. Not like a normal business when you can put things away at the end of the day and say, 'That's it, I'm done.' You're always continuing to have to do something the next day, or it needs to be tackled right away." Faith continued, "The most difficult thing for me is when I'm picking up that phone and you have an agitated elderly on the line, and to try to agree with what they're saying and to float that problem to a supervisor." In the process, Faith said she had "learned to be very patient, and patient with the people that are coming in. Some days it's very hard to come in and put on that happy face. You've got to be personable, and you've got to be able to take a problem and somebody screaming at you and say, well, this isn't really personally they're mad at you, they're just really aggravated, and try to direct that to the right person."[26]

At first, Rosati remembered, ValleyCare had a skeletal staff performing all of the new agency's tasks: "When we opened the doors it was Pat, myself, and

Faith Muller, who was receptionist, bookkeeper, toilet paper purchaser, and coffeemaker, everything. And Pat was everything else, and I was everything else with the home health aides. So that was it. And then we had Betsy Gaudian, the nurse, and we had two homemakers and two home health aides, I think it was, and one patient every other week. And that's how we started."[27]

As the company grew, Diorio recalled, new office staff were hired: "someone who did payroll, somebody who did billing, and a receptionist. Margie always was the homemaker/home health aide coordinator, and initially she scheduled the aides, but in the last several years we also had a scheduler. That's an awful job."[28]

Rosati's several jobs became overwhelming. It became impossible for her to recruit, interview, and orient new aides; troubleshoot for those in the field; and schedule all at the same time. When she gave up her job as scheduler, it provided a new work opportunity for an NVP leader and home health aide, Henrietta Norman, who continued to work half-time as an aide, then transitioned into a full-time office job.

Whether scheduling was an "awful job" or not, it was certainly a tense and tricky one. Matching aides with clients was difficult, particularly for a company that was doing its best to provide both decent jobs and quality care. Public transportation in the Naugatuck Valley was extremely limited. For the patients' sake, it was important to hire aides with reliable transportation. Yet many among the population who most needed the jobs did not have access to cars. Scheduler Henrietta Norman explained that Rosati "tried to hire aides that had the transportation, but some of the aides didn't, and if you had an aide that was available, she couldn't take the job because the job was so far she couldn't get to it on the bus line." At times, the company had to turn down jobs in suburbs and outlying towns because there was no public transportation and no aides with their own.

Other scheduling challenges grew from the nature of the work: "Say if someone called out, trying to find someone to take that person's place and if you got a new case, trying to find an aide that wasn't busy so you can send that aide to cover. That was a challenge in itself, trying to get everybody covered and not leave anybody without some kind of care. Especially in the wintertime, when a lot of aides couldn't get out because of the snow."[29]

Fortunately, the office environment encouraged problem solving. Nurse Maria Gerard confirmed that, "as far as the nurses were concerned, we always discussed all the new clients, any problems. We made time, and I think one of the benefits was because the way the nursing office was set up, all the nurses came to chart in one room" where they all had their desks. "So when one nurse was having a hard time with one client we all knew about it. It was kind of like case conferencing."[30]

The social atmosphere in the office also allowed workers to let off steam in more informal ways. Faith Muller's view was that "though home care is very stressful, sometimes that gives Margie and the office staff a way out. We sit here, we joke around, we laugh, we sing, and that gets us through the day. And by the end of the day, sometimes we don't quit at 4:30, we're here till 5 or 6 at night, because of the kind of business it is. And that's the way for us to release and not get so stressed out about things here." Likewise, Henrietta Norman stated, "The nurses and everybody in there got along well, we would sometimes have lunch together, we'd all buy something and we'd chip in, we'd celebrate each other's birthdays. Sometimes when you'd get kind of overwhelmed you can stop and you go talk to somebody for a couple of minutes and you'd calm down and you'd go back and get a renewed outlook on what you were doing."[31]

One of VCC's chronic problems, however, was attracting and keeping quality office staff. While the agency's efforts made turnover relatively low among the aides, it was high among office staff. As Diorio explained, salaries for all positions were lower than industry standards:

> We were never able to recruit people that I think would have been my first choice, the ideal candidate, because we were small, because it was a constant struggle, because the jobs were more than full time and our salaries weren't competitive.
>
> It wasn't the mission they weren't interested in. They weren't interested in a small company because we couldn't give them the security that they were looking for, and the advancement. I interviewed a lovely young woman, very capable, but she was a young woman who was interested in becoming a supervisor and then a director of clinical services and then the administrator eventually, and she could see there wasn't anything here for her.

Diorio chose one director of clinical services "because she was the only one interested in coming to work for us and I thought, well we need to try this. And why did I choose that office manager, the same thing. Because we needed somebody desperately and she was the only one interested in the job. Now that's not a good reason to choose somebody, but it's realistically what happened."[32]

Improving the Jobs

Providing stable full-time jobs for aides was at the core of ValleyCare's mission, but administrators had to work hard to provide decent schedules. At times, VCC had to struggle both with their contractors and with their clients, even at the risk of rejecting business. According to Pat Diorio:

When we started, of course it was difficult and most of the patients like morning so it's always an uphill battle when you're trying to give people 40 hours in less than seven days a week. In the very beginning when we didn't have a lot of patients, some of the aides even then were getting 35 and 40 hours, but they were working seven days a week, thirty days a month, because they would then pick up, like four hours on a Saturday and four hours on a Sunday to get close to their 40 or 35 hours. Then we got to a period where we had enough patients that we were able to give them 35 or 40 hours in a five-day week, and we did that mostly with aides who could be very flexible. If they couldn't be, it was still hard. What we needed were people who would say yes, I'll take a case from 7 to 8 in the morning to get somebody ready for day care, and then I'll go on to an 8:30 patient, 8:30 to 10:30, and then 10:45 to 12:45 and so on. They also needed to be available in the afternoon.

What we were starting to be able to do is give some of our patients twice a day coverage, but that meant 8:30 to 10:30 and again 3 to 5 or 4 to 6. So those aides who could be flexible and maybe finish at 1 and take a little break and then go back from 4 to 6 were really getting 35 to 40 hours in a 5 day week. And then they worked every fourth weekend and they were averaging out then to the 35 or 40. And some of them were working every other weekend, that was their choice.

All this required nurses and other staff who were with the program, Diorio noted:

> We expected our nurses to understand that one of our goals was to provide full time work for the aides. And we were small enough that we could communicate on a day to day basis with the nursing staff and say, you have a new admission today, and you're going to go out and they're going to want an aide. Do not tell them that they can have an aide at 8 o'clock or 8:30. We have no aides at 8:30. You need to tell them that we'd be happy to send an aide at 1 o'clock for two hours and then if they really prefer morning, as soon as aide time becomes available in the morning, we'll do that. Then what happens is the patient likes the aide, and when another aide becomes available at 8:30 they don't want to change, so then you've got an aide in the morning for your next patient. And that's what we would do. And we would say to the patient, we don't have anybody at 8:30. So you have a choice. Now, if you don't want the 1 to 3, then you need to consider another agency.
>
> CCCI often would call with very specific orders. We didn't have it, we would tell them up front. We do not have an aide that can go in the morning five days a week. And if this patient can't be flexible we can't take this referral. And we wouldn't even take it. And sometimes what would happen is that worker would go back and say to the patient, this is what this agency can do. And we did gather a reputation for providing consistent quality service, so the case managers would often negotiate with those patients and say, it's probably in your best

interest to take ValleyCare because you've already been to another agency and you've seen how they promised an aide 8:30 to 10:30, they don't deliver it, and then they don't deliver consistency, you have a different aide every day.

Diorio and Rosati were deeply disturbed that VCC could not afford to pay better wages. They sought other incentives for staying with the company: "We looked at the wage structure and we tried to structure it as much as we can based on what were prevailing wages, but they were lower than many of our competitors." One of the company's most troubling problems was that it could not pay for health insurance. "A few years later we did through the Chamber [of Commerce] begin offering health insurance, and I think they initially paid $2 a week, but many of the home health aides weren't eligible for it because they didn't work enough hours. You had to work an average of 35 hours a week. And we were never able to offer health insurance where we could pay for the family." VCC provided aides modest sick and vacation pay prorated to their hours of work. It paid mileage and, unlike most other agencies, travel time between patients.

Ultimately, VCC's dedication to its aides had results. According to Diorio, the agency's home health aide turnover was consistently low, roughly 20 percent as compared to the industry standard of 50 to 60 percent. "I think what attracted people was our willingness to work with them to give them full time hours. Many of them were working at other agencies who said they would give them full time hours and they never delivered. And some of them came here and we were able to do that, actually for quite a few of them, and that made a real difference."[33]

ValleyCare Cooperative created jobs for scores of Naugatuck Valley workers, most of whom had lost their previous jobs or were on welfare. It succeeded in managing the company to maximize the quality of the jobs for its workers, turning what were normally irregular, highly casualized jobs into full-time, reliable ones. It also succeeded in providing quality services to clients who often received unreliable care from an ever-changing set of aides.

ValleyCare created a management structure that was accountable both to its worker owners and to the broader community represented by the NVP. It established management practices and a work environment that provided support, enjoyment, and personal meaning and growth to the workforce. It provided employees a voice in every aspect of the company's life and work. Employees shared responsibility both for the company and for the work itself.

ValleyCare thus challenged some of the key sources of powerlessness of the valley's people. It held managers and other economic actors accountable to worker and community needs. It provided broad-based local ownership whose interest lay in reinvestment in the local community. It provided work-ers voice and power in their own enterprise. It mobilized resources, albeit modest ones, to fund local economic development. It cajoled government agencies into playing a supportive role.

In sum, ValleyCare largely succeeded in managing a company for the benefit of its community and its employees. But it did so only within the constraints of the market, which in this case was largely shaped by govern-ment policy. If the market did not make it possible for such a company to pay adequate wages, supply health and other benefits, or provide opportunities for staff career advancement, there was no way the most dedicated workers or managers could overcome its constraints. Even as the company grew, these constraints would prove even more severe.

9. The Demise of ValleyCare

During the second half of its life, ValleyCare faced massive external changes in the home health care industry. At the same time, ValleyCare was grappling with changes in the company culture brought about both by these larger industry trends and by the company's internal growth. In combination, these changes made it increasingly difficult for the agency to realize its goals, led it to adopt drastic survival measures, and ultimately forced it to close.

Decline

Throughout its years of operation, VCC was buffeted by the shifting winds of state and federal health care policies. As early as its second quarter, VCC had suffered the effects of a state budget crisis that led to a cutback in homemaker and companion programs.

As early as 1994, anticipated changes in federal health care policy were also forcing the company to reconsider its strategies. Government-funded health care programs such as Medicare and Medicaid were expected to switch to a managed-care model. Though details were vague, this suggested a new "capitated system" under which agencies would be reimbursed up to a certain amount of money per patient rather than paid per service performed. Hospitals and VNAs appeared to be positioning themselves for national reform by initiating preferred-provider relationships with home health care agencies. Within this system, agencies like VCC would have to submit bids to these institutions, and the lowest bidder providing the highest quality of service would get the contract. An industry consolidation in which larger—and fewer—home health care agencies would survive seemed the likely scenario for the future.

The federal Balanced Budget Act of 1997 implemented the massive budget cuts that many in the health care sector had feared. Congress planned to save some $130 billion on health care over the next five years and instituted huge cuts in Medicare and Medicaid. Reimbursements were indeed placed on a capitated basis, and home health care services were severely curtailed. Massive consolidation began among industry players that left little room for small companies like ValleyCare.

To survive in the new environment, VCC needed to grow substantially, expand its office staff, and become more efficient. VCC's own goals of increasing employment, improving the quality of jobs and wages for its workers, and providing incentives for worker ownership grew even more difficult to achieve.

> Things were changing within our industry from 1995 on, and good people were reluctant to go to small companies, because the handwriting seemed to be on the wall, you needed to be part of a network, you needed to be part of a regional affiliation, [or] you're going to be out of business. There's still talk about, there's going to be two major hospitals in Connecticut, Yale and Hartford, and there's going to be a few large VNAs. The predictions back in '94 and '95 were that there might be five major homecare agencies in the state in the future.[1]

ValleyCare increasingly found itself a bit player within an industry where performance standards kept declining. As companies cut corners with brief and perfunctory nurses' visits and shorter and shorter cases, both the quality of care and the quality of jobs in the companies ValleyCare had to compete with reached a new low.

Whereas VCC's service revenues had grown rapidly in its first few years, multiplying by forty-two between FY 1991 ($18,253) and FY 1994 ($780,503), the agency now began to witness a decline in its earnings. This in turn impacted the worker-owners. Home health aide monthly service hours peaked at more than 4,600 in October 1995, but they began to decline thereafter, dropping to a low of 1,727 in November 1997. Whereas full-time worker-owners had each received a patronage dividend of $314 in 1995 and the agency had netted $15,673, the patronage dividend in the following year had declined to $250, and the net profit of the agency fell to $11,400. The total service revenue of the company was now more than $1 million, but the modest profit was expected to shrink even further as a result of uncollectible debts and ever-dropping reimbursements.[2] The audit for FY 1997 showed a $13,000 loss for the company.[3]

The increasing pressure to cut corners and the difficulty of attracting good staff had an effect in turn on the agency's finances and morale. Diorio noted,

"I think we had about four good years. And then we made the mistake of not being clear about what we needed to function efficiently and effectively. We knew we needed more staff. We as a board didn't make the commitment to finding money to get more staff." The company had to write off more than $50,000 in government billings because a staffer got behind. "And I have to say we attracted some different personalities, which then made it difficult to have a cohesive working together staff. I had an administrative staff part of the time that nobody liked each other and nobody wanted to work with each other. It was a nightmare."[4] Within a couple of years, VCC went through four nursing supervisors.

As VCC entered the second half of its life, its staff struggled not only with the meaning of worker ownership in a tightening cash situation but also with fostering workplace culture among a growing population of employees. Rosati believed, "Unfortunately towards the end in the past couple of years it became harder and harder. We grew a lot more and I can understand how as you grow you really have to concentrate and pay attention at keeping the culture and the philosophy of the company going." Henrietta Norman, who had been at the company since late 1991, also saw these changes and their effects: "In the beginning it was more like a family type thing but as it got bigger it was kind of losing that closeness. You could understand with its growing, but in the beginning you felt a sense of togetherness. People would take time and talk to each other. Sometimes after work we would socialize with each other, but after it got bigger, people had different priorities, it kind of got away from that." The change affected not only "work-type problems" but "personal problems" as well. Before the company grew, "the aides would go in and talk to Margie or talk to me and then they would I guess feel better and they would go back out and start all over again. Some of them had marital problems, some financial, some kids' problems, babysitting problems, those type of things."[5]

ValleyCare administrators also grappled with growing problems in maintaining a racial and cultural balance among the staff. In the initial years, the company had met its goals of dividing jobs more or less evenly among African American, Latino, and European American applicants. Over time, the agency become more and more Hispanic oriented. In some ways, this was a strength, a special market niche that appealed to many VCC contractors and clients, but it troubled agency administrators concerned about human development and a healthy company culture. Diorio remembered, "The last couple of years at least, we had many more Hispanic workers, and relatively few black workers. We had trouble recruiting black workers and keeping them. White workers, we had a fair number. Bordering 50 percent were

Hispanic, but then you'd be talking maybe 30 percent white and 20 percent black." Rosati recalled, "The Hispanics that came were disenfranchised. In any job that they had before, if they had held any jobs, they didn't feel like they were appreciated or valued. And that came across. And we had a lot of success with that population. So I think that that was very good for them, and I think that that's why they told their friends, come to ValleyCare."

In the face of this applicant pool, Rosati's approach to hiring was complicated by the fact that she herself was Puerto Rican:

> It was interesting to see the resentment, a little bit of mistrust. I am Hispanic, that's my culture. Well it was very present in my mind that as part of our commitment to our lenders and to the people that gave us money, to hire people from certain communities. And I was very conscious about keeping a balance that was representative of the community. It was impossible at times. Because I think that the way the Hispanics that came to ValleyCare were made to feel encouraged that population to seek employment more than anybody else. So then I would agonize over what the balance looked like. And it is terrible to purposely have to say, I have to hire from this group.

The difficulty of hiring a racially balanced staff in part reflected what Diorio and Rosati analyzed as different job and survival strategies among different groups. Rosati reflected on the difficulties of hiring and keeping large numbers of African Americans:

> From the African American community we had some of our most wonderful staff. Mabel Sears, Susan Mitchell, Lonnie Jean Hunter, we had lots of wonderful people. But in order to keep the balance that I thought was required, I really had difficulty.
>
> I found a more transient look towards employment. For instance, some of them would sign up with us, then sign up with another agency and they never had enough hours. And then it presented a conflict because if we gave them a case and then another agency that paid 25 cents more than us offered them hours, they would be looking at the total, but not understanding that if they made a commitment to one place, the place would make a commitment to them. It was a more desperate type of look at employment, like the more things that I have on the fire, the better chance I have. And it was the other way around. Because if a person cannot make the commitment, neither is the scheduler going to make a commitment to them. Because if they go, "No, I have another case through another agency," and they call them the next time, it's time that the scheduler is wasting when she knows that she can call somebody else and they'll always say yes.
>
> It was a group with the least backups in their private lives, in their homes, to deal with problems when they arose. I was very concerned about that. I think

most of the black aides were heads of household and the pay scale wasn't as comparable to, say, the VNA. I was head of household, but I also felt a sense of ownership. I'm not saying that I was more dedicated but I was just more involved in the workings, because I knew what NVP was all about, so I knew what they were trying to do. We had some African Americans that really stayed. But the turnover of African Americans was greater than any other.[6]

Henrietta Norman, an NVP leader who became a VCC aide in the fall of 1991, was one of the first African Americans to join the company: "It was more Hispanic patients than any other that we had. So sometimes we would send African Americans and so you can't relate to the patient because you couldn't understand what they were saying, so I think that's kind of discouraging also," she observed. "The Hispanics did stay longer and I really think that's part of the reason. Some spoke English pretty well but [for] some of them the English wasn't all that great so I guess they felt more comfortable working with the Hispanic population. And also when they came into the office they had someone to speak to, Margie was there, and I think that helped too."[7]

In 1996, when the company found itself in increasingly straitened financial circumstances, the worker-owners had to vote upon whether to institute an expected raise that would have augmented their modest wages. The proposal was to have a small increase in March and reexamine the possibility of another raise in June. Rosati had feared what would happen under such conditions, but she was surprised and gratified with the result: "It was explained, it was discussed, and when the vote came, they voted for what was good for the company. And I said, 'Oh my God, it worked! I don't believe it!' That's when it really clicked that it could work."[8]

When June came, the worker-owners' dedication to the company was once again tested. Diorio discovered that the state reimbursement rate upon which the company's profits depended was less than they had hoped. "So we did the calculations, ICA helped us, and we couldn't give a raise. We had to have a meeting of the worker owners, and we said, this is the story, and these are the numbers, and we had three scenarios on the board, and they had it in writing in their hand. I think there were two possible increases, [one] very minimal and then [the other] a little bit more. And then what we needed to break even." She continued, "And it was very difficult, but they unanimously voted 'no raise.' *Unanimously.* Did they like it? No. Did any of us like it? No. Did some of them remember that forever and do they still talk about it? Yes. But when they saw the numbers and we said to them, 'It is your responsibility to vote what's best for ValleyCare,' they unanimously voted."[9]

During VCC's last few years, the company's increasing financial difficulties eroded patronage dividends. Still, substantial numbers of people did make the effort to "own a little piece of the company," as Lillian González had put it. According to Diorio, "We probably have had about 35 people who have become worker owners of ValleyCare; at any particular point in time the largest number we might have had would have been 25. And that might have represented pretty close to half of the workforce."[10]

In a retreat on January 15, 1995, VCC staff and board determined that the agency needed to work on a number of fronts. In addition to improving job conditions, increasing worker ownership, and reducing worker turnover, plans included strengthening its office administration, increasing its visibility to potential referral sources and clients, forming strategic alliances with other health care providers, and considering more subcontracting options. Other ideas for company expansion were also being considered, including broadening the company's geographic service area and creating more career-ladder opportunities for aides through new ventures.

One possibility that aroused interest was an adult day care center for non-English speakers. Such a center would both address the needs of underserved clients and allow Spanish-, Portuguese-, Italian-, and Russian-speaking VCC staff to use their skills and linguistic abilities within a growing array of job offerings.[11] Diorio was enthusiastic about the prospect, feeling it would fulfill many of VCC's goals. "I think there are too many elderly that are at home that have no stimulation. Sometimes their care borders on neglect and it would be a wonderful service for them," she said. "I also saw it as a way to stabilize at least some jobs, because you would be open from six in the morning till six at night, so you had 12 hours of staffing that you could fill. In an adult day care situation you would use aides who were trained similarly to the home health aides, so I didn't really see it as a big change, I saw it more as stability, a decent job, decent hours, possibly full time guaranteed, and then maybe we could tie in a health insurance package for them."

The ICA got a grant to do a feasibility study, but it concluded that such a center was not viable. "They felt that there were existing day cares that had empty slots and at that point there were so many insurances that would not reimburse for adult day care that you had to depend on a private pay market, and this is a generation that doesn't want to pay privately, no matter how much money they have." Unfortunately, "The conclusion of the study was that it was not realistic to begin an adult day care, whether it was to target Hispanic patients or all patients, that we would not be able to break even and on top of it it would create very few jobs."

Lack of money and the constant struggle not to lose ground also deflated VCC's dreams of prospering through geographic expansion. For example, the agency lacked the cash to follow through on a plan to lease cars or buy a van so that aides without cars could take cases in areas that lacked public transportation.

By 1997, ValleyCare Cooperative had to make a difficult decision that would greatly affect its autonomy and ability to shape optimal conditions for its workers and clients. Diorio recalled:

> Medicare was going to make such significant changes in their regulations and in their reimbursement that it didn't seem likely that our company could continue as a licensed, certified agency. And we did a lot of investigation on that and then made the decision to go out of the business as of June 30th, 1998. And it was the right decision. We never would have been able to make it as a licensed, certified agency. We would have needed a lot more staff, which means more cost, at a time when reimbursement has decreased. This way we could scale down our staff and our costs and place our aides with other agencies, and they would do the supervision.[12]

Maria Gerard was then a board member who had to help make this difficult decision. Voting for the restructuring, she said to herself, "I'm going to lose my job, and that was really personal to me, because I felt really good about this company." Nonetheless, "I felt that it was our only option. There were nurses' aides that had started before I did, and there were nurses' aides that had come along after I did, and some people found a place that they enjoyed and they loved their work, and I remember them being so upset when they started to hear talk" about the company closing. "So I wanted to try to do whatever it took to keep people's jobs intact."[13]

Fall

Federal and state cuts to health care had meant consolidation within the industry in which small agencies such as ValleyCare would be squeezed out unless they allied themselves with larger and more powerful actors. After much thought and negotiation, VCC decided to develop a subcontracting relationship with VNA Healthcare, the biggest VNA in the state. Diorio explained: "VNA Healthcare was the agency we chose to try and negotiate a contract with because they were supportive of us as a cooperative, they understood our mission, they supported it. They are the agency that is affiliated with St. Mary's Hospital. They do get patients from Waterbury Hospital, but Waterbury Hospital actually owns the Watertown VNA now. So VNA Healthcare was the logical choice for us and seemed to be a good partner," she said. "It was large enough we hoped that we could get enough business to break even. There also would have been opportunity because their other major branch is in Hartford, and they were having difficulty recruiting aides and keeping aides in Hartford." VNA, however, was itself struggling with the turmoil caused by shifts in government health care policy. It also faced high staff turnover, including the resignation of the company president. The three-month gap before a new president was hired was a critical time for ValleyCare.

At the beginning of July 1998, VCC entered into a subcontracting relationship with VNA Healthcare. Although that meant laying off its nursing staff, VCC hoped the new relationship would still mean high-quality jobs for its aides: "Under the business plan, we were going to be able to continue to provide our aides with decent salaries and decent benefits in this arrangement, if we could get enough volume." Within the new arrangement, VCC would be reimbursed at the rate of $16.50 per hour, a rate that meant economy for VNA as well as acceptable pay for VCC's workers. In the beginning, it seemed that the arrangement might work, although for a reduced staff of paraprofessionals. Ultimately, however, VNA was never able to provide the number of service hours or the quality of jobs it had promised ValleyCare. "We had at our peak, I would say, 65 aides. That would have been probably the '96, '97 time frame. We were probably down to 40 in June of '98. Now I have to say that those 40 may have been doing more hours than the 65 when we were at our peak. I don't believe that we ever did, as a licensed agency, more than 4000 hours a month of home health aide service. As a subcontracting agency, we did close to 5000 hours a month for at least a few months."

Because of government austerity for health care and VNA's own struggle to survive, it was difficult for VCC to obtain the quantity of work it had hoped for. Many aides were working full-time hours at the beginning of 1998. "And if those aides who wanted the hours would work with us and do evening cases and early cases, that's how we were able to continue that. And I would say that there were aides, at least the end of '97, who were still getting good hours, the hours they wanted, and in a decent schedule."

But the VNA arrangement made it far harder for ValleyCare to manage in a way that made the jobs viable for its workers. "I think we did a really good job of scheduling aides in limited geographic areas. We really paid attention to, where is this patient, and we did not expect our aide to go from here to here to here to here. We really planned that." VNA, on the other hand, might give aides far-flung cases of short duration, in some cases with little or no travel-time compensation.

One of the big problems we ran into immediately with the VNA was their requests. We were able to hold them at bay a little bit about our aides going everywhere in the world, because most of our staff don't have decent cars, and to send them to Southbury is just stupid because their car breaks down on the way, and then everybody's aggravated, the patient, the VNA, us. So we said to them, we can't do it. But they were dumping cases on us, six to seven in the morning to get a patient to day care, seven to nine at night to get a patient ready for bed, and no hours in between. Or instead of getting aide service every day, the patients were getting two or three days a week. Recently they started cutting down to one-hour cases.

Not surprisingly, some ValleyCare aides began to rebel against the deteriorating conditions. Diorio vividly remembered one such situation in VCC's last days: "I said to Martha, 'I need you to do a case,' and she said, 'I don't want to. I'm sick and tired of this work and this job.' I said to her, 'What are you talking about?' She said, 'Look at my schedule.' So I opened the book and I looked at her schedule, I thought, holy cow. She would work from seven o'clock in the morning till six o'clock at night Monday, Wednesday, and Friday. On Tuesday and Thursday she had one case, eight to nine in the morning." Martha said to Pat, "'This isn't a good job.' I said, 'You know what, Martha, you're right, this is a terrible job.'"

Top ValleyCare staff and nurses had worked within a framework in which the quality of aides' jobs was considered as important as the quality of patient care. VNA personnel, in contrast, did not accustom patients to the kind of flexibility that would allow aides to piece together full-time schedules. Diorio noted: "That was another thing that the VNA was thinking, 'Well, we have all of these patients that want eight to ten,' and I would say to them, 'but we can't hire 100 aides to do eight to ten, and then they don't do anything else.' We were not hiring more aides until the aides we had had the hours they wanted, if at all humanly possible." Diorio's attempts to fight back met with a lot of goodwill but little change: "It didn't make sense for me [to] continue working on this contract if the jobs weren't going to be decent. I said to the VNA, would you want to work this job for this kind of money? And they started getting the picture."[14]

VNA executives, however, struggling to stay afloat, could not also stay on top of the case assignments in the hands of less cooperative nurses and schedulers: "The nurses are so busy and so stressed, they try and do what the patient wants so that it limits their aggravation. And the aides suffer. That was absolutely unreasonable and should have been squashed. And it wasn't. So it affects the quality of the jobs, the hours we can get. So then the scheduler says, 'I tried to give you ten hours this week, and you didn't take it, so why are you hassling me for more hours?'"[15]

VNA precipitated a financial crisis for VCC in 1998 by reimbursing the agency for its services as much as three months late.[16] And it failed to meet its commitment to helping ValleyCare expand into the Hartford market. "The operational people couldn't make it happen, and they were bombarded with problems and staff changes. Because they really are, I believe at this point, fighting for their own survival." According to Diorio, "I did meet with Ellen Rothberg, the new head of the VNA, and she said to me, 'I'm really sorry this didn't work out, and in a couple of years I'm going to wish you were around.' And I said to her, 'I know you are, I understand this industry, and in a couple of years you are going to be dying to have dependable, flexible home health aides at a good cost.' But they couldn't do it."

By October 1998, ValleyCare Cooperative was contemplating giving up the struggle. In February 1999, it finally closed its doors. But the work was not yet over for some. Within the now silent offices, Diorio and Rosati worked for months to square accounts and to meet their responsibilities to their lenders. As I interviewed her, surrounded by stacks of company records, Diorio observed: "I was so worried about these loans that were given in such good faith. It was pretty scary when we had to close, I thought we might not be able to pay the Adrian Dominican Sisters back. Talk about being upset, not being able to pay the nuns back! But we did. We aren't going to have enough money to pay everybody. What we need to do is be sure how much money we have, so that we can probably pay everybody a percentage. So that's what we're working on now."[17] This meticulous attention to a responsible closing was much appreciated by the ICA and other worker-owner specialists who would be applying for grants and loans from many of the same sources in the future.

"We Were Just Chewed Out by the Big Guys . . ."

For many of those involved in ValleyCare Cooperative, from those who had created it to the agency's administrators, nurses, and aides, its loss was the loss of a dream. But amid the grieving was the sense of having been part of a special experience with elements worth celebrating, ways of working worth passing on, and pitfalls to avoid.

Doreen Filipiak, a working-class single mother who had been instrumental in creating the company, remembered the role of Ethel Spellman, who had been a leader in starting Valley Care:

> To me probably one of the most important parts of it was that it was brought to the forefront by a woman who simply saw a need, she was a nurse, she had been out there in the field and knew that there were people who needed help and at the same time knew that there were women out there who needed jobs, who had no training, who were in situations where they really needed something

that they could count on and something that could offer them the time they needed to work, the flexibility and eventually in time, to be part owner of the company that they worked for. And to think that it was just the thought of one person that created the company that came of it is probably the most important thing that I can think of ValleyCare. When we think of companies we think of big dollars and CEOs and board meetings, we don't think of just a person.

We started with one person, we created a company, we did everything that we set our minds to do and unfortunately other circumstances took it out of our hands. That's the hardest part.[18]

After the closing, Maria Gerard said, "I had forgotten how much I missed ValleyCare." In her new job, she went into a building where she had worked for ValleyCare. "When I went into that building, something came over me, just being in the elevator, and I ran into two clients that I used to take care of. It was a very sad experience because I knew that I probably wouldn't see these clients again, and that ValleyCare was truly gone, it just didn't exist any more. I think when you feel that way about a company you know you've had a good experience." She continued, "I don't think that it was really anything that ValleyCare did wrong, I really don't think there's a lesson to be learned. It was a small agency and I think we were just chewed out by the big guys. I can't imagine ValleyCare surviving if you don't have a contract with Cigna or Aetna or a big agency. And I think that we tried to do what we could. This is what happens when you have a company that has a totally different philosophy and their best interest is not you, it's their company."[19]

Pat Diorio believed that worker ownership was one of the most valuable components of the ValleyCare experience. "I think it had an impact. Those worker owners who did become involved, I think got a great deal from it, and I think it helped them understand the workings of the agency. I think they became sensitive to and really learned about needing to wear different hats, depending upon where you were. When you were a worker owner in voting you had to think about what was best for the agency as opposed to what was best for me as an individual."[20]

While a bit skeptical of loftier goals, Maria Gerard felt that one of the agency's key achievements was the atmosphere it created for its aides: "One of the phrases that used to get passed around a lot [was] empowerment. And I can't say that I ever got the sense that a nurses' aide felt extremely empowered by this company. But I think they probably felt more of a connection than they felt at any other company," she said. "That's probably an important lesson for people to learn, that it doesn't matter what your background is, I think you can make people feel good about where they work if you just present it to them in the right way and if you treat them the right way."[21]

In the contrast between running ValleyCare as a licensed and certified agency and working in a subcontracting relationship with another provider, Diorio was reminded of the special strengths of VCC as it was originally conceived and run:

> I think we did a lot of things really well. And one was putting together decent schedules for the aides. And it wasn't easy. The schedulers and Margie worked very hard on that. I think we did a really good job of matching up the patients and the aides, considering the strengths of the aides and the needs of the patient. I don't think there's a lot of thought to that any more.
>
> I think we did a good job of looking at wages and benefits, and whenever we could we made beneficial changes.
>
> The other thing I think we did a really good job at was keeping the staff informed. Our aides always knew what was going on, whether it was good or bad. And they always had information as soon as we could give it to them. Sometimes we couldn't tell them, but as soon as we were able to tell them, we did. Where I work now, the nurses did not know the [new] supervisor was coming this Monday, until I told them last week. At VNA Healthcare they never know what's going on. And we did a really good job through the use of memos. We pulled together a group of aides, the ones who are involved on the board are more involved worker owners, and they would call aides to give them information so that they could talk to them and the aide could ask questions.
>
> We did a really good job I think of supervising our aides when we had our own licensed agency. The nurse when she went in was there to supervise the aide, to help the aide, and to support the aide. And we also helped many of our aides gain a great deal of competence through the support we gave them, and then the in-services that we provided. So we did a lot. I think when we look at a situation, we always consider what's best for the patient, what's best for the staff, and what's best for the agency.

ValleyCare administrators and outside supporters also took a hard look at the agency's problems. One was clearly undercapitalization. Diorio said:

> It was a lesson that you have to take from ValleyCare. It's one thing to start a company but there needs to be some realistic planning on what kind of ongoing support that company is going to need in their particular industry. If you're making widgets and it's clear that you're going to make a 6 percent profit, that's one thing, but in home care, where it's hard to break even, now it's even worse, we should have had some money there to help us. I don't think it would have taken a lot of money for ValleyCare. To me, 25,000 or even 50,000 isn't a lot of money for a company that had potential revenues of over a million dollars and potential of employing 65 to 75 workers. We were offered more loans, but we didn't have the ability to take those loans and be sure that we could pay them back.

I think we've had incredible support from groups like ICA and NVP and PHI.[22] One of the most difficult things though has been that, although this agency was well-funded initially, there was not enough continued funding to make it—I think it interfered with us being as successful as we might have been. I don't believe that an agency should be started and you should expect to fund a high percentage of its budget forever, I think they should try to achieve break even. But I think there need to be some resources available for the rainy days, and that could have made a difference. There were a couple of years there where maybe $25,000 on a million dollar budget would have made the difference for us. It would have made a difference in our profitability, in our working conditions, it would have made a big difference. And it wasn't a lot of money.[23]

A report prepared for the Lilly Foundation at the beginning of 1995 described cutbacks in many sources of denominational funds.[24] ValleyCare had been fortunate in its start-up because, as a spin-off of a coalition of largely religious groups, it had access to ecclesiastical pots of money that more secular community organizations would not have had. But VCC suffered from the problems of many start-up operations: after an initial flurry of enthusiastic funding, it was difficult to get money when the newness wore off. According to Diorio, "The only additional money that we did get that was substantial was from the Mott Foundation. I think initially we were lucky to fit the criteria that Lilly had. Because you know Lilly has a lot of money. And I think there was real interest in creating jobs. I think as the years went by, there was still the interest, but the money was tighter. There just wasn't as much money out there. Certainly not money that we seemed to be able to get. Because I know ICA and NVP did try."[25]

Unlike powerful agencies such as the VNA, ValleyCare did not have the size or the clout to weather financial storms: "You have your relatively new players within the last 15 to 20 years who are pretty entrenched, like Interim Health Care, which is part of a national chain, and they have money to play with, and they also have a lot of marketing." Rosati noted that the chronic shortage of money aggravated staff difficulties: "One of the most important things is to look at the people that you're hiring. Staffing is incredibly important. And sometimes you're under the gun to hire people that may not be your best choice but you need to have somebody in place right now or the state is going to kill you."[26]

Diorio concurred with some of those who tried to save ValleyCare, including employees of the ICA and the NVP, that the board could have played a stronger role: "In retrospect, I wish we had been able to develop that board more fully, so that we would have had outside community representatives with special expertise, legal, banking, human resources kind of people."[27]

As it was, the agency was heavily dependent on already overbooked outside consultants to provide business advice. There were virtually no members of the board with the needed business expertise. Additionally, an increasingly fractious office staff absorbed Diorio in day-to-day administrative problems. Not only did she not have the internal team behind her to solve the agency's larger problems, but she also was constantly embroiled in the smaller ones.

Clearly, VCC's principal problems were rooted in the public policy context in which it operated, the enormous shifts in health care policy on both the federal and state levels. However, the company had difficulty finding the time and resources to address public policy questions. ValleyCare's mission statement had affirmed that "VCC is committed to working with other health care-related organizations to raise standards of care for the benefit of recipients and workers alike, and to increase the accessibility and affordability of health care for all."[28] In 1991, Connecticut saw state fights over Medicare assignment, ConnPace prescription subsidies, MediGap insurance rates, and Medicaid reimbursement for home health care. VCC's 1991 self-assessment was hopeful that after a short period of internal focus, the agency could get involved in state battles. VCC would begin by lobbying for legislation that would allow agencies to provide their own certification training for home health aides and go on from there to work on improving jobs and services statewide.

But, as Diorio remembered with regret, the always struggling ValleyCare was not able to get as involved in public policy areas as she would have liked, even as the need became stronger for such intervention:

> Through NVP we did do some things. We developed a strong relationship, for instance, with Congressman Maloney. We did have some relationship with a couple of the local [state] representatives, but we never were able to find the time to do what we would have liked to because quite honestly most of us were working much more than full time.
>
> I would have liked to see us work with NVP to present our case to the legislators, so that they could know more about the terrible effects the legislation they were passing was having on us as a company and our workers as employees. I would have liked to develop a relationship with some of the local people because the state has done terrible things, just as Medicare has, to reimbursement. I think it's a good long term plan but we were never were able to spend much time on that. And neither was NVP.
>
> Where I worked and I think we were effective was with the Connecticut Association for Home Care. I was on their board of directors. CAHC and NAHC, the National Association for Home Care, did do a lot of advocating, lobbying, and we were members of both of those groups. They would keep us informed

of what was going on and we would write letters, those kind of things. Some of the few changes that really have been made to improve the jobs for home care workers and reimbursement have been through CAHC and NAHC.[29]

VCC at its peak had provided jobs for some sixty home health aides who performed tens of thousands of hours of service per year. These aides were an ethnically and racially diverse group, many of whom had been on welfare before they started the job. Throughout its years, VCC nurtured its workers within a supportive, educational, and sometimes festive office atmosphere; provided nurses who served as teachers and mentors to the aides out in the field; and worked hard to provide decent schedules for aides and quality care to patients.

The ValleyCare experience vindicated many of the original assumptions on the basis of which the company was founded. It established that a community organization like the NVP could initiate and help maintain a substantial job-creating business attuned to local needs. It demonstrated that making good, high-quality home health care jobs could be the basis for providing high-quality care. It showed that employee ownership provided an effective organizational form for such a company and an effective basis for participatory management. The principal assumption that proved false—and led to the demise of the company—was that public policy would respond to the burgeoning need for home-care services by continuing to expand funding for those services.

ValleyCare showed the potential of NVP's strategies to challenge the economic powerlessness of Naugatuck Valley communities. It showed that community members could initiate and run enterprises that would provide good jobs and meet community needs. Given public policies that supported these objectives and fostered a market to sustain them, it could have provided a starting point for a powerful new strategy for community economic development.[30] Instead, it represents a monument to a visionary and heroic effort blocked by market forces and government policies beyond its control.

Heartbreaking as the demise of VCC was for participants, many look back on the experience with fondness. Margie Rosati reminisced, "I think we're very fortunate. I think it was a very sad thing that we had to close the agency, but this was the best experience of my life, it was in some ways very annoying, and with a lot of growth, and I wouldn't have missed it for the world, in spite of everything." Doreen Filipiak said, unassumingly, "When people talk to me I'll say, 'Oh yeah, I started a company once.'"[31]

10. Brookside Housing Cooperative

During the mid-1980s, Connecticut was hit by a speculative real estate boom that dramatically raised rents and house prices. According to the state Department of Housing, the average monthly rent for a two-bedroom apartment in the central Naugatuck Valley region rose by 176 percent, from $176 to $485, between 1980 and 1986.[1] Rev. Shepard Parsons of the Naugatuck Valley Project said that seven hundred people applied to the Waterbury Housing Authority for Section 8 subsidized apartments in one day.[2] Mike Kearney told Ken Galdston that his brother-in-law was having to move out of Seymour because he couldn't find housing and that many workers at Seymour Specialty Wire were having trouble finding affordable places to live. Waterbury also saw a flood of new condominiums and conversion of rental housing to condos. I heard Theresa Francis of the NVP quip, "They're going to stop calling it Waterbury and change the name to Condobury."

Initially, Ken Galdston was wary of NVP involvement with housing issues. "When it was first suggested that the Project do something about housing I know that I was somewhat skeptical or hesitant. I was very concerned about the Project losing its real focus on jobs which is a critical characteristic of this organization."

At the October 1986 NVP convention, two new leaders began pushing for the project to become involved with housing. One was Geraldine Drabek, a Latin teacher at Holy Cross High School who had moved into the valley from elsewhere in Connecticut. The other was Maryann Maloney, another parochial-school teacher whose pastor at St. Vincent Ferrer Church in Naugatuck, Father Edmund Nadolny, was interested in housing. Any delegate to the convention could submit a resolution on anything, so they put in a resolution saying the project should look at housing as an issue. It passed. Ken noted that the proponents were both women, and that they represented a new generation of leaders in the project, but he was still leery. He knew that organizing projects elsewhere had gotten swamped when they tried their hand at housing development. He told Geraldine Drabek, "Let's put together a housing committee," but "it was just sort of stall for time until we really got some sense of how are we going to handle this."[3] Drabek began recruiting a housing committee, and Ken began looking through his files for materials on housing.

Shamrock Ridge

Early in 1987, the NVP got a call from Fred Perella at the Archdiocese Office of Urban Affairs. A developer named Robert Matthews, who had contributed to the archdiocese and was seen as supportive to its work, was involved in a conflict with his tenants at a Waterbury apartment complex known as Summerset Hills. It was originally built in 1941 as temporary housing for war workers. With 172 units, it was the last large private development in Waterbury with affordable housing for poor and working people.

Matthews had recently bought the development and raised the rents so high that tenants might be forced to leave. The tenants had gone to Green Community Services, a Waterbury social service agency run by Catholic nuns. They had suggested that the tenants form a group and negotiate with Matthews, but he refused to meet with more than one or two at a time and insisted that there be no press. Perella, who knew that the sisters at Green Community Services were experienced with social services but not with organizing, asked if the NVP could become involved. Ken gave some advice, but was reluctant to go further.

Matthews reached a tentative agreement with the tenants, then abruptly sold the complex to another developer named Robert Fedak of Stamford, Connecticut, who changed its name to Shamrock Ridge. (Matthews apparently loaned Fedak much of the money for the purchase and remained a player behind the scenes.) The new owner raised rents 100 percent and started converting the complex to condominiums. Many tenants left; the rest feared they would lose their homes.[4] Of its 172 units, only 72 were occupied in June 1987. When Perella asked the NVP to come to a meeting to discuss becoming involved, Ken took along Geraldine Drabek and suggested that he go to the development and "see what's there."

Ken called Evelyn Lush, the identified leader of the tenants, to come out the next day to look around. She asked him if there was anything they should do before he came. He said it would be good to know how many units were vacant. When he arrived the next day, Evelyn had organized three tenants to go to every house in the 172-unit complex and find out not only which were vacant but also other information, like how many tenants were elderly. When Ken arrived, the information was all typed up. "Meeting Evelyn Lush it was very clear that this is a possible organizer, this is a person whose leadership qualities you can see right away. A part of your job is to find new organizers."

Ken was also struck by the look of the place. "It was large, it was barrack-like buildings, but you could also see how it could lead to a sense of community that you wouldn't get in a normal city block. Evelyn's house showed this combination of a lot of hominess in a real family sense, but also these gaping holes in the ceiling and a clear need for some real repairs." At least one family had been in the compound since 1941; many families had been there forty years; the average residence was more than fifteen years.

From Legal Aid in Norwalk, the NVP learned that Fedak had tried to convert an apartment complex there to condominiums and in the process had repeatedly violated the state's condominium conversion law. He had harassed the predominantly black tenants by stripping television antennas from the roofs without warning, entering apartments illegally, and raising the rents. He was forced to make an out-of-court settlement for hundreds of thousands of dollars. "So we had a great target."

The NVP met with a core group of Shamrock Ridge tenants and encouraged them to create a formal organization. They quickly organized the Shamrock Ridge Tenants Association. They announced themselves to the press, elected officers, paid in ten dollars in annual dues per family, held regular weekly meetings, and sponsored raffles and other fund-raising events. They surveyed housing-code violations and then met en masse with Fedak to demand that he make the necessary repairs. They conducted several actions demanding that city departments enforce health and housing laws at Shamrock Ridge. The NVP brought in representatives from the predominantly black tenant group in Norwalk that had won a battle with Fedak when he had tried to convert their apartments to condominiums; the Shamrock Ridge tenants, despite being predominantly white, were fired up by the meeting.

Meanwhile, the project was trying to think through what its approach to housing should be. Ken summarized the process: "First we've got to look at housing from the perspective of who is winning and who is losing, who is calling the shots, making things happen. There are specific developers, a number of them from outside; there are banks that are financing their deals. There is the role of corporate development, moving corporate headquarters up here." Then there was the question of strategies. "We could become developers ourselves. We could simply take on slumlords and say let's make the housing we have more habitable. We could go after legislation to create more housing programs."

But the NVP was attracted in a different direction. Somewhere in his files, Ken discovered information about the emerging effort to create permanently affordable housing by means of land trusts. Land trusts are essentially organizations that acquire land for a particular purpose. They had traditionally served as a way to permanently preserve land for conservation purposes by deeding the development rights to a conservation organization that agreed to preserve the land without development. They illustrate the principle that ownership is not unitary but in fact a "bundle of rights" that can be disaggregated and distributed in different ways.

Community land trusts (CLTs) use the same idea in reverse. The trust agrees never to sell its land but instead agrees to let it be used only for permanently affordable housing. Houses are then sold to tenants with a first option to buy them back for the original selling price plus improvements and inflation. The house can then be sold to another occupant without their having to pay for any increase in the market value of the land. Housing is thereby protected from speculative increases in real estate values.

Government-subsidized housing typically subsidizes private developers to build housing that can be sold or rented at market rates after a certain number of years; land trusts, in contrast, provided for permanent affordability. As an NVP document later put it, such land trusts are similar to conservation land trusts, except "instead of keeping land for birds and wildlife, a community land trust keeps land and the houses on it affordable for low and moderate income people."[5]

The community land trust idea was pioneered in the 1970s by the Institute for Community Economics (ICE) in Greenfield, Massachusetts. Ken met ICE executive director Chuck Matthei at a conference and was impressed with him and with the idea of CLTs.[6]

In 1986, ICE had helped form the Rose City Land Trust in Norwich, Connecticut's first housing land trust. It was funded by small fund-raisers and loans from ICE. By 1988, it had housed nineteen people in two buildings. Two more land trusts had been started by 1988, and the State of Connecticut had established a fund of one million dollars for nonprofit corporations to acquire and manage land for low- and moderate-income housing.[7]

The proliferation of land trusts and other local attempts to address the need for permanently affordable housing was in part a response to dramatic increases in housing prices, especially in the Northeast. It was also a response to changes in national housing policy. According to State Senator Richard Blumenthal, cochair of the Connecticut General Assembly's Select Committee on Housing, "Almost all the really creative, innovative programs begun by the state this year are in large part a reaction to the federal government's abdication of its responsibility in housing and the very momentous changes to tax laws that have completely undercut the incentives in the private sector" to build low income housing. "The federal government has said, in effect, to the housing advocates 'drop dead.'" But, Blumenthal maintained, state officials would have to address the housing shortage because Connecticut's prosperity relies on adequate housing for the employees that businesses and municipalities need. "There'll be a recognition that the quality of life depends on housing."

Land trusts also provided an alternative to public housing, which had fallen into disrepute. Rick Gaumer of the Rose City Land Trust in Norwich said, "It's very much a community based organization" as opposed to federally controlled high-rise projects. "It gives people a real sense of ownership."[8]

Galdston was intrigued with the land trust idea from the start, and ICE staffers came down and gave several presentations to the NVP and other community leaders. But actually forming a land trust took more than a year. "It took us quite a while to figure out how to integrate the land trust idea with the Project." It was a classic case of the conflict between organizing and economic development. NVP leaders were concerned that if the NVP became too involved with development, that would serve as a brake on their ability to organize and confront around controversial issues, especially if they were taking government money for development. But they were also concerned that if they created a separate development organization, it might go its own way and leave the project without either control or benefit.

Galdston and NVP leaders conferred with land trust organizers in Lowell, Massachusetts, and Brooklyn, New York, as well as with the ICA in Boston. The solution they arrived at was to create a land trust that would be separate from the project but maintain close ties with it. The nine-member board would include the three top leaders from the NVP, with the president of the NVP as president of the land trust. Three board members would be residents of land trust projects—initially tenants from Shamrock Ridge. Three board members, initially chosen by the NVP but eventually by the board itself, would be "outsiders" selected for their technical expertise. The NVP would retain veto power over changes in the bylaws. In April 1988, the NVP formed the Naugatuck Valley Housing Development Corporation. NVP president Shepard Parsons was also chairman of the NVHDC.

The NVP's approach to housing drew on the strategies for worker ownership it had already developed for jobs. As Galdston summarized it, the approach emphasized "broad based local ownership, limited equity cooperatives and a community land trust, which is a way for the entire community to be involved in owning land and therefore helping keep the price of housing down by keeping the land affordable." Then, as with jobs, "you have to get into some specific fights, that's the way we're going to learn, that's the way we are going to make some difference, and Shamrock Ridge is one of them."[9]

Working with the NVP, the Shamrock Ridge tenants began exploring the possibility of buying the complex. The NVP brought in as a consultant Chuck Collins, director of technical assistance for ICE. According to Collins, less than 10 percent of the current residents would be able to buy their units at the current selling price, $62,500 to $77,000. He helped develop a plan for getting low-interest loans from religious organizations and community groups to purchase sixty-six units and having residents use sweat equity to cover some of the costs of rehabilitation.[10] ICE offered to put up nearly $1 million from its own revolving loan fund.

The NVP offered about $55,000 per unit, but the owner wanted $80,000 or more per unit. The tenants' association wanted to buy a contiguous block of apartments, including the land under them, to form a distinct community; the owner wanted to sell units as individual condominiums and retain the land. The NVP sought help from the Connecticut Department of Housing, but it discouraged a tenant buyout. Nonetheless, after extended negotiations, it looked like a deal might be possible—until the landlord again dramatically raised the rents. The tenants responded by setting up a picket line in front of the complex.

The effort in many respects followed the organizing model worked out for employee buyouts. The organized tenants formed the core initiators and decision makers; when obstacles were encountered, support was called in from the wider community. In June 1987, the tenants' association held a public meeting with seventy participants, including Collins, three state legislators, three Waterbury alderman, and a representative of U.S. Congressman John Rowland at the Ancient Order of Hibernian Hall near Shamrock Ridge. Tenant Stanley Fox said, "We're in a countdown of six months to our eventual eviction." Tenant Clayton Murphy, who had lived at Shamrock Ridge for thirty-seven years, said his monthly rent had been raised repeatedly by various owners and had increased $195, to $425, in 1986. One of the representatives promised to set up a meeting with the state housing commissioner. Congressman Rowland's representative said the office would seek help from the U.S. Department of Housing and Urban Development.[11]

At its annual convention in October 1987, the NVP reaffirmed its commitment to housing as a core issue along with jobs. Chuck Matthei, director of ICE, told the NVP delegates that their goals of keeping jobs and finding affordable housing were intertwined. "Workers need decent housing, and those who have homes need decent jobs and both are harder and harder to come by for many longtime residents of the Naugatuck Valley and too many other parts of the country." The "structure of ownership" is responsible for plant closings and layoffs, because the profit motive—not workers' needs—dictates whether a business stays here, closes, or moves elsewhere. The "housing crisis" is similar because tenants, like workers, are not in control. Low- and moderate-income tenants pay a higher percentage of rent than upper-income people and pay in rent "many, many times the original market value" of a house or apartment "without any of the benefits of ownership." Evelyn Lush, president of the fifty-two-member Shamrock Ridge Tenants Association, pressed state housing commissioner John F. Papandrea to help tenants buy and fix up Shamrock Ridge.[12]

Meanwhile, when the owner refused to rescind the rent increase, Shamrock Ridge tenants went to court for a temporary injunction to halt rent increases, backing their claim with evidence on the conditions in the buildings and with public meetings and a turnout of fifty or so tenants at the court hearings. The judge issued an injunction to provide time to determine whether the rent increases were fair based on thirteen factors laid out in a little-used state law that allowed judges to act as a fair-rent commissioner in municipalities that lacked a Fair Rent Commission. The new co-owner of Shamrock Ridge, Robert Fedak, said that negative publicity had stopped some people from buying condominiums in the development and said the company, Fedkin, was considering filing a lawsuit for defamation of character and economic damages caused by the lost sales.[13]

After months of hearings and negotiations, lawyers for the two sides unexpectedly reached an agreement. Tenants would not have to pay more rent until a list of repairs was completed and certified. Then rent increases would be implemented gradually, based on the ability of individual tenants to pay. No existing tenant would be evicted. The owner could go on selling unoccupied units as condos. The judge, who had encouraged concessions, said, "This looked like an impossible situation a couple of months ago." Evelyn Lush said, "Tenants have rights. So do landlords, but in this case the tenants were being taken for a ride. You have to stand up for what you think is right."[14]

Fort Hill

At the October 1987 NVP convention, Galdston was approached by Father Edmund Nadolny, head of the Father Nadolny Good News Fund (GNF), a

New Britain–based nonprofit, about the possibility of cooperation. Shortly thereafter, the Good News Fund learned of the availability of a piece of land known as Fort Hill and asked the NVP if it would be interested in developing it jointly. The land was controlled by a developer named Anthony Silano who had previous ties with Father Nadolny but also had a reputation for ties to an organized crime family; Silano was also trying to put together a billion-dollar Egyptian Theme Park near Las Vegas.

A group from the NVP took a look at the land and began discussions about possible joint development. The social service organization Green Community Services of Waterbury joined the discussions. (Later it would pull out of the deal.) So did consultant Pat Spring of Co-Opportunity, a statewide technical-assistance provider for limited-equity co-ops, who had been developing mutual housing for ten years, with projects in Meriden, New Britain, Hartford, and Bridgeport. Ultimately, all agreed to cooperate on a joint project at Fort Hill. An NVP staffer later estimated that two-thirds of the control of the project lay with Silano and his staff and Father Nadolny's developer, Irv Rhodes, less than a third with the NVP and the Shamrock Ridge tenants.[15]

Meanwhile, Galdston had met a woman who was organizing a group of disabled people for United Cerebral Palsy in Waterbury. He and Carol Burkhart did a presentation on the affordable housing plans, and representatives of the group began meeting with them. Soon representatives of the disabled became a central part of the emerging coalition, and providing barrier-free apartments became a central part of the Fort Hill plan.

The plans for the Fort Hill development were presented to one hundred Shamrock Ridge tenants at a meeting July 20, 1988, at the Hibernian Hall. A cluster of duplexes and townhouses called Fort Hill Park would be built on twenty-seven acres near Thomaston Avenue and Fort Hill Road in Waterbury. It would include ninety-six two-, three-, and four-bedroom units that would be owned by a mutual housing association created by the Father Nadolny Fund. Thirty co-op apartments would be developed by the NVP and located on a land trust. Sixteen co-ops would be sponsored by Green Community Services based on sweat equity contributed by families earning twenty-two thousand dollars or less annually. The plan would include fourteen handicap-accessible units. Units would be completed for thirty Shamrock Ridge tenants before their rents were scheduled to increase 110 percent the following spring. The plans, according to the *Waterbury Republican-American*, "brought claps, whistles and a standing ovation from the anxious crowd."[16]

Carol Burkhart invited Merrill Gay, an organizer for CCAG who would later become an NVP housing organizer, to attend the meeting to see how NVP organized. He later recalled:

There were about sixty tenants there and a bunch of elected officials and some folks from the Institute for Community Economics who were there to give a presentation about land trusts, which I'd never heard about before.

The gist of it was: "The reason that you folks are getting forced out is because real estate driven speculation is making this unaffordable for you. Every time a piece of land underneath rental property gets sold, every time the building gets sold, there is a new mortgage and the rents have to go up."

The high cost of housing in Connecticut is basically because of the high cost of land.

So the idea is to separate the value of the land from the value of the houses by having a non-profit hold title to the land and giving the residents a lifetime lease. It means that the first person who moves in is going to be able to get a house for the value of the house, not the value of the house and the land, which makes it affordable for the first person.

Then with the ground lease there is a limited equity formula that says that when you sell your house, you can get the value of what you have put into it, plus some percentage of the market value increase. So the second and the third people who buy the house are able to afford the house.

This contrasted with subsidized purchase, in which the first owner could sell the house and land for market value and pocket any speculative gains. It also contrasted with subsidized rental housing, in which the developer could raise rents or sell the property after a period of years, similarly pocketing any speculative gains. In either case, the price of the house would soar for the next purchaser.

Initially, according to Merrill Gay, the NVP's assumption was that individuals would acquire individually owned homes on the land trust. "A land trust owns the land, and then a home-owner builds a house on top of it." But it became clear that most of the Shamrock Ridge tenants were "not bankable"— their incomes and credit records would not support individual mortgages. The solution was to build co-ops, rather than individually owned houses, on the land trust. "The only way to do it was with a co-op where you get a blanket mortgage and where you're proving to your lender that you've got a reasonable plan for keeping your units occupied and people paying monthly carrying charges," Gay said. "It's not so much that each one of these people is bankable, but that I've got eight people who've agreed to live in these eight units and I have a waiting list of fifteen people more, so that if any one of these people can't pay his rent, I can put somebody else in. And therefore, I'm bankable."

Gay told the story of Dick Dolan, a Shamrock Ridge tenant for the past forty-eight years who said, "My grand-kids kid me, 'Granddad, why did you wait until you're eighty-two to buy a house?'" But he looks at it as, "This is the first time I ever could own my own house, and I'm almost eighty-two." As Gay said, "This was basically turning people into their own landlords. They were co-op owners, but then they write themselves a lease so they're both tenants and landlords at the same time."[17]

Support for housing co-ops had recently been written into Connecticut law. A Hartford group called Hogar del Futur, "Home of the Future," had lobbied through the state legislation for a Limited Equity Co-op program. Co-Opportunity, a spin-off, became the official technical-assistance provider for the program.

Low-income housing projects in Connecticut have often been blocked by the opposition of neighbors. The NVP was tipped off by a city development official that the Waterville Community Club, representing an area near Fort Hill, had tried to block previous projects; he put them in touch with the club's leadership, and a series of informal meetings ensued. In August 2008, the Waterville Community Club hosted a community meeting to let Fort Hill–area residents give their views on the project. Questions were raised: Would there be inadequately controlled blasting? Would there be traffic problems? Above all, would there be the problems of drugs and crime associated with public housing projects? Father Nadolny, who was taking the public lead on the Fort Hill development, explained that it would be owned by the Mutual Housing Association and run by committees on supervision, selection, inspection, recruitment, training, and enforcement; the Waterville Community Club could place members on those committees. Father Nadolny emphasized that the project was "affordable" housing, not "low-income" housing, although it would include some units for low-income people. The fifty Waterville residents at the meeting voted unanimously to endorse the proposal.[18]

The NVP turned to seeking funds for its part of the project. It recruited Margaret Baldridge—widow of Malcolm Baldridge, a Waterbury notable who had served as president of the Scovill Manufacturing Corporation and U.S. commerce secretary—as chairwoman of the Fort Hill Project. Ken Galdston told a meeting that the forty-six units to be developed by the NVP and Green Community Services' developer, CREDO, would need $3,430,000 in financing. Nearly $3 million would come in loans and grants from the state. A local bank would loan $500,000. The state wanted $80,000 to be raised locally to demonstrate community support. Project supporters agreed to seek donations from service organizations, churches, synagogues, and private developers.[19]

Meanwhile, the project moved through the state funding process. The Department of Housing gave its approval.[20] But an application for bonding was found incomplete, and the State Bond Commission did not act on it. The NVP corrected the application, but it also began mobilizing to put political pressure on the state. Twenty-five people led by Rev. Shepard Parsons went to Hartford to deliver a petition with three hundred signatures urging Governor William O'Neill to accelerate financing for the project. An accompanying letter said, "I am sure I do not need to remind you of the desperate need for this type of housing in Connecticut. Every day's delay is a serious hardship to these families."[21]

But the bonding process continued to stall. In January 1989, a growing state deficit led state officials to halt votes on seventy bonding projects, including Fort Hill. In February, the NVP held another community meeting to press for action. One of the speakers was George Nevins, a retired Scovill brass worker who had moved in with his daughter at Shamrock Ridge when the rent on his own apartment exceeded what his Social Security and pension could pay for. "There's a lot of people out there, young couples with families as well as older people, who just can't afford decent housing anymore," he told the meeting. State Representative Doreen DelBianco, an NVP ally, said, "It's a crazy climate up in Hartford these days with people very anxious about the budget." Six state legislators, including a Republican state senator, all pledged to help the Fort Hill project.[22] Several followed up with a meeting with the governor's staff.[23]

The pressure paid off. In February, state housing commissioner John Papandrea announced that the project had been placed on the State Bond Commission agenda, virtually guaranteeing its approval. At $17,015,700, it was the largest bonding request for housing in nine years, representing nearly 20 percent of the state's budget for affordable housing. After the commission voted to approve the bonding, twenty supporters who had attended the session celebrated with champagne and prayers in the atrium of the Legislative Office Building.[24] Shepard Parsons said, "It's the culmination of what has really been a two-year struggle. It's very exciting for us."[25]

Early in 1989, Galdston relocated to Massachusetts, but he continued to play a guiding role for the next half year. That summer, Rev. Kevin Bean came on as executive director. Bean had a wide range of experience in religious-based organizing and was well known in Connecticut for his work on "economic conversion," designed to reduce the state's dependence on military production. In September 1989, Merrill Gay, an organizer for the Connecticut Citizens Action Group with experience in tenant organizing, was hired as housing organizer.

In March 1989, a tenant selection committee chaired by Richard Eigen, executive director of the Valley Regional Planning Agency, was ready to screen applicants.[26] By June, fund-raising efforts began to pay off: the Waterbury Foundation and the Catholic Archdiocese of Hartford each pledged $10,000, and the Waterbury Board of Realtors pledged $5,000 in long-term low-interest loans.[27]

A July headline read, "Fort Hill Project Right on Target." NVP executive director Kevin Bean said, "The project will go out to bid in mid-August, we'll have 90 days to make decisions, and we could break ground in November." Action on approvals for subdivision, traffic, and storm-water easements were expected from the city engineer within the week. The project would be completed in 1989, and occupancy might even begin early in the year.

There was one small cloud on the horizon. An anonymous Shamrock Ridge tenant told a reporter that he had been told that city officials were delaying the project approvals because it would interfere with a trash-to-energy plant they hoped to put near the site. But Arnold Piscotti, executive assistant to Mayor Joseph J. Santopietro, said, "That's a rumor and there is no truth to it." Kevin Bean commented, "We've heard that, but I have no comment. The bottom line is there is $17.2 million in state money for affordable housing in the city, a major investment. Any opposition to that on a political level would be rather silly, and I hope we won't meet any."[28]

Stiffed

Despite Kevin Bean's optimistic prediction, the NVP began to investigate the rumors. In September, it issued a press release headed, "Suspected City Sabotage at Fort Hill." In it NVP president Shepard Parsons and vice president Theresa Francis said Mayor Santopietro told them in May that he opposed the project but would not say why. "The Naugatuck Valley Project has since learned that several important contributors to the mayor's campaign fund own property adjacent to the Fort Hill site upon which they hope to build a trash-to-energy plant." Theresa Francis identified Kenneth Devino, who gave $1,000 to Santopietro, and John Hychko, a friend of the mayor's, who wanted to build a trash-burning plant on land he owned near the Fort Hill site. She accused Santopietro of having a "hidden agenda" to stop Fort Hill even while he claimed to support affordable housing. NVP leaders accused Santopietro's officials of making public records, such as those concerning the trash-to-energy plant, difficult to access. Santopietro, Hychko, and Devino all denied the charges.[29] Two days later, the Shamrock Ridge Tenants Association, no doubt hoping to lock him in, seized on the mayor's denial to issue a press release, saying they were "very happy to hear of the mayor's support for the Fort Hill housing development."[30]

The delays, however, continued. When state traffic officials required a traffic light at the corner of Thomaston and Fort Hill avenues, Fort Hill supporters asked the Waterbury Board of Finance to pay the estimated $55,000 cost. Twenty-five supporters attended the meeting with handmade badges saying, "Give Fort Hill the Green Light." Instead, Mayor Santopietro told the board to refer the question to the Police Board, which it thereupon did. He also said that it would be financially unsound to make any decision until after February 15, four months later. Shamrock Ridge Tenants Association president Stanley Fox told the Board of Finance, "You've shown where you stand on affordable housing." He later released a statement saying, "The city's commitment to $17.2 million in affordable housing was being tested in our request for $55,000 to cover the cost of a light—and the city failed the test."[31]

In the context of soaring housing costs, the state legislature passed a law requiring large municipalities to vote whether to establish Fair Rent Commissions if they did not have them already. (Waterbury was the only large Connecticut city without one.) The commissions could hear individual cases but could not impose rent-control ceilings on classes of apartments. The NVP voted at its 1989 annual convention to make a Waterbury Fair Rent Commission one of its priority issues.[32] Ronald Napoli, an NVP leader turned alderman, proposed a seven-member commission that would investigate complaints and rule on rent increases. When a representative of the Waterbury Chamber of Commerce said at a hearing that controlling rents in Waterbury would discourage developers from renovating houses, Stanley Fox of the Shamrock Ridge Tenants Association shouted, "Who was talking about rent control here?" Rev. Campbell Lovett, an NVP leader, drew applause when he called for the aldermen to give a voice to people who now had no say in a crucial matter.[33] The aldermen, however, voted eleven to two against the Fair Rent Commission.

Meanwhile, time was running out for Fort Hill. The state Department of Housing set a November 3 deadline for the project to go out to bid, warning that the developers risked losing state funds if the deadline wasn't met. The Board of Aldermen needed to give final approval at its October 23 meeting. But the city engineer had to complete her plan and allow fifteen days for appeal before the meeting. Stanley Fox complained that the city engineer was stalling by requiring site reviews by geologists even though state engineers had already approved the site. (When the city engineer described Fort Hill as "the most difficult site I've seen since I've been in Waterbury," the *Waterbury American* newspaper pointed out that "she began her job as the City Engineer last March.") Fox added that the delays were making it difficult for tenants to remain at Shamrock Ridge. "Rents that used to be a $150 dollars a month three years ago are $600 now." On October 12, Kevin Bean warned, "If we can't get this thing finished by the middle of next week, the Fort Hill site will go down the tubes."[34]

The city set October 16 for a meeting to resolve outstanding issues. But when representatives of the NVP, the Good News Fund, and the Shamrock Ridge Tenants Association arrived, they were told it was a private meeting between city attorneys and those of Anthony Silano, owner of the Fort Hill property. "This is what happens when you let lawyers run meetings," Theresa Francis commented sourly. "We should not let them do this." Tenant representative Dick Dolan said, "The whole thing looks like a big stall."

The groups thereupon walked upstairs to the Corporation Counsel chamber. The Corporation Counsel told them, "I happen to think that it's practical for the size of the group to be limited." Alderman Robert Giacomi added, "What use are thirty people in the meeting? Will they provide technical expertise?" The lawyers finally admitted Theresa Francis, Father Edmund Nadolny and an associate from the Good News Fund, and a representative of the state Department of Housing, but closed the meeting to the press.

Kevin Bean pointed out, "All they have to do is stall us for two more days, and the Fort Hill site is dead." He said if that happened, another site would be sought, but the state funding was earmarked for Fort Hill. He added that Fort Hill was almost unique among affordable housing projects in that local citizens supported it. Stanley Fox, reached for comment, pointed out that the city engineer was free to sign off with stipulations. Theresa Francis said later in the day, "Mr. Giacomi took me on personally. He berated me about statements I made to the *Waterbury Republican*. He wanted to know why I wasn't at the Board of Finance meeting to ask for a traffic light for the project." The *Republican-American* article pointed out that Theresa Francis's husband had died two days before that meeting.[35]

Meanwhile, behind the scenes the NVP had been getting indications ever since August that the state was getting cold feet about the Fort Hill site.[36] On October 26, the NVP received a letter saying the state did not want it to build there. On November 1, state Department of Housing Commissioner John Papandrea announced that the Fort Hill site was scrapped. He stressed, however, "The development remains a very serious and real commitment on the part of the Department of Housing. We are simply looking at another site that hopefully would have far fewer problems." He promised not to divert funds allocated to the project to other purposes. Merrill Gay, housing director for the NVHDC, summarized the state's concerns: the expense of building on a rocky ledge–filled site, delays that might mean for getting city permits, and the possibility that a trash-burning plant might be built near the site. He said other sites were available and the project might be able to go forward on the same timeline.[37]

Brookside

Even as it struggled to develop Fort Hill, the NVP had been looking into alternative sites as well. The state Department of Housing encouraged them to investigate existing condo developments, many of which had gone on the ropes as the real estate boom of the mid-1980s turned into a massive real estate bust. Neither the NVP nor the Shamrock Ridge tenants thought much of the fifteen or so condos they visited. The NVP maintained a folder with a variety of contacts they received from developers and landowners offering them alternatives; it was simply labeled "Sharks."

The NVP and the GNF finally homed in on a site known as Brookside in the northwestern part of Waterbury for a scaled-down version of the development. It had already received many of the necessary approvals, and the NVP was assured that final approval would be eased by the owner's close relations with the mayor. On January 9, 1990, the NVP and GNF and their architect presented preliminary drawings for Brookside to the state Department of Housing. The 102 townhouse units would cost less than $100,000 per unit, including land costs, compared to the $120,000 cost of the 140 duplex units originally planned for Fort Hill—the state had urged that the cost-per-unit be reduced to less than $100,000. Merrill Gay said, "We have a site that is much more buildable and that will bring down the costs." He declined to identify the site publicly because the land had not yet been bought.[38]

On January 23, Father Nadolny publicly announced that a 102-unit affordable housing complex would be built at Brookside. The GNF and the NVP would each develop 51 homes. The GNF's units would be mutual housing; the NVP's would be a land trust and 3 limited-equity housing cooperatives with 16 or so families in each. The two-, three-, and four-bedroom units would be for families with annual incomes under $35,000 per year; 10 percent would be wheelchair accessible. Father Nadolny said he had already received more than 1,400 inquiries from people interested in living in the project. Construction would start in May, and tenants from Shamrock Ridge would be moving in before the end of the year.[39] Stanley Fox told an NVP meeting that occupants of the new development would never be forced out of their homes because they could not afford a rent increase or because their homes had been converted to condominiums. "It's a very exciting development and it's going to keep affordable housing in Waterbury's future."[40]

Meanwhile, the remaining Shamrock Ridge tenants were, not surprisingly, getting discouraged. Merrill Gay reported, "It was their third winter and people were pretty down." To build morale, "We organized a pancake breakfast fundraiser that raised seven or eight hundred bucks to help people get through the winter as far as paying fuel bills when there was a hardship, and we brought them in right away into the design process." The tenants met with the architect and put their feedback into the design process. They met almost weekly with the land trust board over detailed plans.

The NVP, which was now a bigger player in a smaller project, began to take more leadership in the development process, and the project began moving rapidly forward without obstruction. In March, bids went out on schedule for construction for opening April 16 at the NVP headquarters.[41] The low bid was $1.6 million lower than expected, reducing the per-unit cost from $98,000 to $83,000. The NVP began taking applications for homes.[42] The project was placed on the agenda of the Bonding Commission and on April 30 was voted $8.2 million. The NVHDC's share for its 48 units included $2,779,965 in grants and a forty-year $1 million no-interest loan. Stanley Fox of the Shamrock Ridge Tenants Association said, "I think it's a victory not only for us but the Naugatuck Valley Project as well." By December, Merrill Gay reported that Shamrock Ridge tenants "can go see how this housing is going up and pretty soon they are going to start going out to the site every week to do insulation."[43]

Each family was required to put in 300 hours of work for sweat equity. Eighty hours were for thirty-four weekly classes to learn how to manage a co-op and to get the members working together as a group; 220 hours were for insulating and painting the units. I remember getting a call from Theresa Francis seeking volunteers to help put in sweat equity for families that were unable to do so themselves; I went down to the Brookside site and pitched in along with others on unskilled construction work.

The Department of Housing wanted the development to have at least 20 percent nonwhite residents. The NVP decided it wanted to go beyond that to represent the racial breakdown for its target group, those with incomes below the median for New Haven County, which at that time was $42,000 for a family of four. That meant approximately 20 percent black and 20 percent Hispanic. Most of the places for whites were already filled by tenants from Shamrock Ridge. Residents also had to be matched with homes on the basis of number of rooms and need for barrier-free access.

The carrying charges for rent and utilities depended in part on the size of the apartments. But they were also scaled for income, so that no family would be charged more than a third of their income. How adjustments would be made in the future was left open.

A couple of informational meetings and articles in local newspapers brought a flood of applicants for apartments. Ellie Santana, an NVP leader from the Spanish Action Council, went door-to-door to people who she knew needed better housing and had them fill out applications, resulting in a strong representation of Latino and Latina applicants. As Merrill Gay described it, she told people, "Hey! You live in a dump, don't you? Why don't you fill out this application and we'll get you into better housing!" The NVP went to NAACP meetings and informed black churches, but did not have the same kind of self-recruitment within the black community. Some observers wondered how white families would react to the high proportion of nonwhites, but by Merrill Gay's estimate, only a couple out of forty-eight white families withdrew applications because they were uncomfortable with the racial composition of the group.[44]

Nearly one hundred people attended the groundbreaking ceremony June 11. A news article about the event described the first shovel full of dirt as a "symbol of hope" for three of the participants in particular. Michael Valuckas, who had helped design the handicapped units and had applied for one of them, said a unique aspect of the handicapped units is "they will be integrated throughout the site, not confined to one unit." Lucille Connor, who was hoping her family might be picked for one of the units, said, "My husband Oliver and son Kenneth are very excited about moving here and owning our own home. We've been priced out of the housing market." Evelyn Lush of the Shamrock Ridge Tenants Association said, "with a huge grin," according to the article, "Becoming a tenant of the Brookside Development will mean never worrying about rent increases again."[45]

Prospective residents continued contributing sweat equity to the project. Victor Aviles, who had painted, insulated, and landscaped for his 300-hour down payment on a four-bedroom apartment said, "This is a dream come true for me and my family. No longer will we be under the threat of a landlord raising the rent." Soon tenants were moving in. Evelia Rosado and her three children were among the first. "We lived on Laurel Street for nine years. Here it is beautiful, but there it was noisy and we couldn't sleep at night." She said being an owner of the co-op was like being a member of a big family. "Everyone knows each other. It's real nice."[46]

On September 25, 1991, after four years of struggle, the dedication ceremony was finally held. Andre Giroux, president of the Naugatuck Valley Project, commented, "The residents have taken on certain responsibilities to be a part of this development as well as the pride that goes along with homeownership."[47]

On July 14, 1991, barely a month after the groundbreaking at Brookside, an investigative report on the front page of the *Waterbury Sunday Republican* revealed the secret history of the Fort Hill site.[48] The NVP had been correct in its belief that Mayor Joseph Santopietro was sabotaging the project for devious reasons, but the reasons turned out to be even more devious than the desire to install a trash-to-energy plant nearby.

The key player was Richard Barbieri, president of Security Savings and Loan in Waterbury and a close associate, fund-raiser, and political contributor of the mayor. Barbieri owned a site known as Lake Pointe in Waterbury's North End. He had made plans with the nonprofit Neighborhood Housing Services to build an eighty-four-unit affordable housing project there and had received extensive support from Mayor Santopietro for the project. But all the state money available for affordable housing in Waterbury had been allocated to Fort Hill. The city's yearlong stalling on permits killed off the Fort Hill project and thereby freed up that money for Lake Pointe.

After the demise of Fort Hill, less than half of the $17 million that had been allocated to it by the state was transferred to build Brookside. Much of the rest was given for the Lake Pointe project; $3.8 million of its state funding went directly to purchase Barbieri's land. The minutes of the Housing Department's applications review committee stated that the money for Lake Pointe came from "a previous allocation for Fort Hill Park, which has been cancelled."

Santopietro, Barbieri, and their associates became targets of federal investigations. Kevin Bean met several times with FBI agents to share information the NVP had gleaned. On September 25, 1991, the day of the Brookside dedication ceremony, Mayor Joseph Santopietro was arrested on federal corruption charges.[49] According to the twenty-nine-count indictment, he had met over dinner at a Naugatuck restaurant with Richard Barbieri and agreed to use his and his party's political power to aid their development projects. Over the next three years, he received $170,000 in money, loans, and property in return. Mayor Santopietro and six other Waterbury public officials were convicted on charges of bribery, bank fraud, embezzlement of federal funds, and tax evasion for their dealings with Security Savings and Loan. Barbieri was sentenced to five years in prison; Santopietro was sentenced to nine.

The Land of Ever After

Late in 1991, Kevin Bean reflected on the present and future of Brookside:

> It is fascinating to go up there, because there is not only this beautiful housing, but you go there—school is letting out and you see two school busses full

of kids, and so many people, there are 375 people. It is now the most diverse community in Waterbury, about one-third white, one-third black, and one-third Hispanic.

There are some wonderful and very strong leaders who have come out of good organizing in the Project. You have a Theresa Francis, a Mary Ann Maloney, a Henrietta Norman, a Debby DuPont, a Marita Fernandez, and a lot of others living in that community, whom you would want living in whatever community you lived, knowing that they would be pillars of stability.

After noting that the NVP and the Good News Fund had "different visions of what this land trust was to look like, who had control, what the community involvement really would be," Kevin looked into the future: "In order to prevent this from turning into a slum, and ever turning into a badly organized housing development, there is still a lot of on-going organizing that has to take place at Brookside. In order to really build a community, really empower the families to see the cooperative structure, the sharing of ways of conflict management and just how you really live out your lives in a very diverse community."[50]

An undated draft request for proposal (RFP) for residents' training indicates that Kevin Bean's concerns were not misplaced. Indeed, it suggests that Brookside suffered both from conflict between its codevelopers and from many of the problems that might be anticipated in a population drawn from low- and moderate-income inner-city residents and a structure that required intense mutual cooperation. The document noted that challenges facing Brookside residents ranged from "organizing to force contractors to fix freezing pipes" to dealing with "potential youth gang members who surfaced at a teenage graduation party." The biggest challenge, however, was "the need for individual co-op families to get along with each other and effectively manage their cooperatives."

Some problems resulted in part from divisions between residents in the NVHDC and the GNF units. The GNF members were given "a great deal of misinformation by the GNF staff re: the role of cooperatives." NVHDC co-op members "began their training months before the GNF members; many of the NVHDC members have established relationships with the NVP (some are either current or past NVP leaders)." Prior to becoming co-op members, the GNF attempted to evict a number of families without adequate due process; several GNF co-op members had even sued the GNF for violating the Connecticut security-deposit law.

There were also social problems. There was "a large percentage of co-op residents who are self-proclaimed substance abusers." There were "clear racial tensions between some co-op members (some members have never lived in integrated neighborhoods)." There was divisiveness between "co-op members with formal secondary education and less educated members." There were "ongoing questions about who is responsible for common maintenance and groundskeeping responsibilities." There were many children but "no recreational facilities on site," leading teenagers to congregate on the premises at night. The RFP sought training sessions on "conflict resolution (how to work together productively)," "racial and cultural differences," and "how to work with youth from different backgrounds."[51]

In 1994–95, Father Nadolny pulled out of Brookside. The mutual housing was turned into three housing co-ops. Brookside became a single complex with six co-ops linked by an "All" committee with representatives from each.

Perhaps more surprising than the presence of the problems listed in the RFP is how well Brookside has dealt with them in the long run. A series of interviews conducted with residents in 2009, more than twenty years after the first tenants moved in, indicates not only that the enterprise has survived but that, in the midst of a devastating national and local housing crisis and a major economic recession, it is still solvent, still self-managed, and still providing decent housing and a secure community for low- and moderate-income families at below-market rates.

Not that Brookside is without its problems. James Beck, who moved into Brookside when it was first built and is currently president of his co-op, chair of the "All" committee, and a member of the land trust board, is acutely aware of them. He notes that not everyone takes their fair share of management responsibilities. The six co-ops tend to go their own way without adequate information sharing and cooperation. Housing maintenance costs are soaring, leading to significant increases in carrying charges. Flaws in the original construction are also becoming apparent, creating additional expenses. Although the co-ops are good at coming together to meet an emergency, they are not so good at anticipating problems and addressing them proactively. But Beck also notes some of the positive aspects. "There's never been a race problem in the community. We've never had gangs. I cannot think of one instance where there's been a race issue between residents. We're ethnically diverse, certainly religiously diverse, sexual orientation diverse; it has never been an issue, which is quite amazing. I think that's because we know our neighbors and they're involved in the selection process."[52]

Derricia Parker heard about Brookside from a coworker, moved there in 2002, and eventually became president of her co-op. She recalls that the application process was friendly. "Sitting around with people and meeting my neighbors, my potential neighbors, I thought was comforting. It wasn't harsh or cold. The people who interviewed me became my friends. I see the same thing on the selection committee. Having new members coming in and you want them to 'oh, come meet this person, meet this person.'" From the training program, "You learn so much. I better understood co-op living and what they meant in the interview process about this being a stepping stone to ownership because there's a lot of responsibility that comes with co-op living." She continues, "I'm comfortable with letting my kids go outside, and staying out there. Usually kids all over the place. Which is why we are really into visitors. We want to know who's coming in and out of the units. Why is this person always outside? Because our kids are out there. The older kids look after the younger kids and it's a pretty nice place."

The community is largely crime free. "There's sometimes mischief like there's been issues with cars being egged. I think the worst thing I've heard since I've been here in the seven years: Someone used to keep his car running in the mornings in the winter and one of his kid's friends took the car and joy rode. That's the worst thing that I've heard." She is aware of only one instance of drug dealing; the family was informally confronted and chose to move away.

Carrying charges remain significantly below market-rate rents. "We remind them when they are not paying their carrying charges. We are like, 'Well, if you leave here, guess what? You're going to be paying double.' We tell them that if we lose this place, if we go into receivership, we can be paying double."

For many residents, co-op ownership is a step toward individual home ownership. "In my co-op we've had maybe four people go out and buy homes in the seven years since I've been here," Parker says. Asked what Brookside stands for, she replied, "Community and advancement. Because we want someone that is coming from the crappy neighborhoods that this is better than what you have and then we want to see you leave here and be able to go on to something better than this, have your own home. Those are the two words I would use to describe it."[53]

The NVP strategies that eventually created Brookside countered many of the sources of powerlessness faced by people in the Naugatuck Valley. By forming an organized group, the Shamrock Ridge Tenants Association, residents were able to negotiate directly with landlords, city and state officials, and developers, establishing a degree of accountability that was entirely lacking for individual tenants. By using creative means of ownership like land trusts and cooperatives, people in need of housing but unable to afford it were able to build and control their own housing development. They were able to mobilize a wide range of resources, ranging from the contributions of local religious, civic, and business organizations to the State of Connecticut to their own sweat equity. By means of the land trust, they were able to counter the speculative dynamics of the housing market to ensure permanent affordability; by means of the co-op structure, they were able to counter the financial industry's exclusion of lower-income people from the mortgage market. Despite enormous obstacles, ultimately they were able to win funding and approvals from city and state government.

Brookside was made possible by a strategy of organizing people to meet their own needs. Kevin Bean emphasized what made the NVP's approach different from other groups involved in housing development: "Our true strength was the fact that we were a community-based organization and that we had tenants that were driving this along. Because if we didn't have tenants driving, we didn't have real people that we could bring to the meetings at the state. Even the so-called technical meetings. The State would say, 'Oh, well, they really don't need to be here. This is a technical meeting.' And we'd say: 'This is their housing.' That kept this thing alive."[54]

11. Economic Democratization from Below

The NVP efforts recounted in this book have sometimes been disparaged as "social experiments that failed." But it would be closer to the truth to say that those initiatives that failed were crushed by the policies of neoliberal globalization that dominated the world for the past three decades. Now it is neoliberal globalization that has proved to be a failed experiment, wreaking devastation on the entire world year by year and culminating in the "Great Recession" that reached a crescendo in 2008–9.

How can we now find taking-off points for new experiments that can test alternatives to the "let the market decide" neoliberal dogma? The strategies developed by the NVP in the 1980s can provide one touchstone from which to go forward.

One of the NVP's original godfathers, sociologist Fred Perella, described it as "an embryonic sign" of what had to develop in the future on a much broader basis "for this society to survive and be strong."[1] But what does that "sign" signify?

In contrast to more common approaches to economic problems, the NVP's goal was neither to increase the power of government over the economy nor to reduce the role of government in favor of unconstrained markets. Rather, it sought ways that grassroots people and organizations could affect economic forces and decisions themselves. It took the underlying idea of participatory democracy—that people should control the decisions that affect them—and tried to apply it in the economic sphere. It pursued economic democratization from below.

This chapter reviews the strategies the NVP used in the experiments described in this book, in later activities, and in projects considered but not realized. It supplements these with ideas and experiences from initiatives elsewhere. It aims to analyze NVP strategies, but also to suggest what further development of an NVP-type process of economic democratization from below might entail. This chapter revisits the "sources of powerlessness" described in chapter 1, and it examines the ways in which NVP strategy attempted to address such problems as the concentrated control of property rights, the undesirable side effects of economic decisions, and the lack of accountability of public institutions. It compares and contrasts NVP strategies with traditional trade union strategies. It looks at related strategies that have been tried or considered elsewhere.

Accountability

Who was responsible for coping with deindustrialization? For much of the Naugatuck Valley's history, a civic leadership of local industrialists had used their economic, social, and political power to preserve and develop the valley's economic base. But after the middle of the twentieth century, their power, resources, and commitment eroded. Plant closings affected congregations, unions, community groups, government, and virtually all other institutions in the valley, but no institution had clear responsibility for addressing them. Unions represented many of the workers most directly affected by particular closings, but U.S. courts had held that employer decisions to close businesses are "peculiarly matters of management prerogative."[2] Corporations had even less accountability to local communities than to their workers.

Although the NVP worked with, included, and depended on unions, it organized people along different lines than traditional forms of unionism. Unions generally are based on uniting in one organization workers who are selling their labor power in the same or related markets. Craft unions unite workers in the same occupation, industrial unions those in the same industry, enterprise unions those with the same employer. Union members are presumed to have common interests rooted in their shared position in the labor market.

Plant closings, housing, and related issues affected workers but also the wider community. They went beyond workplace conditions and the relation of one group of workers to one employer. The NVP brought together a range of people whose interests might vary far more than workers in one craft, company, or industry but shared a wider common interest in relation to issues like plant closings and housing, whatever their personal workplace, employer, and class.

Although the core of the NVP's constituency was composed of people who would usually be described as working class, it included small-business people and middle-class suburbanites. Although it was largely grounded in the economic interests of its working-class constituency, it also included many people whose motivations for involvement were partly or predominantly noneconomic. Because it represented a geographical region, it drew on shared local interests but lacked the intense and multifaceted geographical boundary–spanning common interests of workers who share a craft, employer, or industry.

This structure of interests was reflected in the NVP's form of organization. Unlike a union or a political party or interest group, it did not form an organization of individual members who shared an identity. But unlike many networks, it was not just a vehicle for information exchange. The NVP exemplified what is sometimes known as a "structured network." It included complex interests and constituencies. It built on, but did not eliminate, distinct interests of constituent elements. Its function was not only expressing but actually constructing common interests. To do so, it not only articulated but created shared frames.[3]

Like unions, the NVP tried to establish a degree of accountability to its constituency by entering bargaining relationships with other actors. Unions strive to win "recognition" from employers—essentially an agreement to engage in an ongoing bargaining relationship in which the employer "recognizes" the union as the representative of its employees. This employer-employee relationship was formalized by the National Labor Relations Act. But the NVP, unlike legally recognized trade unions, had no legally guaranteed right to bargain with anyone.[4] Nonetheless, faced with a problem, the NVP's typical first step was to ask for a meeting with those it identified as part of the problem.

To win recognition, and to exert bargaining power, unions utilize dependence of employers, dependence of politicians, and institutionalized rights created in the past by utilizing these dependencies. The NVP also used pressure to establish bargaining and bargaining power. In Seymour and Century, it used petition campaigns and mobilization of allies to put pressure on corporations to negotiate. In cases like Talley, it exerted pressure for a meeting through publicity in the media. In the Century campaign, it used public exposure of the company. In Seymour, it used its role as a potential buyer, backed by community support, to establish negotiations with owner National Distillers. At Shamrock Ridge, it used the power of tenants to withhold rent, expose predatory landlords, and provide a financial base for new housing. Although the project's sources of bargaining power were often far more limited than those of unions, in many instances it was able to establish a bargaining relationship that allowed an exercise of collective power vis-à-vis an antagonist.

Ownership

The factories whose closing threatened the valley were private property. They were not owned by those affected by their closing—not even by local capitalists. In most cases, they were owned by national and increasingly global corporations for which, as the NVP often emphasized, they were but a speck on a balance sheet. Such owners had little interest in the well-being of the valley, and valley residents had few channels to affect their behavior.

At one time, the ownership of industry was a major issue for American workers. In the nineteenth century, unions like the Knights of Labor advocated worker cooperatives as a means by which the system of wage labor, with an employing class owning the means of production and a working class of their employees, could be abolished. But in the twentieth century, trade unions generally tried to represent the interests of workers as workers rather than change their class status.[5] This approach was reinforced by labor law, which drew a sharp line between labor and management. Although some U.S. unions at times advocated nationalization of their enterprises, they have rarely proposed that they be taken over by their workers.[6]

From its inception, the Naugatuck Valley Project focused on the ownership of enterprises. It declared its objective as "broad-based local ownership," which it maintained would lead to economic decisions in the interests of the valley's people. It attempted to implement this objective through worker and worker-community ownership of enterprises.

Ownership, however, turned out to be not a single thing but a complex set of relationships, what is sometimes called a "bundle of rights."[7] The NVP's approach to unbundling and distributing those rights became increasingly sophisticated as it accumulated experience.

Seymour Specialty Wire, for example, appeared to represent a fairly simple transfer of ownership from one entity, a corporation, to another, an ESOP that owned all the company's stock. But even in this case, "ownership" involved differentiated rights. Power over company decisions was quite distinct from claims on its profits or "usufruct." Worker-owners had no vehicle for directly controlling the company. Rather, all company employees voted for the board of directors on a one person–one vote basis. The board hired a company president who was responsible for all decisions concerning the business. Ordinary workers had no formal means as owners to influence decisions that affected them except to vote for different representatives on the board of directors.

As the loans were paid off, individual employees were credited with shares of the company's stock in an individual capital account in proportion to their earnings. They could not sell their shares in the open market, however, but only to the ESOP, and only when they left the company's employ.

SSW's structure redistributed ownership rights to current employees, but it remained a private company that did not provide any new rights to the broader community or society. Legally, the fiduciary responsibility of company officials remained to maximize the private profit of the company—even against the broader environmental interests of the community and even against the interest of its worker-owners in stable employment.

In subsequent efforts, NVP projects used the "unbundling" of property rights to pursue a new balance among individual, group, and social control and benefit. At ValleyCare Cooperative, the structure of Class A stock owned by the employees and Class B stock owned by the NVP provided a vehicle for asserting social interests other than profit maximization. The NVP's veto power over basic decisions provided an accountability structure for ensuring the enterprise's public purpose of providing good jobs and quality care while also involving the NVP in a continuing support role.

The Brookside housing development represents an even more sophisticated distribution of ownership. At Brookside, the land is owned as a community land trust by a nonprofit organization, the Naugatuck Valley Housing Development Corporation, established for the public purpose of providing permanently affordable housing. The housing itself is owned and managed cooperatively by the residents. Residents have well-protected use rights and acquire limited equity in their homes over time.[8] They can pass use rights and accumulated equity on to family members or other heirs but cannot sell them to anyone but the co-op. The Naugatuck Valley Housing Development Corporation retains a residual oversight authority to ensure continuing affordability and financial responsibility. Rather than hiring professionals to manage the project, a strong emphasis has been placed on training residents in the skills necessary for self-management. The structure works effectively to prevent speculation and ensure permanent affordability for the housing while also providing residents with the security of ownership and the benefits of an equity stake.

VCC and Brookside embodied alternative ownership models that combined direct control by participants with vehicles for social oversight. This approach treats property as a "bundle of rights" that can be distributed to different parties representing different interests. It provides a means for balancing particular and broader community and social interests.[9]

Restrictions on the right to sell can take various other forms. Laws governing nonprofits typically provide that they cannot be sold and that if they are liquidated their assets must be donated to other public purposes. An agreement the NVP helped the union negotiate with Reymond Bakery in Waterbury, providing workers the "first option to buy," represented transfer of a piece of the property-rights bundle to the employees.

The issues of property ownership have been among the most difficult for democracy to deal with. The NVP's emphasis on broad-based local ownership, its "unbundling" of different aspects of ownership, and its innovative techniques, such as worker ownership, land trusts, and housing co-ops, suggest that there are far more options available than the poles of private and state ownership. Exploring them may open new strategies both for social movements and for democratic societies.

The Workplace

Naugatuck Valley workers faced the legacy of a century-long management effort to separate mental from manual work and to concentrate knowledge and control in the hands of a managerial cadre. This division was symbolized at SSW by the way employees referred to management as "upstairs" and production workers as "downstairs." Established roles emphasized management's authority and workers' obedience—an emphasis that generated interminable class conflict and left little room for shared responsibility.

In nineteenth-century industrial workplaces, in contrast, skilled workers and their craft unions controlled much of the work process, helping to determine training, job content, production processes, work pace, and other features of production. In particular, they insisted that work be done by "all-round craftsmen" and that jobs not be "diluted" so they could be performed by less-skilled workers. Twentieth-century industrial unionism, however, accepted "management's right to manage" to a greater degree, while insisting on work rules that imposed a degree of fairness on workplace practices. American labor law allows unions to bargain over "working conditions" but not to interfere with "management's right to manage."

When SSW reopened as an employee-owned company, workers were astonished to learn that nothing seemed to have changed in the workplace itself. The boss was still the boss; workers were still workers; the office was still "upstairs" and the shop "downstairs." An attempt was made to "retrofit" the existing structure with an employee participation program called Workers Solving Problems. Its initiators intended it to institute a degree of direct accountability of managers to workers in the workplace. But passive resistance by middle management successfully sabotaged that effort. SSW union leaders were interested in introducing forms of job restructuring that would allow workers in effect to manage their own jobs. But instead, a conventional redesign was instituted by industrial consultant Universal Scheduling. Conventional patterns of labor-management conflict continued throughout the life of the company.

The SSW experience indicated that worker ownership did not necessarily change work relations. Partially in response to this experience, VCC incorporated an elaborate phased three-year training plan for employee participation and ownership designed to systematically transform internal governance roles. Implementation of the plan was spelled out as a key responsibility of management, and the NVP remained involved in the process. While there was no attempt to eliminate the distinction between managers and workers, there was a far more open boundary between them. Formally, worker-owners voted on key business decisions, including budgets and raises, and participated in evaluations of staff. Informally, managers maintained an "open-door" policy and tried to communicate in a way that ensured "no surprises." These patterns were facilitated by the company's small size and perhaps by the cultural styles of a female and service-providing workforce.

There are a variety of approaches for reducing the division into managers and workers still further. The NVP got a taste of such an approach when the Reymond Bakery turned to its workers to lead a complete reorganization of the production process in an attempt to save the company from closing. Strategies for "worker self-management" reverse the specialization promoted by Frederick Winslow Taylor's principles of "scientific management" and integrate productive and managerial labor. Advocates of "participatory economics" promote "balanced job complexes" that equalize work by including a mix of routine and creative activities in each job.[10]

Resources

Individuals and groups in the valley had extremely limited resources for efforts to save or create jobs. In the 1990s, the net worth of the least-affluent 90 percent of Americans barely equaled the top one-half of 1 percent. Few Naugatuck Valley workers owned more than a car and some equity in a home. Few had other resources beyond their ability to work. Local businesses, governments, churches, foundations, and other conceivable sources of funding for responses to deindustrialization were pinched by economic decline.

The primary labor-movement strategy for increasing workers' resources is to raise wages. Unions also promote redistributive public policies for taxes, health care, Social Security, and broad economic policies designed to promote full employment. Unions have sometimes used control of capital to affect industry conditions, such as the use of loans from the Amalgamated Clothing Workers bank to regulate conditions in the garment industry.[11] Recently, unions have experimented with "capital strategies" that use funds controlled by unions and allies to influence corporate policies, primarily regarding union recognition rights.

Because of its emphasis on broad-based local ownership, finding resources with which workers and community groups could acquire enterprises was a significant NVP concern from the first. In the SSW buyout, a 10 percent wage cut provided the initial equity. Bank loans were, for a brief time, readily available from conventional capital markets, in part because leveraged buyouts were a hot and profitable product, in part because of the tax benefits available for loans to ESOPs.

This proved to be an exception, however. The unequal distribution of wealth means that ordinary people usually lack the resources to establish nongovernmental organization– and co-op-owned enterprises. Therefore, such enterprises generally require the transfer of resources from other sources. But conventional sources make investments solely for the purpose of maximizing financial return. NVP enterprises were intended to end up in the black, but they pursued other goals in addition to profitability.

The sources of funds used by NVP-initiated projects were varied, but they boiled down to donations, private loans and investments, and the government. At SSW, employee purchase was made possible by city and state grants for feasibility studies, a bank loan, a state loan guarantee, and a note from the seller. At VCC, private foundation grants to the NVP contributed most of the start-up funding, while government-provided fees for services furnished the bulk of revenue. At Brookside, state bonding provided the principal funding, supplemented by donations and sweat equity.

Three other ways to secure capital were developed by the NVP, though never actually utilized. With encouragement from the NVP, the State of Connecticut established a revolving fund for investment in employee buyouts. The possibility of a revolving fund for employee buyouts, based on local banks' Community Reinvestment Act (CRA) obligations, was explored. Religious and other organizations pledged to move several million dollars in deposits into NVP-designated banks if necessary to encourage financing of buyout deals.

In 1993, the State of Connecticut established another source of resources for community-based initiatives, the Community Economic Development Fund.[12] The CEDF was designed to provide development funding and technical assistance to public, for-profit, and nonprofit enterprises in the state's poorer communities. It offered business and community revitalization loans; loans to "peer lending groups"; support for business incubators; development of commercial real estate for businesses owned, operated, or employing residents of target areas; and technical capacity training.

I helped to plan and lobby for the program, and I drew heavily on the NVP experience in shaping it. The CEDF established social criteria for the activities it funded, focused on those that contributed to its seven goals: (1) job creation and skill development for the unemployed and underemployed and persons receiving public assistance, (2) leveraging of private and community investment, (3) community participation in decision making, (4) the establishment of self-sustaining enterprises, (5) improvement of the physical environment of the community and the state, (6) promotion of affirmative action and equal employment opportunities and minority-owned businesses, and (7) coordination with the *State Plan of Conservation and Development* and local, regional, and state strategic economic development plans.[13] A few years after it was founded, the CEDF helped fund the NVP's efforts to clean up polluted "brownfield" industrial sites in the Naugatuck Valley.

Some related approaches to securing capital have been used by similar groups elsewhere. ACORN and others have used the CRA to force local banks to expand investment in impoverished communities. Chicago's South Side Bank and various credit unions have provided funding for housing and economic development. Public entities like the Steel Valley Authority have used or threatened to use the power of eminent domain to acquire resources needed for community economic purposes. In some cities, the concept of "linkage" has been used to require developers using downtown space and amenities to invest in affordable housing and other needed community facilities.

Various proposals have been made over the years to expand such mechanisms. A Massachusetts bill, for example, proposed to extend CRA requirements to business investment and to insurance companies. During the savings and loan crisis of the 1980s, the Financial Democracy Campaign proposed that the properties acquired in the savings and loan bailout serve as the basis for creation of a public-purpose banking system.[14] The labor-based capital funds authorized by Canadian provinces, such as the Quebec Solidarity Fund, provide models that many in the United States have sought to import.

The redistribution of resources to underaddressed social needs and interests is also a vehicle for correcting the biases of purely market systems.

NVP model projects like Brookside and VCC were designed to meet multiple criteria and provide multiple benefits to various constituencies whose needs were not met by the unmodified market. Vehicles for subsidizing prosocial enterprises, like the Steel Valley Authority, Greater London Enterprise Board, and Connecticut Community Economic Development Fund, can serve as ways to compensate for externalities, maldistribution of resources, and inability to mobilize unused resources.

Sweat equity provides another source of resources, which may be quite extensive in a community with high unemployment. Tenants at Brookside, for example, were required to provide a certain number of hours of labor on the co-ops, which in turn was credited to them and the project as equity. The 10 percent pay cut that served as the down payment for SSW was, in effect, sweat equity.

Another approach to utilizing unemployed labor capacity was the "service credit" program that the NVP explored in connection with VCC. A burgeoning model in the 1980s, service credits provide a synthesis of volunteerism and barter. Individuals perform volunteer labor and are credited with "service credits"—sometimes known as "time dollars." They can collect their "credit" at a later time from someone else's donated labor. As home health aide Doreen Filipiak explained, "I would go into someone's home and I would do whatever they need for two or three hours out of the day. And that would be put in a book. If I were to get sick or in an accident and I needed help, someone would come to my home and give me back those two or three hours."[15] Unfortunately, the possibilities could not be fully explored before ValleyCare was forced to close.

During the Great Depression, hundreds of thousands of people survived in part because they exchanged services, often through structures established by organizations of the unemployed;[16] in 1933, there were ninety self-help cooperatives with twenty-five thousand participating families in Los Angeles County alone. In 1934, the Ohio State Relief Commission used relief funds to support a dozen factories in which unemployed men and women made clothing, furniture, and stoves for the unemployed. Other states soon followed suit, and by the end of the year an estimated 15 percent of employment under the Federal Emergency Work Relief Program was in such enterprises.[17] Upton Sinclair's once famous Depression-era plan, End Poverty in California (EPIC), was based on providing jobs and meeting public needs by government support for such worker self-help co-ops.

Other nonfinancial resources were also important for NVP projects. Above all, knowledge was essential to their success. Some professional consulting was purchased from organizations like the ICA and ICE. Some was donated.

The Connecticut Economic Development Fund was structured to provide a source not only for funding but for technical expertise as well. Both governmental and nongovernmental organizations designed to promote local economic development, ranging from the Mondragon cooperatives to the Greater London Enterprise Board, provide a combination of technical expertise and funding.

The various forms of funding for community- and co-op-owned enterprises provide a potential vehicle for correcting the maldistribution of wealth by redistributing it. Used more extensively, they could generate a growing "third sector," neither governmental nor private for-profit, which could address unmet social needs and mobilize underutilized resources while redressing the imbalance in ownership of social resources.[18]

Markets

Economic democratization is not just about the control of individual firms. The interaction among firms can also lead to problems that need to be countered. Each firm pursuing its own interests may engage in interactions that are destructive for the interacting firms, for other people, or for society as a whole.[19]

Naugatuck Valley employers typically blamed plant closings on "market forces"; the demand for their products had decreased or relocated, or wages, electricity, and other costs were less elsewhere. And indeed, the destruction of valley residents' jobs and economic security was often less the effect of malevolent intentions than the side effect and interaction effect of myriad decisions made by multiple players for reasons that often had nothing to do with those the decisions ultimately affected. Scarcity and glut, boom and depression, globalization and corporate restructuring were all unintended side effects and interaction effects over which valley residents had little control.

In an interdependent economy, economic democratization requires change not just in individual firms but also in markets. This typically involves institutions and actions not shaped by the profit-maximizing imperatives of the market. Traditionally, the state has been seen as the primary agent for such activities. But they can also be conducted through voluntary nonmarket initiatives that change the way markets work.

Unions have always had to deal not only with their members' immediate employers but also with markets. Workers work for a particular employer, but each employer is embedded in markets that link them with other firms with whom they buy and sell. Indeed, trade unions originally developed in large part to counter the tendency of firms competing in a market to drive down labor costs, sometimes dubbed by labor the "race to the bottom." Unions address this through strategies designed to modify the labor market by removing labor costs as a factor in interfirm competition. This generally involves contracts or contract patterns that cut across firms. That in turn may require institutions for joint bargaining; unions have often stimulated the formation of employer associations of firms operating in a particular labor market.

NVP strategies aimed to affect markets through changes in ownership, company policies, public policies, and forms of direct cooperation. Although these efforts involved both the market and the government, they also involved a nonmarket, nonstate way of coordinating production with need by a direct linking of producers and consumers.

From its inception, the NVP's vision was to create not isolated companies functioning independently in the market but rather a cluster of linked enterprises and institutions that would jointly transform the economic life of the valley. The closest its founders had to a model was the image they had of the Mondragon cooperative movement.[20] Though such a vision was not realized, a number of elements of the NVP strategy went beyond individual firms to affect market interactions.

A fundamental goal of VCC, for example, was to restructure the home health care labor market; employee-ownership, it was hoped, would make possible a decasualization of the workforce, which would in turn create upward pressure on wages, benefits, and work-life patterns for the industry as a whole. Although VCC did not grow large enough or last long enough to have such an effect, the "sectoral strategy" of its big sister Cooperative Home Care Associates had a significant impact on the home-care industry in New York.[21]

A key goal of the Brookside land trust was to provide permanently affordable housing. This required insulating housing from the speculative character of the real estate market. Putting land in a trust dedicated to the public purpose of long-term affordability protected it from speculative booms and busts.[22]

A variety of NVP actions around supermarkets, transportation, and other services have used social pressure to affect firms in ways that are different from "market signals." As defense downsizing followed the end of the cold war, the NVP worked with the union at Textron-Lycoming, a large producer of tank engines in Stratford, to try to persuade management to engage in planning for conversion to nonmilitary production. Corporate management showed little interest, but local managers in fact began to cooperate; massive downsizings ultimately made the effort moot.

The NVP also tried to establish vehicles that affected markets by facilitating information sharing and joint action. Often referred to as "networks," such vehicles bring people together in ways that are not driven by market forces but can affect them. Such networks bring together different needs and the different groups of people concerned with them. VCC was created as a result of identifying both a need for higher-quality jobs for low-income workers and a need for higher-quality home health care. Its planning process brought together representatives of possible users and providers directly, not through the market. While the resulting company functioned within the home health care market, and had to seek viability within market constraints, its decisions continued to be shaped directly by employees and community representatives.

Such a linking of a community's need for jobs and consumers' need for services has continued to motivate NVP initiatives. For example, the NVP is currently establishing a medical interpretation program in Naugatuck Valley hospitals and exploring a "de-construction" company that will provide training and jobs for dismantling and recycling superannuated buildings in a safe and environmentally friendly way.

Cooperative Home Care Associates in New York took the process of directly linking groups that otherwise might relate only through the market several steps further. For example, it helped establish a "home-care network" to lobby in New York State for a restructuring of the entire home-care market. Then it actually created its own market in the form of an HMO, Independence Care System, which links providers and users of home health care services.

The NVP also tried to initiate what has become known in economic development circles as "networked production." The NVP brought together Naugatuck Valley mayors and development officials with consultants from Mt. Auburn Associates to try to develop a regional strategic-planning process for the valley. Elsewhere in New England, Mt. Auburn Associates had identified key industries for local development and established cooperative networks among small manufacturers and local educational institutions. Such strategic planning is in effect an attempt to counter the lack of planning that characterizes a market economy.

This effort was stymied by the orientation of development agencies toward marketing town properties rather than toward strategic development, the competition among towns for private investment and public development funds, the division of the valley between two state planning regions, and the interest of public officials in protecting their own administrative turf. Ironically, the idea of industrial clusters was subsequently picked up and implemented by Republican governor (and soon-to-be-convicted felon) John Rowland.

Such an approach has been carried much further by the "industrial-sector service centers" established by the regional government in the Emilia-Romagna region of northern Italy. These centers for such industries as ceramics, textiles, footwear, construction, and farm machinery make it possible for small employee- and family-owned local businesses to cooperate and thereby gain economies of scale in the global economy. They help make it possible for small companies to bid together on big contracts. They also provide hundreds of small businesses with research, purchasing, education, training, workplace safety, technology transfer, marketing, distribution, and exporting services.[23]

In its campaigns against plant closings, the NVP utilized a computer program that calculates the side effects and interaction effects of plant closings. It revealed that the loss of one factory job often led to the loss of several additional jobs in supplier and service industries. This research—and the job-saving campaign it encouraged—represents a beginning effort to identify and compensate for such side and interaction effects. Such a mapping of interactions might well be combined with emerging approaches to "social audits" and "stakeholder accounting" that are increasingly used to evaluate the impact of firms' decisions on those they affect.

Many side effects and interaction effects of what firms and markets do reach beyond the realm of economics and the market. Environmental effects are a prime example. Many NVP activities have targeted such larger environmental questions. The decline of brass and related industries left a string of more than 180 contaminated "brownfield" sites up and down the Naugatuck River. An ongoing NVP campaign has worked to clean them up and to redevelop them for worthwhile community purposes. As trash-to-energy plants were proposed in several towns, the NVP worked with local environmental groups to challenge the siting of such facilities in the deep, narrow, already-polluted Naugatuck Valley. The NVP has also participated in the Center/Edge Project, a program developed by the Hartford Catholic Archdiocese to address the long-term development of economic and environmental relations among cities, suburbs, and rural areas in Connecticut.

For markets to serve rather than undermine democracy, they require a transparency based on people's right to know about processes and decisions that affect them. Although both SSW and VCC were based on thoroughly researched business plans, and both produced quality products initially adapted to their markets, both were ultimately destroyed by changes in their markets that neither they nor similarly placed conventional firms could anticipate or affect. Only with far more access to information about the conditions faced by other companies and the decisions they were making could these challenges have been addressed.[24]

The Government

Whereas in principle local, state, and national governments are "of the people, by the people, and for the people," in practice the government was often unavailable or ineffective as a vehicle for addressing the problems of deindustrialization in the valley. The law protects corporations and other forms of private wealth against government interference. The threat of relocation gave companies unequal bargaining power vis-à-vis governments. Politicians and political parties were dependent on campaign contributions from those with wealth and were often affected by outright corruption. The political arena represented a profoundly uneven playing field in which even the interests of the great majority might face an uphill battle.

American trade unions have traditionally addressed governments by "rewarding friends and punishing enemies" in the political process with funding, staff, and volunteers. In most places this strategy has included a long-term alliance with the Democratic Party. The NVP, in contrast, is nonpartisan, does not endorse candidates, and does not allow holders of and candidates for public office to serve as officers. In general, it pursues an arm's-length relationship with politicians. But affecting government officials and institutions has been a core part of its strategy.

NVP leaders characteristically developed particular demands to place on politicians. Its first public policy campaign was to save the University of Connecticut branch in Torrington from shutdown. Another early campaign was to make state economic development funds available for employee-buyout feasibility studies. Over the course of two decades, the NVP has engaged in literally dozens of such campaigns. Some were closely involved in its efforts to save and create jobs in the valley. It sought a state loan guarantee for the purchase of SSW and state assistance in dealing with financial problems at SSW and VCC. It sought state funding for summer job programs for youth and Spanish-language translators in valley hospitals. It tried to draw officials of valley cities and towns into a regional economic planning process.

Other campaigns aimed to make the valley a better place to live, indirectly contributing thereby to its economic betterment but more directly to the well-being of its people. The Project pushed for cities to support brownfield cleanup. It opposed locating a trash-to-energy plant in the valley. It sought state bonding for the Brookside housing development. It tried to redesign Waterbury's property-tax system to protect poor neighborhoods from drastic property-tax increases and consequent abandonment. It worked intensively with residents of Berkeley Heights, a Waterbury public housing project, to demand that the housing authority rehabilitate the project utilizing plans originated by tenants for redesigning entryways to make the projects safer and less inviting for drug sales.

The NVP's nonpartisan stance meant that it could not use the traditional political means of providing money and assistance for politicians' campaigns. Instead, it drew on its legitimacy as the accepted spokesperson for a broad sector of the community, its ability to design and focus attention on its concrete proposals, and its capacity to mobilize public support for its campaigns.

Campaigns typically start with "listening meetings" designed to identify issues of concern to the community. These meetings are complemented by extended work in NVP committees to develop positions and strategies. This process also produces leaders able to articulate the positions. These positions then receive endorsement from the council or convention of the organization, which in turn represents a wide swath of organizations in the community. Campaigns then typically demand meetings with public officials. If meetings are denied or delayed, the NVP network and the media are informed. They are similarly informed of the results, satisfactory or unsatisfactory, of such meetings. When the results are not satisfactory, petition drives, constituent phone calls, public actions, and similar pressure techniques are utilized. Politicians are often invited to participate in "accountability sessions" at major NVP events, such as conventions and assemblies, where they are asked to respond to highly structured questions about their support for NVP positions in front of hundreds of community members.

In a setting where the political system is often dominated by private interests, and where politicians have frequently been found guilty of corruption, these efforts represent an attempt to hold government officials and institutions accountable to a broader constituency. In relation to the political system, as in relation to the economic system, the NVP represents an effort to use a network of voluntary relationships to democratize a system that often facilitates the self-aggrandizement and domination of special interests. Political democratization is often a condition for economic democratization.

A Social Learning Process

Establishing accountability, redistributing ownership, restructuring work roles, garnering resources, transforming markets, and democratizing governments are all essential aspects of economic democratization from below. They are to a degree interdependent aspects: redistributing ownership is likely to have a limited effect if work roles remain the same, for example, and governments are unlikely to be democratized if the control of wealth and corporations remains highly concentrated. NVP strategies operated on all these fronts. Taken together and carried to their logical conclusion, they and similar strategies developed by others could lead to substantial improvement in people's daily lives and substantial change in people's control over the conditions that affect their lives.

Of course, not all economic problems are likely to be countered "from below." This is particularly clear for those that involve interaction effects. For example, some overall regulation of growth and investment rates at a national and today an international level seems necessary to address systemic "macroeconomic" problems like inflation and stagnation. This is illustrated by the failure of SSW, which reflected in part the inability to control an out-of-control market in which neither conventional nor employee-owned companies were likely to thrive. Economic democratization from below no doubt needs to be complemented by democratization from above at a national and global level.

Nonetheless, any economic change that does not include a dimension of democratization from below is likely in the end to leave ordinary people and communities powerless, whatever arrangements are made at higher levels. And even change at higher levels can involve a devolution of power and initiative to lower levels, like, for example, the Wagner Act and the Community Reinvestment Act. In the long run, economic democratization is likely to require a "war on two fronts": both from below and from above.

NVP efforts should be seen in the context of other experiments in economic democratization from below. NVP leaders were most familiar with, and inspired by, the Mondragon cooperatives of Spain. But in some ways what they were trying to do more closely resembled the cooperatives of the Emilia-Romagna region in Italy, where intensively networked co-ops form much of the backbone of the highly successful local economy. The province of Quebec provides an example of a multifaceted effort to move in that direction, combining a labor-based investment fund that is the largest provider of growth capital in the province; other funds that specialize in financing employee-owned and green businesses; cooperative associations that actively promote, develop, and help fund new co-ops; government development agencies that invest in worker- and locally owned socially responsible companies; and provincial support for the development of a cooperative and nonprofit "third sector." Venezuela's "Bolivarian revolution" has used its extensive oil revenues to finance 6,840 cooperatives that employ 210,000, many producing for the government; to provide public funding for such efforts through public and highly regulated private banks; and to reopen closed factories under the control of their workers.[25]

The NVP's strategies described in this book represent an early attempt to explore similar possibilities in the United States. They by no means represent the last word in developing such an approach. They provide grist for an ongoing collective learning process about how people can organize themselves to think and act. The NVP may be above all an example of the social learning process that can make economic democratization from below possible.

12. Afterstories

The era of deindustrialization recounted in this book was just a moment in the history of the Naugatuck Valley, the NVP, and the individual lives that intersected with them. This chapter follows a few threads of what has happened to them since.

The Valley

There was no resurrection in the Naugatuck Valley.[1] Twenty-five years after the closing of its major industrial employers, it remains a "victim of the Rust Belt." But life goes on, and the valley has continued to experience major changes in social geography, demography, economy, class, and community life. It has seen residential, commercial, and industrial suburbanization. Now, according to the Central Naugatuck Valley Regional Planning Agency, Waterbury is "changing from a center city surrounded by residential suburbs to a metropolitan area with dispersed employment and homogeneous housing developments."[2] The valley is also seeing a new immigration; nearly one-third of Waterbury's people now speak a language other than English at home.

Between 1970 and today, the economy of the Naugatuck Valley was transformed. The closing of the three major brass companies—American Brass, Chase Brass and Copper, and Scovill Manufacturing—left only a few hundred brass workers where tens of thousands had labored before. Between 1970 and 1998, manufacturing employment in the Waterbury region decreased from about half to about one-quarter of all jobs, due both to the decline of the brass industry and to the general shift from manufacturing to service work in the U.S. economy.[3]

As industrial employment declined, the region saw a corresponding growth of service jobs from half to three-quarters of its employment. These jobs are highly diverse, ranging from teachers and nurses to janitors and waiters to medical specialists and financial analysts. There is no longer a single type of work or single type of worker that typifies the region's economy. While service jobs run from very low to very high pay, the overall shift from manufacturing to service employment has resulted in a significant decline in real incomes.

Even during the national boom years of the 1990s, the valley continued to lose ground economically. Waterbury's budget deficit was so deep that the state had to take over its finances. Housing values dropped 25 percent during the 1990s. The city entered a cycle of rising residential taxes and residential abandonment that was difficult to reverse. This was part of a broader pattern faced by many though not all cities in the Northeast.

In the midst of the collapse of the brass industry in the mid-1970s, Waterbury's unemployment rate reached 15 percent. In the first years of the twenty-first century it fell to a rate of around 4–7 percent, far closer to the national average. This is not because there are more jobs in the city of Waterbury, however, but because a growing number of Waterbury residents are taking jobs outside the city, plus a national trend toward decreased participation in the labor force.[4] By 2010, the Waterbury labor market had Connecticut's highest unemployment rate, 12.6 percent. *Forbes* listed it as one of America's "10 worst cities for jobs." The city lost 14.7 percent of its jobs between 1998 and 2009.

In the summer of 2009, at the pit of the "Great Recession," the NVP launched a "Listening Campaign" to take the "pulse of the valley." More than three hundred people participated in focus group–style house meetings to tell their stories about how they are being impacted by economic adversity. A few examples:

> Our family lost our farm. We had to move in with other family members.
> I've applied for hundreds of jobs that I am well qualified for. They never say it, but I know it's age discrimination when they don't hire me, or even grant me an interview. I'm fifty-five years old.
> We are working under stress and tension, waiting to see who gets laid off next.
> I am worried and nervous about the crime wave of criminal activity in my neighborhood.
> My husband and I are working longer hours and are not able to spend much time with our children. We feel this is deteriorating our family relationships.
> My daughter was attending an after-school program that was recently cut due to lack of funding. Now I have to pay for day care for her.
> My health care premiums are going through the roof, and my co-pay costs have increased dramatically, too.

Naugatuck Valley towns in the brass era were marked by an easily identified group of entrepreneurs who themselves managed and largely owned the major companies. After these companies were taken over by or themselves became national corporations, their owners and managers became part of a national corporate elite that shaped America—including the Naugatuck Valley—both directly and through its influence on the federal government.

In the last quarter of the twentieth century, the Naugatuck Valley's development seemed less a product of decision than one of drift. It was as if the "visible hand" of corporate and governmental management had been replaced by the invisible hand (or perhaps foot) of blind social forces. In part, this is the result of neoliberalism and the abandonment of government efforts to manage social problems; in part, it reflects the dis-integration of an organized national economy by globalization; in part, it reflects the related move from vertically and horizontally integrated national corporations to global corporations that have stripped themselves down to "core functions" and outsourced most of their activity to competing suppliers around the globe. Whatever the causes, the effect is that it can be hard to know who would actually have the power to determine what happens in the valley even if they could somehow be persuaded or pressured to act one way rather than another.

Today's corporations generally don't employ large numbers of workers in particular locations over an extended period of time. Rather, they shift their operations around the globe and outsource much of their production on a short-term basis. The world is surely still differentiated between those who own the means of production and those who sell them their labor power. But in the valley, power over social decisions and processes does not lie so directly with the immediate employers as it did in the past.

Into the early 1970s, a large proportion of the Naugatuck Valley's workers were organized in unions that possessed considerable economic bargaining power and social influence in the life of the community. The demise of the valley's large industrial employers has eliminated the main power base of organized labor. By the early 2000s, only a small proportion of workers in either manufacturing or the service sector were organized in unions, and their power was correspondingly reduced. Unions are now well organized in the public sector. Other than that, Naugatuck Valley workers are no more organized than they were in the nineteenth century.

Workers are also sharply divided between a poor urban working class that is primarily African American, Latino, or immigrant and a suburban working class that is white, culturally separated from the inner city, and substantially better off. The working class has also become more highly differentiated occupationally, with no equivalent of the semiskilled manufacturing workers who formed the center of gravity of working-class organization during much of the twentieth century.

In sum, what was once a rather direct relation between an employing class and a working class has become extensively mediated. At the same time, workers have lost many of the institutions that protected them from the full impact of the market. Their labor is less and less anything but a commodity. This is particularly clear in the loss of job-security provisions and the rise of temporary, part-time, contract, and other forms of contingent work.

The region has been deeply abused by its political system. Two of Waterbury's recent mayors have spent years in jail on charges of corruption and other criminal behavior. Waterbury failed to revalue its taxable property for twenty years, leading to blatant unfairness and a wrenching adjustment when revaluation finally occurred. Its city plan had not been revised for thirty years, and new kinds of businesses couldn't be established simply because zoning regulations had not been updated to include them. Its political administrations have frequently exhibited a depth of incompetence and corruption that has been compared to a third-world country.

The Naugatuck Valley still faces hard times. But anyone in day-to-day contact with the region knows that it is full of life. One of the most striking evidences of that vitality is the resurgence of citizen initiative at the neighborhood level. Virtually every neighborhood in Waterbury now has its own organization, and they insist on playing a role in police, park, development, social policy, environmental, and other decisions that affect their neighborhoods. In some cases, this activity has moved beyond pressuring city agencies to actively planning and implementing extensive programs for neighborhood regeneration. This activity reflects a strong sense that people have a right to participate in decisions that affect them. This contrasts with the period before the 1970s, when there was much less feeling of a right to participate in decisions about such then important matters as highways, urban renewal, and the location of development.

There have also been efforts to fill the gap in civic leadership. The Naugatuck Valley Project itself was one. In the 1990s Waterbury also developed a Waterbury Vision Committee with a broad base and several hundred active participants to try to provide a response to the city's economic, social, image, and self-image problems.

The Naugatuck Valley region seems to face Janus-like in two directions. On the one hand, it has to address the realities that all American communities face in the present and future, including globalized competition, political incapacity, social instability, and economic and environmental crisis. On the other hand, it is still very much engaged with both the negative and the positive aspects of the past. It faces old polluted factory sites, a workforce trained for jobs that no longer exist, housing and neighborhoods suffering from decades of disinvestment, and a large job gap due to the loss of its major employers. But it also possesses globally competitive small manufacturers spawned by the brass industry, magnificent brass-era homes and public buildings, vibrant neighborhoods, and families and ethnic communities with a long-term commitment to and identification with their hometowns.

In 2004, I taught a course on the past, present, and future of the city of Waterbury at the new Waterbury campus of the University of Connecticut.[5] My students were well aware of the problems of the city, and most of them regarded it with disdain for its poverty, bigotry, isolation, shabbiness, lack of opportunity, and political corruption. But as part of the course, we brought in a wide range of community residents—from nonprofit housing developers to civil rights activists to NVP community organizers—who were involved one way or another with trying to improve the economic, political, social, and cultural life of the community. Over the course of the semester, the change in the students' attitudes was palpable. They still saw it as a community beset by problems inherited from the past and aggravated by the present—but also as a community filled with people struggling to make a better life for themselves and each other.

The NVP

The NVP has continued as a vital part of Naugatuck Valley life for twenty-five years. As it completed its first quarter century, it continued to provide a way for poor and working people in the valley and their allies to organize themselves and express their interests. Its activities reflected both the NVP's own traditions and the changes in the valley.

The NVP has persisted largely because it has adapted to the new conditions of the deindustrialized region. Its focus changed from saving jobs to meeting the wide array of needs of poor and working people and ensuring that they are represented in decisions affecting the valley. Its core constituency shifted from the older, predominantly white ethnic working class to the African American, Latino, and new immigrant population that moved into the towns along the Naugatuck River. As the Catholic parishes of the older white communities declined, the NVP developed ties and membership among the Latino and African American evangelical churches. Convention programs are now printed in English and Spanish, and many events include Spanish interpretation.

Ken Galdston left the valley in 1989 but continues to perform a mentoring role from a distance. A series of experienced organizers have succeeded him. A special element of continuity has been provided by Carol Burkhart, now Carol Burkhart-Lyons, who has served on the staff through much of that period and recently retired as director and lead organizer.

The range of NVP activities has been wide. In an effort to save some of the remainder of the region's industrial economy, the NVP worked with local manufacturers and the Waterbury adult education program to establish a Multi-Metals Training Center that has trained and placed hundreds of workers in the eyelet and screw machine industries. To challenge blight in Waterbury neighborhoods, the project organized a network of inner-city neighborhood leaders, held an antiblight "Badder Homes and Gardens" tour, and secured a city blight officer and a new police headquarters. Faced with the first Waterbury tax revaluation in twenty years, which threatened to shift the tax burden to residential property owners with a likely consequence of tax delinquency and abandonment, the NVP conducted an economic-impact study and encouraged the city to create a $2.5 million tax circuit breaker for low-income families. Concerned with the area's lack of opportunities for youth, the project initiated a youth center and a youth leadership training program that brought together eighty young people from diverse backgrounds from ten different towns in the valley.

Of the hundred or more campaigns the project has conducted over the past twenty years, three that are currently ongoing can provide a sense of its trajectory and its interaction with the development of the valley.

The brass and other industries that abandoned the Naugatuck Valley left behind as a memento nearly 200 contaminated industrial sites. The NVP has seen the cleanup and redevelopment of these brownfield sites as a way to link a range of concerns and constituencies. Those who live near the sites face direct health effects. The contaminated real estate could, if cleaned up, serve as a major economic resource and contribution to local tax bases. Appropriate development of the sites could provide jobs and housing. Cleanup itself could provide a source of jobs. Availability of inner-city sites could provide an alternative to the sprawl that is transforming more rural parts of the region. The NVP's approach was summed up in the slogan "Create Jobs That Save Our Environment."

The NVP's initial strategy was to create a coalition to secure federal pilot status and funding for a regional effort to clean up and redevelop abandoned and polluted industrial sites, supported in part by the Connecticut Community Economic Development Fund. In response to local initiative, the federal Environmental Protection Agency (EPA) designated the Naugatuck Valley a regional brownfield remediation pilot area, allocating eight hundred thousand dollars for the Valley Brownfields Pilot Program. It identified 189 polluted industrial sites in a forty-five-mile region of the valley. As of 2005, a dozen of the sites had been remediated.

The NVP's next move was to try to connect the need for brownfield cleanup with the need for jobs. It entered agreements with two of the valley's Workforce Investment Boards to create an Environmental Remediation Technician Training Program at the Naugatuck Valley Community College. The program trained fifty-seven technicians and placed forty of them in its first two years. The NVP is now seeking EPA support for a Brownfields Job Training and Development Demonstration Pilot in the valley. It is also seeking a policy of preference for local workers in environmental remediation efforts.

The NVP identified specific sites for remediation and development. In 2000, it participated in the redevelopment of the historical Plume and Atwood plant in Thomaston. Now it is seeking sites in Waterbury's predominantly Hispanic South End. According to NVP jobs committee member Steve Shrag, "That area looks like a war zone." The goal is "to take that clearly blighted area and re-invigorate it while giving people jobs."[6]

The brownfield program is hoping to draw in additional allies and sources of support in the future. The NVP has worked with state and regional antisprawl efforts, such as the Catholic Archdiocese–initiated Center/Edge Project, to include brownfield remediation as part of their program. And it is trying through Connecticut's congressional delegation to access Department of Defense resources to help clean up the sites of former military contractors.

The immigrant population has more than tripled in many valley towns. In response, the NVP hired a Latina organizer, Rev. Elizabeth Rosa, who was deeply connected in the local community as a social worker and copastor of a Waterbury church. She recruited a Latino Hispanic Resource Committee in the lower valley that eventually formed a center with an office in Derby. Rosa organized twenty house meetings and focus groups with more than two hundred attendees to identify Spanish-language services that needed to be made available. Dozens of bilingual interpreters were trained to run these meetings.

The house meetings identified the greatest need as interpreters in hospitals, which had little or no trained bilingual staff. The project conducted a prefeasibility study for a medical interpretation initiative, based on the familiar NVP premise that meeting local community needs could also be the basis for creating good-quality local jobs. After meetings with officials of valley hospitals, the NVP established the Health Care Interpretation Project. So far, it has secured two foundation grants totaling more than one hundred thousand dollars to provide a certification-training program in using medical terminology in a variety of languages and establish round-the-clock interpretive language services at local hospitals and other health care facilities.

In the late 1990s, long before subprime mortgages became headline news, NVP activists got wind of horror stories about poor people who had been sold houses on what appeared to be favorable terms only to find that they had purchased broken-down wrecks whose real condition had been concealed by cosmetic repairs and whose mortgages were far more expensive than they could afford. In 2002, one such victim, Luz Lebron, shared her problem with NVP staffers Elizabeth Rosa and Carol Burkhart-Lyons. Rosa and Lyons invited Luz Lebron and Tim Norieka, another victim, to share their stories with the NVP president, Rev. Earle Sanford. After researching the situation and discovering several more victims, the NVP decided at its 2002 annual convention to make predatory lending one of its key issues for the coming year.

The NVP housing and predatory-lending committee followed several strategies characteristic of the NVP's approach. They involved those directly affected by the problem, they reached out to a network of allies, and they confronted those in a position to do something about the problem. The predatory-lending campaign also illustrates the effort to modify markets—in this case the housing market—through social action.

One common obstacle to predatory lending campaigns is that the victims are often burdened with shame at what they experience as a personal failure. The committee made extensive efforts not only to document the shady lending practices but also to provide victims the support they needed to go public. Meanwhile, the committee met with potential allies, such as Waterbury Neighborhood Housing Services, ACORN, the University of Connecticut at Waterbury, and their state senator and two U.S. congresspersons.

After meeting with the state banking commissioner and state Consumer Fraud Division attorneys, the NVP finally presented two cases to the staff of Connecticut attorney general Richard Blumenthal. After a series of further meetings with the NVP, the attorney general sued three politically well-connected real estate agents and their companies on behalf of nineteen victims the NVP had recruited to be part of the case. Most were low-income families who spoke little English and had poor credit histories. Seventeen had suffered foreclosure.

After the suit was brought, nearly fifty more victims stepped forward. This was made possible by the NVP's deep roots in the community. Norberto Zorrilla, for example, whose life was devastated by a housing scam, got connected with the NVP through the Church of God, where he played guitar at services.

Richard Anthony, one of the victims, told his story at the 2003 NVP convention. He and his wife had bought a home from a real estate company that had discouraged them from hiring their own attorney or inspector. "The joy we felt at that time was short-lived," Anthony told the convention. The house was full of leaks, and the heating ductwork needed to be replaced. After paying for repairs, the family couldn't pay the mortgage, and the lender foreclosed on their house. "I felt that I failed my family," Anthony concluded. "But now we have come from being a victim to being a fighter."

Early in 2004, the NVP marched into city hall to demand help for victims on the verge of losing their homes. City officials offered to channel funds from the Department of Housing and Urban Development to provide emergency grants. By March, special-needs grants had been made available through Neighborhood Housing Services.

The NVP continues to hold regular meetings with the victims-turned-fighters. They have found three pots of rehab money. NVP ally Neighborhood Housing Services is making available Federal HOME (Home Ownership Made Easy) Funds. The NVP uncovered a second HOME Fund in the city of Waterbury Development Corporation and pressured the agency to research the rules and adapt them so it could help the victims. NVP staff and the victims created their own "Adopt a House Fund" that helps the victims pay back taxes, water bills, rent deposits, or mortgage payments.

In April 2006, the attorney general reached a $750,000 settlement on behalf of nineteen home buyers brought to him by the NVP. One of them, NVP leader Constance Hunter, said, "I'm just enthralled and hopefully by the summer families will be blessed."[7]

These victims are now seen as experts on predatory lending. The attorney general has asked them to help on a state task force to stop predatory lending statewide. They are now working with banks, financial companies, and Fanny Mae to find a long-term solution to halt the exploitation of the subprime lending market.

In 2009, the NVP celebrated its twenty-fifth anniversary. I worked with a "history committee" of current and veteran NVP activists to develop a participatory history project to present the NVP's experience back to the local community. We organized a history exhibit at the Mattatuck Museum, developed a Web site on the NVP's history (http://www.brassvalley.org), and

held a reunion of people who had been involved with the NVP over the past
quarter century. The exhibit closed with a quote from Father John Cooney,
the president of the Naugatuck Valley Project: "It is often said that history
repeats itself, and in today's very difficult and uncertain economic times many
people are feeling fearful and alone once again. We hope that the stories of
everyday citizens who successfully worked together to address job loss, lack
of affordable housing, predator lending, and a host of other issues in the
Naugatuck Valley can inspire hope."[8]

Ken Galdston

At the start of 1989, Ken Galdston married Jan Saglio of the ICA. He left the
NVP staff and moved to the Boston area, partially to join his new wife, partly
in accord with the Alinskyite principle that an organizer should stay with a
particular organization for only a finite period of time.

Ken Galdston soon began organizing in the declining industrial region
around Lawrence and Lowell, Massachusetts. In 1989, the Merrimack Valley Project was formed, very much on the model of the NVP. It included
churches, unions, and community organizations.[9] It fought to save manufacturing jobs, led a resident buyout of a 160-unit housing project in Lawrence,
and sought increased funding for inner-city firefighting, community policing,
and after-school programs.

Meanwhile, his vision expanded to creating a network of such projects
for deindustrialized regions throughout New England. These regions shared
important traits in common, including loss of economic resources; weakened
civic culture and political participation; segregation by income, race, and
ethnicity; renewed immigration; and the growth of contingent work and
multijob families.[10] In 1995, the NVP and three other groups formed the
InterValley Project to provide joint leadership and staff development and
build a regional network. In 1997, the IVP established a board of directors
and membership-dues structure and hired Ken Galdston as full-time director
and organizer. The IVP continues to seed new organizations in industrial
areas throughout New England.

The IVP projects, like the NVP, use community and citizen-action organizing techniques with an emphasis on pursuing broad-based local ownership. These groups typically bring together African American, Hispanic,
and working-class white Roman Catholic congregations, Jewish synagogues,
unions, tenant associations, and community groups. Galdston provides a
source of guidance, support, and coaching for the individual projects. I have
witnessed how useful it has been for the NVP to have such outside mentoring

for dealing with both strategic planning and sticky personnel problems that have arisen over the years.

The IVP provided introductory training sessions for more than 1,000 leaders and Advanced Leadership Institutes for more than 240 experienced leaders and organizers. It has organized special training events for religious leaders, labor leaders, project board members, and leaders working on parallel issues. The IVP provides monthly organizer meetings, and Galdston makes semimonthly field visits to the projects. An Apprentice Organizer Program trains and places organizers within the network.

The Merrimack Valley Project stimulated the formation of a City Commission on Immigration in Lowell. It organized the Temporary Workers Association, which won passage of a Massachusetts Fair Transportation Act that caps transportation charges for seventy-one thousand temp workers. It pressured the Gillette Corporation to meet with it to discuss improving wages and job quality for one thousand temp workers at razor packing subcontractors.

The Rhode Island Organizing Project, initiated in 1991, campaigned to triple the state housing trust fund, change tax laws to deter real estate speculation, and extend benefits for legal immigrants. The Pioneer Valley Project, started in 1994, negotiated student transportation, policing reform, and union organizing rights with the City of Springfield; increased funding for library branches in poor neighborhoods; and created "Deconstruction Works," a worker-owned company that provides training and skilled jobs for inner-city workers who dismantle buildings in a careful, environmentally sound way. The Granite State Organizing Project, begun in New Hampshire in 1998, organized to win benefits and job training for 500 workers laid off by Tyson Foods. Emerging projects include the Kennebec Valley Organization initiated in 2002 and an upper Connecticut River Valley organization formed in 2005 by groups in New Hampshire and Vermont.

In 2004, IVP leaders joined with other organizations to launch the New England Joint Action (NEJA) Campaign. Their first project involved pressuring New England government officials to protect and expand federal funds for affordable housing, education, and employment training. A total of 850 leaders from around New England attended the first NEJA Regional Assembly in 2005. The IVP hopes the NEJA can serve as the basis for developing a regional economic development strategy.

Theresa Francis

As she had prophesied, the failure of the Century buyout by no means put an end to Theresa Francis's activities with the NVP. Mike Kearney recalls, "I went with her on numerous corporate money campaigns in the Valley. She put her fist on that table and some of the bank presidents and company presidents that she sat across from or the personnel managers—they blushed when Theresa started talking. Supper Club was another of her pet projects. Every place you turned, your heard Theresa's name or you saw Theresa involved. Whether it was fighting with the seniors on the health issue, or the schools."[11]

Until her death untimely death from cancer—and indeed even after—Theresa Francis exemplified what the NVP was as a human enterprise. I spent hundreds of hours with her in interviews, community meetings, and work projects, and I never ceased to learn more from her about what grassroots community leadership really means.

Theresa Francis exemplified the idea that good community leaders are above all people who help other people to act. She was legendary for her ability simultaneously to pressure community members to do the right thing and to give them the support they needed to do it. A feisty leader from Independence Northwest recalled, "I worked with her at one of the leadership conferences. She and I were both presenters. For a guy who likes to talk, as soon as you put me in front of people the mouth and the brain are not in sync and I start stuttering. And I started. And she says, 'Start over. Talk clearly. This will work.' And it did."

A woman from an NVP member organization said, "I would be the last person in the world to get up and read a paper in front of a group. She said to me, you don't have to be nervous: they're all friends. So I got up and did. So another meeting came along, about Hamilton Park. And I had written a little bit about the homeless. That is what I was supposed to read. So there I am reading, and again I'm still nervous. But she got me to do it."

Kathy Francis, an NVP leader who became Theresa's daughter-in-law, remembered, "When I first started with NVP and I had to get up and do some speeches or presentations, I rehearsed with her so I felt a little more comfortable. And I'd make sure I'd sit next to her before I had to get up so she could give me some encouragement. One of the things I asked her, how do you do it? She said, you always wear long skirts. I said, what do you mean about long skirts? 'Cause then they can't see your knees shake."

Theresa Francis was able to help others overcome such insecurities in part because she experienced them herself. My impression was that her ability to exemplify and inspire courage and self-confidence resulted from her deep feeling of both her own worth and that of other people. She assumed that people had both the ability and the goodness to do things that they did not know they were capable of doing. Many of those who found encouragement from Theresa Francis remember her confronting their sense of inadequacy by telling them, "God didn't make no junk." It was an adage she used to bolster herself as well.

Theresa Francis's methods of getting people to do things could be highly unusual, to say the least. I remember when she wanted to get an advertisement for an NVP ad book from Bergin Brothers, the long-established Irish funeral home whose proprietors had served for two generations as Waterbury mayors. Not long after her husband's death, she went to one of the Bergin brothers at the funeral home. She said, Look, the family's been buried at Bergin's for years, but if you want me, you're going to have to buy an ad or else we'll take our trade elsewhere. She got the ad.

Theresa was known for her frankness. NVP organizer Patty White recalled a meeting with state officials and potential investors at the Connecticut Department of Economic Development. "They were all posturing about what could be done to save Seymour. It went on for an hour and a half maybe. Then Theresa, in Theresa's style, sat up and basically said, let's cut the bullshit, what's the deal that we're going to get? And all these men—she cut it so clearly for people. That was the end of the meeting."

She was also known for her willingness to confront powerful officials. Patty White remembered, "Shortly thereafter we found out that Governor Weicker was going to be at the library in Watertown. Ginny and Theresa and I at Theresa's urging got in Ginny's van and rode over there. The two old ladies, you know, they got Governor Weicker and twisted their fingers in his face, telling him, you'd better do something to save Seymour Specialty Wire!"

Often her confrontation of the powerful and her encouragement of the timid went hand in hand. Rev. Shepard Parson, who served for a time as NVP president, reminisced about attending a fund-raiser for a local politician with Theresa:

> We'd been trying for weeks to get a meeting with the mayor for what was then Fort Hill [later Brookside housing development]. We were trying to get approvals. We kept being thwarted at every turn. We had done our power analysis and figured out who owned property next to it, but we couldn't get this meeting with the mayor. I don't know how I ended up at a table with Theresa. My back was to the door. I'm eating my salad, Theresa's kind of picking at hers, and all of a sudden her eyes light up. "There's the mayor!" I immediately got more interested in my salad. "We've got to go talk to him!" She was like a great running back. She sees just the slightest opening in the line and she runs right at it. She grabbed me. He saw us coming and tried to slip on and she blocked his way. I'm kind of, "Hi, hello Mr. Mayor." She's in this man's face. "Where have you been? We've been trying to get this meeting. You keep avoiding us. We've got our power analysis. We know who's got property next to this. You need to

sit down and talk to us." So then he pulled out his calendar—"OK OK OK OK." He gave us a meeting. And she was back and had a great meal. And I was so upset I could hardly eat for the rest of the evening.

NVP leader Andre Giroux recalled a similar combination of confrontation and inspiration:

I was involved with Theresa the last couple of years on health care. We were going to the legislature to see if we could get some movement. This was her mission—to bring this up to the legislature. [If a legislator went] for a breath of fresh air or a smoke out in the hallway, Theresa was there confronting them. And she blocked their way. Very soon what happened was, all the other people from senior groups that were going to Hartford representing other groups followed what Theresa was doing. She led the pack and they all followed her, and after a while they started doing exactly what Theresa was doing. They were all following her example and getting courage from her.

He also recalled that she would drive to the state legislature in Hartford without a spare tire because she couldn't afford one.

Theresa Francis played a significant role in the development of the NVP's Brookside co-op housing land trust and pitched in to provide sweat equity for herself—and for other future residents who were unable to do so. Andre Giroux observed:

She had that organizing experience and derived a lot of strength from it, but I wonder sometimes if she wasn't happiest when she worked the paintbrush with the other people working on sweat equity at Brookside. I didn't hear her sing, but I think inside she was singing, as she saw people doing manual labor and taking pride in the things that they were doing. And if there was too much paint that got splashed on the varnish of those railings, you heard about it from Theresa, because she prided in doing wonderful work. I think it stimulated other people, who were always thinking, we're going to live here, we're going to be here. Every time she would say she was going to be there on Wednesday and Thursday, she was there. I think that was a boon for other people: to show that they had to be committed too. That was not only talking with your mouth, but talking with your person. That was easy to understand.

I helped organize a series of Brass Valley Music Festivals in Waterbury to present the music of the region's many ethnic groups; the NVP became a principal sponsor, and Theresa became a performer, a volunteer, and, ultimately, the coordinator. As so often, she was able to articulate the essence of what people were trying to do: "It's like the squares of a quilt. You get all of these beautiful squares, and they're off by themselves. And they don't get woven together. When you put them together, you give everybody a chance to see what the other group is doing, and you develop an affinity for all the different traditions that you might not come in contact with. It was the greatest thing to see what somebody else was doing, and to hear the richness of their music and their dance."

Mike Kearney said, "To me she never thought about herself. She was always there for everybody else." But to me that was not the whole story. Theresa always believed in having a good time. When she found out that her cancer was probably not going to be successfully treated, the first thing she did was to take a jaunt to Connecticut's new Foxwoods Casino. Part of her ability to put pressure on people and have them come away loving her more lay in that infectious sense of joy, sometimes even gleeful complicity, that underlay even her scolding. She did not believe that guilt should be the great motivation of life—just a little seasoning to make things go along. "It's important," she said of the Brass Valley Music Festival, "to get together for your happy things."

Theresa's involvement with the NVP continued until the end of her life.

> I got sick, I had a series of operations, cancer of the uterus. ValleyCare cooperative came up and they evaluated the case, they talked to my doctor, my surgeon, and for eight weeks they came up and irrigated this big wound on the stomach. So they would have to come twice a day and help it to close naturally so you wouldn't get any infection. It's a tough darn job. Messy. So like they have to do some tough, tough things that people are not likely to feel comfortable doing. Christmas time I wanted to be with my family. They even came out to Bethlehem to treat me. They were very accommodating and became very close. They were half of the cure, because they smiled and they said, take one day at a time, you're going to be OK.[12]

At her memorial, one of her home health aides from ValleyCare recalled how appreciative she could be. "What did you do to my bed? It was like getting into a cloud." She died in the care of ValleyCare.

Shortly before her death, Theresa Francis was asked what she thought heaven would be like. She answered that she was sure she would see God, and then see all the friends and loved ones who had died before her. And after a while she thought she would probably go to God and tell him that if there was any organizing that needed to be done in heaven, she was ready to help pitch in.

If God has any organizing to be done in heaven, I'm sure Theresa is doing it.

Notes

Prologue

1. Thomaston children's chant quoted in Agnes O'Brien Crowe, interview. For a slightly different version collected by the Works Progress Administration in the 1930s, see "Seth Thomas Clock Company," manuscript, Record Group 33, WPA Records (CT), box 206, file vi, Connecticut State Library, Hartford.

2. Mary Tycenski, interview.

3. James Wilson, interview.

4. Matthew Monahan, interview; Francis Kane, interview.

5. "Clock Burning Symbolizes Loss of Seth Thomas," *Hartford Courant,* April 11, 1983.

Introduction

1. For an account of the Brass Workers History Project, see Lynne Williamson and others, "Using Ethnography to Enhance Public Programming," in *Ethnographer's Toolkit,* ed. Jean J. Schensul and Margaret D. LeCompte, vol. 7, *Using Ethnographic Data* (Walnut Creek, Calif.: AltaMira, 1999), 130–50 and references on 177–78. For products of the project, see Jeremy Brecher, Jerry Lombardi, and Jan Stackhouse, comps. and eds., *Brass Valley: The Story of Working People's Lives and Struggles in an American Industrial Region,* Brass Workers History Project (Philadelphia: Temple University Press, 1982); and *Brass Valley,* produced by the Brass Workers History Project and Connecticut Public Television (1982). The project's papers and interview recordings are archived at the Mattatuck Museum in Waterbury, Conn.

2. Ken Galdston, interview, December 18, 1985.

3. Waterbury, Conn.: Naugatuck Valley Project, 2009.

4. See, for example, Jeremy Brecher and Tim Costello, eds., *Building Bridges: The Emerging Grassroots Coalition of Labor and Community* (New York: Monthly Review Press, 1990);

Jeremy Brecher and Tim Costello, *Global Village or Global Pillage: Economic Reconstruction from the Bottom Up* (Boston: South End Press, 1994); and Jeremy Brecher, Tim Costello, and Brendan Smith, *Globalization from Below: The Power of Solidarity* (Cambridge, Mass.: South End Press, 2000).

5. Fred Perella, interview.

6. *A Profile of the Central Naugatuck Valley Region, 2002* (Waterbury, Conn.: Council of Government of the Central Naugatuck Valley, 2002), 27.

7. *The State of Working Connecticut, 2001* (New Haven: Connecticut Voices for Children, 2001), 5.

8. Today's economic adversity is generating a new interest in democratic economic alternatives. See, for example, Gar Alperovitz, *America beyond Capitalism: Reclaiming Our Wealth, Our Liberty, and Our Democracy* (Hoboken, N.J.: Wiley, 2004); and Richard D. Wolff, *Capitalism Hits the Fan: The Global Economic Meltdown and What to Do about It* (Northhampton, Mass.: Interlink, 2010), which advocate new forms of democratic enterprise to address unemployment and inequality. In the University Circle neighborhood in Cleveland, the employee-owned Evergreen Cooperative Laundry has been opened as the start of the Cleveland Foundation's new strategy to use community-based green enterprises as a vehicle for neighborhood renewal.

9. Theresa Francis, video interview.

Chapter 1: Roots of Powerlessness in the Brass Valley

1. Principal sources for the history of Waterbury and the Naugatuck Valley include Joseph Anderson, ed., *The Town and City of Waterbury* (New Haven: Price and Lee, 1896); and William J. Pape, *History of Waterbury and the Naugatuck Valley* (Chicago: S. J. Clarke, 1918). The Mattatuck Museum and the Silas Bronson Library hold a great deal of additional material in their collections.

2. Anderson, *Town and City of Waterbury*, 1:149.

3. Ibid., 502.

4. Timothy Dwight, *Travels in New England and New York* (Cambridge, Mass.: Belknap, 1969).

5. Principal sources for Waterbury and Naugatuck Valley industrial history include William G. Lathrop, *The Brass Industry in the United States: A Study of the Origin and the Development of the Brass Industry in the Naugatuck Valley and Its Subsequent Extension over the Nation* (1926; reprint, Mount Carmel, Conn.: William G. Lathrop, 1980); and Cecelia Bucki and the staff of the Mattatuck Historical Society, *Metals, Minds, and Machines: Waterbury at Work* (Waterbury, Conn.: Mattatuck Historical Society, 1981). Additional background is provided in unpublished research reports prepared by Jeremy Brecher in 2003 as background for the Mattatuck Museum's permanent history exhibit Coming Home: Building Community in a Changing World and available at the museum.

6. *Brass Valley*, produced by the Brass Workers History Project and Connecticut Public Television (see introduction, n. 1).

7. Pape, *History of Waterbury*, 1:2.

8. Anderson, *Town and City of Waterbury*, 1:401–2.

9. A classic discussion of this transformation is Richard L. Bushman, *From Puritan to*

Yankee: Character and the Social Order in Connecticut, 1690–1765 (Cambridge: Harvard University Press, 1967).

10. For the history of workers in the Naugatuck Valley, see Brecher, Lombardi, and Stackhouse, *Brass Valley* (see introduction, n. 1). For a classic study of the transformation of work and workers in early industrial America, see Herbert Gutman, *Work, Culture, and Society in Industrializing America* (New York: Alfred A. Knopf, 1966). For comparisons with other industries and regions, see, for example, Alan Dawley, *Class and Community: The Industrial Revolution in Lynn* (Cambridge: Harvard University Press, 1976).

11. Joseph Anderson, *History of the Soldiers' Monument in Waterbury, Connecticut* (Waterbury, Conn., 1886).

12. Charles S. Johnson, Director, Department of Research and Investigations, "The Negro Population of Waterbury, Connecticut," *Opportunity* (National Urban League) 1, nos. 10–11 (1923).

13. Much of this history is documented in the Mattatuck Museum's African-American History Project.

14. Constance McL. Green, *History of Naugatuck, Connecticut* (New Haven: Yale University Press, 1948), 121, 143.

15. *Fibreboard Paper Products Corp. v. NLRB*, 379 U.S. 203 (1964).

16. For a contemporaneous interpretation of deindustrialization, see Barry Bluestone and Bennett Harrison, *The Deindustrialization of America: Plant Closings, Community Abandonment, and the Dismantling of Basic Industry* (New York: Basic Books, 1982). For an effort to understand economic globalization that was stimulated in part by the experience of industrial decline in the Naugatuck Valley, see Brecher and Costello, *Global Village or Global Pillage*. For additional perspectives on deindustrialization and the American working class, see, for example, John Hinshaw, *Steel and Steelworkers: Race and Class Struggle in Twentieth-Century Pittsburgh* (Albany: SUNY Press, 2002); David Bensman and Roberta Lynch, *Rusted Dreams: Hard Times in a Steel Community* (New York: McGraw-Hill, 1987); Thomas Sugrue, *The Origins of the Urban Crisis* (Princeton: Princeton University Press, 1996); and Thomas Dublin and Walter Licht, *The Face of Decline: The Pennsylvania Anthracite Region in the Twentieth Century* (Ithaca: Cornell University Press, 2005). For the relation between corporate strategy and the effects of deindustrialization on working-class communities, see Charles Craypo and Bruce Nissen, eds., *Grand Designs: The Impact of Corporate Strategies on Workers, Unions, and Communities* (Ithaca: Cornell University Press, 1993).

17. Frank Santaguida of Century Brass quoted in the *Hartford Courant*, March 19, 1985.

18. James Wilson, interview.

19. Howard Ploman, interview.

20. Perella, interview.

21. For collections of case studies of such efforts, see Brecher and Costello, *Building Bridges* (see introduction, n. 4); and Bruce Nissen, *Fighting for Jobs: Case Studies of Labor-Community Coalitions Confronting Plant Closings* (Albany: SUNY Press, 1995). For the Youngstown campaigns, see Staughton Lynd, *The Fight against Shutdowns: Youngstown's Steel Mill Closings* (San Pedro, Calif.: Singlejack Books, 1983); Thomas G. Fuechtmann, *Steeples and Stacks: Religion and Steel Crisis in Youngstown* (New York: Cambridge Univer-

sity Press, 1989); Sherry Lee Linkon and John Russo, *Steeltown U.S.A.: Work and Memory in Youngstown* (Lawrence: University Press of Kansas, 2002); Terry Buss and F. Stevens Redburn, *Shutdown at Youngstown: Public Policy for Mass Unemployment* (Albany: SUNY Press, 1983); and Dale Hathaway, *Can Workers Have a Voice?* (University Park: Pennsylvania State University Press, 1993). Those seeking more information on these efforts will find little recent historical research; they were, however, covered extensively at the time in the *Labor Research Review* and *FIRR News*.

22. See Barbara Richards, "The Community-Labor Alliance of New Haven," in *Building Bridges,* ed. Brecher and Costello.

23. Produced by Jan Stackhouse and Jerry Lombardi, these are now in the archives of the Mattatuck Museum, Waterbury, Conn.

24. *Union Leader* (March 1983).

25. Jerry Harrington, interview.

26. For a parallel interpretation of power and powerlessness in another industrial region, see John Gaventa, *Power and Powerlessness: Quiescence and Rebellion in an Appalachian Valley* (Urbana: University of Illinois Press, 1980).

27. John T. Cumbler, *A Social History of Economic Decline: Business, Politics, and Work in Trenton* (New Brunswick: Rutgers University Press, 1989).

28. *Fibreboard Paper Products Corp. v. NLRB.*

29. *Textile Workers Union v. Darlington Manufacturing Co.,* 380 U.S. 263 (1965). For a valuable discussion, see Terry Collingsworth, "Resurrecting the National Labor Relations Act: Plant Closings and Runaway Shops in a Global Economy," *Berkeley Journal of Employment and Labor Law* 14, no. 1 (1993).

30. Whether the high-flying speculative managers of the 1980s actually served the interests of their stockholders rather than their own self-aggrandizement would be a worthy topic for investigation. Their behavior often seemed to illustrate Charles Lindblom's concept of "extended authority," in which authority granted for one purpose is used by those who received it for other purposes—generally their own. See Lindblom, *Politics and Markets* (New York: Basic Books, 1977).

31. Gar Alperovitz, "Memorandum to President-Elect Clinton," *Tikkun* 7, no. 6 (1992): 16. Inequality has increased substantially since that time.

32. Lathrop, *Brass Industry in the United States,* 111.

33. The evolution of property ownership forms in early Waterbury, and the conflicts it entailed, is traced in considerable detail in Anderson, *Town and City of Waterbury.*

34. Under the doctrine of a right to a "fair rate of return," property rights were further extended beyond "doing what I want with what is mine" to a right to profit, in effect a claim on the total social product.

35. This provides another illustration of Lindblom's concept of "extended authority."

Chapter 2: Banding Together

1. Campaign for Human Development, *Poverty in American Democracy: A Study of Social Power* (Washington, D.C.: United States Catholic Conference, 1974).

2. Perella, interview.

3. For other examples of communities attempting to develop responses to plant closings

and deindustrialization in the same era, see, for example, Eric Mann, *Taking on General Motors: A Case Study of the Campaign to Keep GM Van Nuys Open* (Berkeley and Los Angeles: University of California Press, 1987); Jeanie Wylie, *Poletown: Community Betrayed* (Urbana: University of Illinois Press, 1989); and William Serrin, *Homestead* (New York: Times Books, 1992).

4. Perella, interview.

5. Saul D. Alinsky, *Rules for Radicals* (New York: Random House, 1971), 12–13. For a full biography of Alinsky, see Sandford D. Horwitt, *Let Them Call Me Rebel: Saul Alinsky, His Life and Legacy* (New York: Alfred A. Knopf, 1989). For other interpretations of organizing, see, for example, Frances Fox Piven and Richard Cloward, *Poor People's Movements: Why They Succeed, How They Fail* (New York: Random House, 1977); Harry Boyte, *Backyard Revolution* (Philadelphia: Temple University Press, 1980); and Rick Fantasia, *Cultures of Solidarity: Consciousness, Action, and Contemporary American Workers* (Berkeley and Los Angeles: University of California Press, 1988).

6. Galdston, interview, November 19, 1985.

7. Ibid.

8. Perella, interview.

9. Memo to Hank Murray, Fred Perella, and Miles Rapoport from Ken Galdston, October 12, 1982, NVP Collection, Mattatuck Museum, Waterbury, Conn.

10. Galdston, interview, November 19, 1985.

11. For additional information on LEAP, see Bruce Shapiro, "Connecticut LEAP: A New Electoral Strategy," in *Building Bridges,* ed. Brecher and Costello (see introduction, n. 4).

12. Galdston, interview, November 19, 1985.

13. Andrew Walsh, "Peter Rosazza," *Hartford Courant,* May 15, 1983.

14. Peter Rosazza, video interview.

15. Galdston, interview, November 19, 1985.

16. Rev. Tim Benson, interview.

17. "Naugatuck Valley Project" (handout, October 12, 1982), NVP Collection, Mattatuck Museum, Waterbury, Conn.

18. From the substantial literature on the Mondragon cooperatives, a good introduction is William Whyte and Kathleen King Whyte, *Making Mondragon: The Growth and Dynamics of the Worker Cooperative Complex* (Ithaca: Cornell University Press, 1991).

19. Galdston, interview, November 19, 1985.

20. "Ken Galdston: Activity since Last Meeting" (handout, February 10, 1983), NVP Collection, Mattatuck Museum, Waterbury, Conn.

21. See "Early Warning Signals" (handout, n.d.), NVP Collection, Mattatuck Museum, Waterbury, Conn.

22. Galdston interview, November 19, 1985.

23. Ibid.

24. Rosazza, video interview.

25. Galdston, interview, November 19, 1985.

26. Campbell Lovett, interview.

27. "Proposed Interview Questionnaire" (handout, June 8, 1983), NVP Collection, Mattatuck Museum, Waterbury, Conn.

28. Lovett, interview. This presentation occurred at a somewhat later time but was typical of Galdston's approach.

29. "ICA: Consultant's Statement of Capability" (handout, n.d.), NVP Collection, Mattatuck Museum, Waterbury, Conn.

30. Galdston, interview, November 19, 1985.

31. Ibid.

32. Ibid.

33. Ibid.

34. Benson, interview.

35. Galdston, interview, November 19, 1985.

Chapter 3: Buyout

1. The material on Seymour Specialty Wire in this book is based in part on "Upstairs, Downstairs: The Rise and Fall of 'Seymour Specialty Wire: An Employee-Owned Company,'" a study conducted by the author under a grant from the Cooperative Charitable Trust. See the report for additional information on research methodology. See also Jeremy Brecher, "Upstairs, Downstairs: Class Conflict in an Employee-Owned Factory," in *Building Bridges,* ed. Brecher and Costello (see introduction, n. 4).

2. Pape, *History of Waterbury,* 1:372–73 (see chap. 1, n. 1); Seymour Manufacturing Company, *Facts about Seymour* (Seymour, Conn.: Seymour Manufacturing, n.d.).

3. Ed Labacz, interview.

4. Ibid.; Brecher, Lombardi, and Stackhouse, *Brass Valley,* 106 (see introduction, n. 1).

5. Ken Galdston, *Worker Ownership: Presentations from Chicago Innovative Enterprises Conference* (Chicago: Midwest Center for Labor Research, n.d.), 11.

6. Galdston, interview, December 18, 1985.

7. Mike Kearney, video interview.

8. Kearney, interview, May 12, 1986.

9. Galdston, interview, December 18, 1985.

10. Ibid.

11. Kearney, video interview.

12. Galdston, interview, December 18, 1985.

13. Ibid.; Benson, interview.

14. Galdston, interview, December 18, 1985.

15. Benson, interview.

16. Ibid.

17. Galdston, interview, December 18, 1985.

18. Ibid.

19. Ibid.

20. Galdston, *Worker Ownership,* 13.

21. Benson, interview.

22. Roland Cline, interview, May 20, 1986.

23. Galdston, interview, December 18, 1985.

24. Cline, interview, May 20, 1986.

25. Jan Stackhouse, "Seymour Specialty Wire: An Experiment in Industrial Democracy" (New York University Graduate School of Business Administration paper, 1987), 26.

26. Ibid.

27. Galdston, interview, December 18, 1985; anonymous office worker, interview.

28. Ken Galdston, "Organizing Report for Sponsoring Committee Meeting," July 5, 1984.

29. Kearney interview, May 12, 1986; anonymous office worker, interview.

30. Galdston, interview, December 18, 1985.

31. Ibid.

32. Stackhouse, "Seymour Specialty Wire," 27.

33. Quoted in ibid., 2. There is a large literature on employee ownership and ESOPs. See, for example, John Logue, Jacquelyn Yates, and William Greider, *The Real World of Employee Ownership* (Ithaca: ILR Press, 2002).

34. Stackhouse, "Seymour Specialty Wire," 2–3.

35. "Popular ESOPs Get Tax Aid," *New York Times,* March 21, 1987, cited in ibid., 3.

36. Cline, interview, May 20, 1986.

37. Ibid.

38. Cline, interview, May 12, 1986.

39. Kearney, interview, May 12, 1986.

40. Carl Drescher Jr., interview.

41. Cline, interview, May 12, 1986.

42. Rosazza, video interview.

43. Chapter 6 recounts the subsequent history of Seymour Specialty Wire as an employee-owned company.

44. Benson, interview.

Chapter 4: Organizing

1. There is an extensive literature on community organizing. See, for example, Robert Fisher and Peter Romanofsky, *Community Organizing for Urban Social Change: A Historical Perspective* (Westport, Conn.: Greenwood Press, 1981); Robert Fisher, *Let the People Decide: Neighborhood Organizing in America* (Woodbridge, Conn.: Twayne, 1997); and Heidi Swarts, *Organizing Urban America: Secular and Faith Based Progressive Movements* (Minneapolis: University of Minnesota Press, 2008). The account given here also draws heavily on extended discussions with Ken Galdston, many of which were recorded and are available in the Naugatuck Valley Project collection at the Mattatuck Museum.

2. Galdston, interview, March 23, 1988; Peter Rosazza, interview, March 21, 1986.

3. Rosazza, video interview.

4. For Ken Galdston's reflections in choices about levels of militancy, see his interview of April 14, 1986.

5. Rosazza, video interview.

6. Galdston, interview, March 23, 1988.

7. Ibid.

8. Ibid.

9. Ibid.

10. Benson, interview.

11. Ibid.

12. Ibid.

13. Ibid.

14. Galdston, interview, March 23, 1988.

15. Frederick J. Perella Jr. to Archbishop John F. Whealon, July 1, 1983.

16. Galdston, interview, November 19, 1985.

17. Ibid.

18. Benson, interview.

19. Galdston, interview, November 19, 1985.

20. Benson, interview.

21. Ibid.

22. Perella to Whealon, July 1, 1983.

23. Benson, interview.

24. Galdston, interview, March 23, 1988.

25. Ibid., December 18, 1985.

26. Benson, interview.

27. Ibid.

28. Ibid.

29. Galdston, interview, November 19, 1985.

30. Carol Burkhart, interview.

31. Ibid.

32. Ibid.

33. Ibid.

34. Galdston, interview, April 14, 1986.

35. Ibid.

36. Ibid.

37. Burkhart, interview.

38. Galdston, interview, April 14, 1986.

39. Ibid.

40. Ibid.

41. Ibid.

42. "Long-Range Goals" marked "Draft" (November 7, 1986), NVP Collection, Mattatuck Museum, Waterbury, Conn.

43. Galdston, interview, April 14, 1986.

44. Ibid.

45. Benson, interview.

Chapter 5: Century Brass

1. Brecher, Lombardi, and Stackhouse, *Brass Valley,* 232–42 (see introduction, n. 1).

2. Theresa Francis, interview, May 19, 1986.

3. Ibid.

4. Galdston, interview, December 18, 1985.

5. Mark Pazniokas and G. Philip Morago, "Brass Union Rallies behind Fiery Chief," *Hartford Courant,* undated clipping.

6. Galdston, interview, December 18, 1985.

7. Ibid.

8. Ibid.

9. Ibid.

10. Francis, interview, May 19, 1986; Galdston, interview, December 18, 1985.

11. Carol Burkhart-Lyons, memorial service for Theresa Francis.

12. Francis, video interview. See also Galdston, interview, February 24, 1988.

13. Galdston, memorial service for Theresa Francis.

14. Francis, interview, May 19, 1986.

15. Ibid.

16. Ibid.

17. Ibid.

18. Ibid.

19. Jeremy Brecher, "Century Brass Closing," 15, NVP Collection, Mattatuck Museum, Waterbury, Conn.

20. Francis, interview, May 19, 1986.

21. Ibid.

22. Ibid. See also Industrial Cooperative Association, "Century Brass General Products Division: Phase 1 Feasibility Study" (November 1985), NVP Collection, Mattatuck Museum, Waterbury, Conn., which identifies the same difficulties.

23. Galdston, interview, February 24, 1988.

24. Jeremy Brecher, note on discussion with Ken Galdston, early June 1989, and discussion with CCAG staff.

25. Lovett, interview.

26. Francis, video interview.

27. Lovett, interview.

28. Francis, interview, May 19, 1986; Francis, video interview; Lovett, interview.

29. Galdston, interview, October 16, 1987.

30. "Century: Clergy in Dark about Us," *Waterbury Republican-American,* May 12, 1986.

31. Campbell Lovett to Jeremy Brecher, March 25, 2006.

32. Lovett, interview; Francis, interview, May 19, 1986.

33. Lovett, interview; Lovett to Brecher, March 25, 2006; Lovett, interview.

34. Francis, interview, May 19, 1986.

35. Lovett, interview.

36. Ibid.

37. Ibid.

38. Galdston, interview, April 14, 1986.

39. Galdston, interview, February 24, 1988.

40. Ibid.

41. See, for example, letter from Attilio D'Agostino to Theresa Francis, October 16, 1987, expressing shock at an alleged mishandling of money, and Francis's reply of January 28, 1988, NVP Collection, Mattatuck Museum, Waterbury, Conn.

42. Galdston, interview, February 24, 1988.

43. Ibid.

44. Attilio D'Agostino, video interview.

45. "Century Workers Say No to Buyout," *Waterbury Republican-American,* May 30, 1987; Galdston, interview, February 24, 1988.

46. Galdston, interview, February 24, 1988; Lovett, interview.

47. Francis, video, interview.

48. Lovett, interview.

49. Galdston, interview, February 24, 1988.

50. Ibid.

51. Lovett, interview; Galdston, interview, February 24, 1988.

52. Galdston, memorial service for Francis.

53. Francis, interview, May 19, 1986.

54. Ibid.

Chapter 6: *The Life and Death of Seymour Specialty Wire*

1. Brecher, Lombardi, and Stackhouse, *Brass Valley,* 129 (see introduction, n. 1).

2. Sam Kwochka, interview.

3. Brecher, Lombardi, and Stackhouse, *Brass Valley,* 133; Kwochka, interview.

4. With the authority often went the power to compel favors from workers unrelated to work functions. Such abuse was a major motive for unionization in the brass mills.

5. Kearney, interview, June 1, 1990. These reflections came in the midst of a discussion of the resistance to Universal Scheduling.

6. Anonymous Seymour worker, interview.

7. Tom Stundza, "Watch for Supply Volatility in 1991," *Purchasing,* March 7, 1991, 72B1–72B6.

8. Tom Stundza, "Purchasing Deluge Will Ebb Slightly in '93," *Purchasing,* March 4, 1993, 34B6–34B7.

9. "Transplant Brass Mill Comes to Iowa," *Purchasing,* May 17, 1990, 31.

10. "Metal Chips," *Purchasing,* undated clipping.

11. *Purchasing,* March 7, 1991.

12. Ibid.

13. Ibid.

14. Ibid.

15. *Purchasing,* April 5, 1990.

16. Ibid.; *Purchasing,* March 7, 1991.

17. Figures in this paragraph from "Business Plan," 5, NVP Collection, Mattatuck Museum, Waterbury, Conn.

18. Anonymous Seymour worker, interview.

19. Kearney, interview, June 1, 1990. I conducted interviews with Michael Kearney approximately once a year over the entire life of Seymour Specialty Wire. These interviews cover many aspects of each period in detail. Kearney was well situated to observe various aspects of the company: he was a board member for all but one brief period; he was first a worker in the mill and president of the union, then a salaried manager working in the mill; and throughout, he played a role in NVP jobs programs and national networks concerned with employee ownership.

20. Ibid.

21. Personal communication from participant.

22. Ibid.

23. Harrington, interview.

24. Drescher, interview.

25. Kearney, interview, June 1, 1990.

26. Drescher, interview; anonymous Seymour worker, interview.

27. Kearney, interview, June 1, 1990.

28. See ibid. for more on Universal Scheduling.

29. Prior to Universal, there were no computers in the mill (Kearney, interview, September 27, 1991).

30. Drescher, interview.

31. Kearney, interview, June 1, 1990.

32. Kearney, interview, November 16, 1987.

33. Kearney, interview, June 1, 1990.

34. Ibid.

35. Ibid. In April 1990, an experienced production-control person evaluated the system. His report stated in part, "The manufacturing computer systems are good, but of little immediate value because of lack of data input. . . . Approximately 40 interrelated data bases and approximately 40 different menus. To me the most important step for utilizing the system is to hire a data input clerk. Data must be input on a timely basis for management to use reports for decision making. Today too much control is dependent upon 'MBWA,' management by walking around." He further found, "Concurrently with a data entry clerk must be the establishment of cut off times when data is available for generating reports. . . . In fact, the time requirements for data input for system integrity will impact most departments and this demand, which initially will be looked upon as an infringement, will not be embraced with open arms" (NVP Collection, Mattatuck Museum, Waterbury, Conn.).

36. The election was in February 1989 (Kearney, interview, June 1, 1990).

37. Ibid.

38. Ibid.

39. *Purchasing,* March 4, 1993; *Purchasing,* April 5, 1990.

40. See Kearney, interview, June 1, 1990. Acceptance of the wage cut was based in part on an agreement to bring Roland Cline back in at company expense. See ibid.

41. Ibid. Kearney points out that employees on salary could not make use of these tactics.

42. Kearney, interview, June 1, 1990; Kearney, interview, September 27, 1991.

43. Kearney, interview, June 1, 1990.

44. Ibid.

45. Jerry Harrington to Pauline Lounsbury, December 7, 1992, NVP Collection, Mattatuck Museum, Waterbury, Conn.

46. Ibid.

47. Kearney, interview, June 1, 1990.

48. Ibid.

49. Harrington, interview.

50. Kearney, interview, September 27, 1991.

51. Kearney, interview, June 1, 1990. Layoffs took place December 25, 1989.

52. Ibid.

53. Ibid.

54. Ibid.

55. Kearney, interview, September 27, 1991.

56. Kearney, interview, June 1, 1990.

57. Resolution of February 20, 1990. See also Harrington to Lounsbury.

58. Harrington to Lounsbury.

59. *Purchasing,* November 22, 1990. Complaint letters from customers in the company papers indicate that quality and on-time delivery remained serious problems. A February 20, 1991, memo to Jerry Harrington from Frank Lang, head of sales, says, "We cannot continue to have an on time delivery performance of less than 50%, accept approximately $100,000 per month of returned material and measure our customer response time in half days or days and still obtain business" (NVP Collection, Mattatuck Museum, Waterbury, Conn.).

60. Kearney, interview, June 1, 1990.

61. Kearney, interview, September 27, 1991.

62. Ibid.; Pauline Lounsbury, "When the Cure Is to Fix It," undated clipping.

63. Kearney, interview, September 27, 1991.

64. Ibid.

65. Ibid.

66. Harrington, interview.

67. Harrington to Lounsbury. Kearney maintains that these claims are "blown way out of proportion" (Kearney, letter to *Waterbury Republican-American,* December 28, 1992).

68. In late 1990, Larry Motel was elected union president. At the February 1991 board election: Harrington and Motel, automatic. Don Colson, Mike Kearney, Paul Wojahowski, Linda Baldino, Jimmy Lewis, elected. John Harlor, retired director of human resources for Polaroid, added as outside director and made chairman. Joe Lombardo, outside director. In other words, two hourly workers were elected. See Kearney, interview, September 27, 1991.

69. Harrington, interview.

70. Kearney, letter to *Waterbury Republican-American.*

71. Minutes of January 22, 1991, board meeting, NVP Collection, Mattatuck Museum, Waterbury, Conn.

72. Harrington to Lounsbury; Kearney, letter to *Waterbury Republican-American.*

73. Meeting of the Trustees of the Seymour Specialty Wire Co. E.S.O.P. Trust, February 21, 1991, NVP Collection, Mattatuck Museum, Waterbury, Conn.; Mark Rosenbaum, Foothill Capital Corporation, to Jerry Harrington, May 21, 1991, NVP Collection, Mattatuck Museum, Waterbury, Conn.

74. Kearney, interview, September 27, 1991.

75. "Seymour Specialty Wire Company Presentation to State of Connecticut Department of Economic Development, May 31, 1991," 16, NVP Collection, Mattatuck Museum, Waterbury, Conn.

76. Kearney, interview, September 27, 1991.

77. Ibid. Such realities indicate one of the difficulties in trying to quantify the dynamics of a situation like Seymour Specialty Wire.

78. Jeremiah Harrington to Employees, September 13, 1991. There were charges that layoffs involved favoritism and discrimination against "troublemakers" (Kearney, interview, December 6, 1991).

79. Kearney, interview, December 6, 1991.

80. A UAW international representative servicing the SSW local was among those propounding this view.

81. Ibid.

82. *Purchasing,* March 4, 1993.

83. Kearney, interview, December 29, 1992. Such charges would be difficult to prove or disprove definitively. In the event, no such purchase occurred.

84. Later, the ESOP was reconvened and a new board elected.

85. Ibid. Thanks to Mike Kearney, a substantial part of the company records were saved.

86. David Duke, interview.

Chapter 7: Founding ValleyCare Cooperative

1. Ken Galdston, "Organizing Report for Sponsoring Committee Meeting" (March 14, 1984), NVP Collection, Mattatuck Museum, Waterbury, Conn.

2. Chapters 7, 8, and 9 on the history of ValleyCare are based in part on *Valley Care Cooperative: A Retrospective,* prepared by Jeremy Brecher and Ruth Glasser for the Cooperative Charitable Trust. Ruth Glasser conducted many of the interviews and contributed to the analysis. For an interesting comparison, see Annelise Orleck, *Storming Caesars Palace: How Black Mothers Fought Their Own War on Poverty* (Boston: Beacon Press, 2005).

3. Doreen Filipiak, interview.

4. Carol Burkhart, "Home Health Care Outline" (November 16, 1987), NVP Collection, Mattatuck Museum, Waterbury, Conn.

5. "Naugatuck Valley Project Home Health Care Prefeasibility Workplan" (March 16, 1988), NVP Collection, Mattatuck Museum, Waterbury, Conn.

6. Information in this and preceding paragraph is from the VCC generic grant proposal, NVP Collection, Mattatuck Museum, Waterbury, Conn.

7. "Preliminary Research on Homemaker/Home Health Aide Market" (March 28, 1989), NVP Collection, Mattatuck Museum, Waterbury, Conn.

8. "Preliminary Research," 9; VCC generic grant proposal.

9. "Valley Care Cooperative, Inc., Revised Business Plan" (June 21, 1990), 19, NVP Collection, Mattatuck Museum, Waterbury, Conn.

10. Ibid.

11. Rosati, interview.

12. Ibid.

13. Ibid.

14. Filipiak, interview.

15. "Lilly Progress Report" (October 31, 1990–June 30, 1991), NVP Collection, Mattatuck Museum, Waterbury, Conn.

16. Rosati, interview.

17. Ibid.

18. *Waterbury Republican-American,* April 25, 1991.

19. The VCC also expected additional funding from the Mott Foundation pending its March 1992 CHCA review.

20. Pat Diorio, interview, August 4, 1999.

21. "Lilly Progress Report."

22. Diorio, interview, August 4, 1999.

23. Ibid.

24. "VCC Program Report for Lilly Endowment" (January 1, 1992–June 30, 1992, dated August 19, 1992), NVP Collection, Mattatuck Museum, Waterbury, Conn.

25. Susan Wefald, Staff Director of the NVP, to Mark Weinheimer at Lilly Endowment, April 30, 1993, NVP Collection, Mattatuck Museum, Waterbury, Conn.

26. David Scheie, "Rainbow Research Report" (January 25, 1993), 2, NVP Collection, Mattatuck Museum, Waterbury, Conn.

27. Annual report (year ending June 30, 1995), NVP Collection, Mattatuck Museum, Waterbury, Conn.

28. Valley Care Mission Statement excerpt, annual report (1992), NVP Collection, Mattatuck Museum, Waterbury, Conn.

29. "Lilly Progress Report."

30. "VCC Self-Assessment" (November 1991), NVP Collection, Mattatuck Museum, Waterbury, Conn.

31. Rosati, interview.

32. "Worker Ownership and Participation Plan for VCC" (May 9, 1991), NVP Collection, Mattatuck Museum, Waterbury, Conn.

33. "Draft Replication Group/VCC Assessment: Worker Ownership" (September 17, 1991), NVP Collection, Mattatuck Museum, Waterbury, Conn.

34. Plan outlined in "Worker Ownership and Participation Plan for VCC."

35. From "Lilly Report" (January 1992–June 1992, sent August 19, 1999), NVP Collection, Mattatuck Museum, Waterbury, Conn.

36. Rosati, interview; Lillian González, interview; quote from inside cover, 1992 annual report, NVP Collection, Mattatuck Museum, Waterbury, Conn.

37. Rosati, interview.

38. González, interview; Rosati, interview.

39. Rosati, interview.

40. Scheie, "Rainbow Research Report," 3.

41. "Lilly Report" (submitted April 30, 1993), NVP Collection, Mattatuck Museum, Waterbury, Conn.; Valley Care Cooperative Second Annual Meeting Minutes, NVP Collection, Mattatuck Museum, Waterbury, Conn.

42. "Lilly Report" (submitted April 30, 1993).

43. Rosati, interview.

44. Valley Care Cooperative, Second Annual Meeting Minutes, NVP Collection, Mattatuck Museum, Waterbury, Conn.

45. President's letter, in annual report for 1994, NVP Collection, Mattatuck Museum, Waterbury, Conn.

46. As per report submitted January 30, 1995, for the period June 1 to December 31, 1994, NVP Collection, Mattatuck Museum, Waterbury, Conn.

47. "Lilly Report" (January 30, 1995, to reflect second half of 1994), NVP Collection, Mattatuck Museum, Waterbury, Conn.

48. Diorio, interview, August 4, 1999.

49. González, interview; Norman, interview.

50. Maria Gerard, interview.

51. Rosati, interview.

52. Diorio, interview, August 4, 1999.

53. Filipiak, interview.

54. Rosati, interview.

Chapter 8: Taking Care of Business

1. Filipiak, interview.

2. ICA, "Taking Care of Business" (1991), NVP Collection, Mattatuck Museum, Waterbury, Conn.

3. For more on the character of home-care work, see Ruth Glasser and Jeremy Brecher, *We Are the Roots: The Organizational Culture of a Home Care Cooperative* (Davis: University of California Center for Cooperatives, 2002).

4. Francis, VCC slide-show script; note from NVP to Karen Jacobson, Adrian Dominican Fund, September 22, 1990, NVP Collection, Mattatuck Museum, Waterbury, Conn.

5. Letter from David M. Scheie, project associate of Rainbow Research, Inc., to Carol Burkhart-Lyons, October 25, 1990, NVP Collection, Mattatuck Museum, Waterbury, Conn.

6. Rosati, interview.

7. See Lilly quarterly reports, NVP Collection, Mattatuck Museum, Waterbury, Conn.

8. VCC slide-show script.

9. "VCC Self-Assessment" (November 1991), NVP Collection, Mattatuck Museum, Waterbury, Conn.

10. See Brecher and Glasser, *We Are the Roots,* for extensive discussion of CHCA training.

11. Rosati, interview. Willow Street is the main thoroughfare of Waterbury's Willow/Plaza neighborhood, an area in the city's North End that is plagued by drugs and prostitution.

12. Up until 1993, as will be explained later.

13. "VCC Self-Assessment"; Rosati, interview.

14. Rosati, interview.

15. Diorio, interview, August 4, 1999.

16. Gerard, interview.

17. Anonymous home health aide, quoted in "ValleyCare Annual Report, 1992," NVP Collection, Mattatuck Museum, Waterbury, Conn.

18. Henrietta Norman, interview.

19. González, interview.

20. Norman, interview.

21. C-Town is a Hispanic supermarket chain.

22. Rosati, interview.

23. Norman, interview.

24. Gerard, interview.

25. Rosati, interview.

26. Faith Muller, VCC slide-show script.

27. Rosati, interview.

28. Diorio, interview, August 4, 1999.

29. Norman, interview.

30. Gerard, interview.

31. ICA, "Taking Care of Business"; Norman, interview.

32. Diorio, interview, August 4, 1999.

33. Ibid.

Chapter 9: *The Demise of ValleyCare*

1. Diorio, interview, April 14, 1999.

2. ValleyCare Cooperative Board Meeting Minutes, May 3, June 18, 1996, NVP Collection, Mattatuck Museum, Waterbury, Conn.

3. VCC Board Meeting Minutes, January 30, 1998, NVP Collection, Mattatuck Museum, Waterbury, Conn.

4. Diorio, interview, August 4, 1999.

5. Rosati, interview; Norman, interview.

6. Diorio, interview, August 4, 1999; Rosati, interview.

7. Norman, interview.

8. Rosati, interview.

9. Diorio, interview, August 4, 1999.

10. González, interview; Diorio, interview, August 4, 1999.

11. "Lilly Report" (January 30, 1995, for the period June 1 to December 31, 1994), NVP Collection, Mattatuck Museum, Waterbury, Conn.

12. Diorio, interview, August 4, 1999.

13. Gerard, interview.

14. Diorio, interview, August 4, 1999.

15. Diorio, interview, April 14, 1999.

16. Ibid.

17. Diorio, interview, August 4, 1999.

18. Filipiak, interview.

19. Gerard, interview.

20. Diorio, interview, August 4, 1999.

21. Gerard, interview.

22. PHI (Paraprofessional Healthcare Institute) is a policy organization affiliated with Cooperative Home Care Associates.

23. Diorio, interview, August 4, 1999.

24. "Lilly Report" (January 30, 1995, for the period June 1 to December 31, 1994), NVP Collection, Mattatuck Museum, Waterbury, Conn.

25. Diorio, interview, August 4, 1999.

26. Rosati, interview.

27. Diorio, interview, August 4, 1999.

28. "VCC Mission Statement," NVP Collection, Mattatuck Museum, Waterbury, Conn.

29. Diorio, interview, August 4, 1999.

30. For public policy options supportive to such efforts in the health care industry, visit the Paraprofessional Healthcare Institute, a policy center affiliated with Cooperative Home Care Associates, at http://phinational.org/.

31. Rosati, interview; Filipiak, interview.

Chapter 10: Brookside Housing Cooperative

1. Greg Mizera, "2 of 3 Unsure of View on Forming Rent Panel," *Waterbury Republican-American,* October 31, 1989.

2. *Waterbury Republican-American,* February 16, 1989.

3. Galdston, interview, May 25, 1988.

4. Greg Mizera, "Shamrock Ridge Tenants Seek Help," *Waterbury Republican-American,* June 10, 1987.

5. Naugatuck Valley Project, Request for Proposal, "Training for Residents of Brookside Cooperatives Located in Waterbury, Connecticut" (n.d.), NVP Collection, Mattatuck Museum, Waterbury, Conn.

6. Galdston, interview, October 26, 1989. For historical background on ICE and community land trusts, see http://en.wikipedia.org/wiki/Community_land_trust. For a review of the academic literature pertaining to limited equity co-ops in the early 2000s, see Susan Saegert and Lymari Benitez, "Limited Equity Housing Cooperatives: Defining a Niche in the Low-Income Housing Market," *Journal of Planning Literature* (May 2005).

7. Greg Mizera, "Coalition Hopes to Use Land Trusts to Create Housing," *Waterbury Sunday Republican,* June 5, 1988.

8. Ibid.

9. Galdston, interview, October 26, 1989.

10. Mizera, "Shamrock Ridge Tenants Seek Help."

11. Ibid.

12. Amy LaRoche, "Coalition to Focus on Housing," *Waterbury Republican-American,* October 26, 1987.

13. Greg Mizera, "Shamrock Ridge Tenants Get Judge to Halt Rent Hike," *Waterbury Republican-American,* January 28, 1988.

14. Jane Lerner, "Agreement Allows Tenants to Stay at Shamrock Ridge," *Waterbury Republican-American,* May 24, 1988.

15. Kevin Bean, interview, April 9, 1990.

16. Roberta Baker, "Tenants Unveil Alternative Housing Plan," *Waterbury Republican-American*, July 20, 1988.

17. Merrill Gay, interview.

18. Bob Perry, "Waterville Group Supports Plan to Build Duplexes," *Waterbury Republican-American*, August 5, 1998.

19. Greg Mizera, "$80,000 Needed for Housing Venture," *Waterbury Republican-American*, September 14, 1988.

20. State support was part of a new Department of Housing Land Trust/Land Bank program and a Limited Equity Cooperatives/Mutual Housing Association program approved by the legislature in 1987. See Andrew Baker, "Community Land Trusts Are Keeping Some Housing 'Forever Affordable,'" *Hartford Commercial Record*, May 31, 1991.

21. "Petitioners Seek Financing for Waterbury Housing," *Hartford Courant*, November 3, 1988.

22. Bill Leukhardt, "Fort Hill Housing Supported," *Waterbury Republican-American*, February 8, 1989.

23. John Pirro, "Funding Endorsed for Fort Hill Project," *Waterbury Republican-American*, February 24, 1989.

24. Ibid.

25. "Supporters Hail State Funding of Fort Hill Project," *Waterbury Republican-American*, February 26, 1989.

26. Jacqueline A. Viggiano, "Valleyites Are Eligible to Apply for Area Co-op," *Ansonia Evening Sentinel*, March 25, 1989.

27. Greg Mizera, "Sponsors Pledge $25,000 toward Affordable Housing," *Waterbury Republican-American*, June 6, 1989.

28. Frank Juliano, "Fort Hill Project Right on Target," *Waterbury Republican-American*, July 24, 1989.

29. Greg Mizera, "Housing Plan's Supporters Blame City for Delays," *Waterbury Republican-American*, September 29, 1989.

30. "Santopietro Lauded for Fort Hill Support," *Waterbury Sunday Republican*, October 1, 1989. See also letter to the editor, "Support Proposed Subdivision," from Stanley Fox of the Shamrock Ridge Tenants, to the *Waterbury Republican-American*, October 4, 1989.

31. Greg Mizera, "Police Commission Gets Request to Aid Fort Hill," *Waterbury Republican-American*, October 6, 1989.

32. Mizera, "2 of 3 Unsure."

33. Bill Leukhardt, "Tenants Cheer, Landlords Pan Proposal for Fair Rent Board," *Waterbury Republican-American*, December 1, 1989; Robyn Adams, "Sleep-in at City Hall Vowed If Fair Rent Agency Fizzles," *Waterbury Republican-American*, December 2, 1989.

34. Brian Stuart, "Fort Hill Developers Worried," *Waterbury Republican-American*, October 12, 1989.

35. Joe Unfried, "Meeting between City, Housing Officials Private," *Waterbury Republican-American*, October 17, 1989.

36. Bean, interview, April 9, 1990.

37. Robyn Adams, "Fort Hill Housing Project Is Scrapped," *Waterbury Republican-American*, November 1, 1989; Robyn Adams and Greg Mizera, "Fort Hill Housing Proj-

ect Scrapped; State Seeks Another Site," *Waterbury Republican-American,* November 2, 1989.

38. Frank Juliano, "Affordable Housing Plan Gets Second Look," *Waterbury Republican-American,* January 9, 1990.

39. Greg Mizera, "Groups Plan to Build Affordable Housing," *Waterbury Republican-American,* January 24, 1990.

40. Greg Mizera, "Affordable Housing Planned by Groups," *Waterbury Republican-American,* January 26, 1990.

41. Bob Perry, "Low-Cost Housing Bids Sought," *Waterbury Republican-American,* March 19, 1990.

42. Greg Mizera, "Housing Complex Expected to Get State Funds," *Waterbury Republican-American,* April 26, 1990.

43. Greg Mizera, "State Approves Housing Bond," *Waterbury Republican-American,* May 1, 1990; Gay, interview.

44. Gay, interview.

45. Robyn Adams, "Ground Broken for Cooperative Housing," unidentified clipping in NVP Collection, Mattatuck Museum, Waterbury, Conn.

46. Robyn Adams, "'Sweat Equity' Pays for City Residents," *Waterbury Republican-American,* June 25, 1991.

47. Robyn Adams, "Home at Last," *Waterbury Republican-American,* September 26, 1991.

48. Mike McIntire, "State Money, Public Housing, Waterbury Politics," *Waterbury Sunday Republican,* July 14, 1991.

49. George Judson, "Waterbury Mayor Charged with Corruption," *New York Times,* September 26, 1991.

50. Bean, interview, May 11, 1990.

51. Naugatuck Valley Project, Request for Proposal, "Training for Residents."

52. James Beck, interview by Lucien Lafreniere and Jeremy Brecher.

53. Derricia Parker, interview by Lucien Lafreniere and Jeremy Brecher.

54. Bean, interview, April 9, 1990.

Chapter 11: Economic Democratization from Below

1. Perella, video interview.

2. See chapter 1.

3. For an extended analysis of the role of structured networks in social movements, see North American Alliance for Fair Employment, "Making Networks Work," http://www.fairjobs.org, and references cited there.

4. This was also the case for trade unions prior to the National Labor Relations Act (Wagner Act).

5. A few unions, such as printers, retained a place for cooperatives within their structure.

6. Exceptions include the IWW and at some points part of the UMW, calling for "the mines to the miners." See Jeremy Brecher, *Strike!* (Boston: South End Press, 1997).

7. This approach to property as a "bundle of rights" that can be distributed among vari-

ous actors was classically formulated by Adolph Berle and Gardiner Means in *The Modern Corporation and Private Property* (New York: Macmillan, 1933). That such property rights are a product of and dependent upon authority relations, rather than somehow originating in the market, is forcefully brought out by Charles Lindblom in *Politics and Markets* (see chap. 1, n. 30).

8. The theoretical significance of leases as a vehicle for disaggregating and assigning various sorts of use and usufruct rights has been explored by Roberto Unger. Shortly before his political demise, Mikhail Gorbachev was advocating the leasehold as a form for combining the benefits of social ownership with those of decentralized economic initiative.

9. Combining control of an enterprise's day-to-day life by participants with control of its core decisions by a wider community organization was a theme in Dan Swinney, Miguel Vasquez, and Howard Engelskirchen, "Towards a New Vision of Community Economic Development," distributed by the Federation for Industrial Retention and Renewal. (A more recent paper developing some of the same themes is Dan Swinney, "Building the Bridge to the High Road," available at http://www.clcr.org/publications/btb/contents .html.) Staughton Lynd has suggested that alternative enterprises should be owned by nonprofit organizations with the public purpose of providing jobs and needed goods and services (see Lynd in *Building Bridges,* ed. Brecher and Costello [see introduction, n. 4]). This is essentially the model of Brookside and of the initial phase of VCC. What would happen if this model were applied to industrial enterprises like SSW remains to be seen.

10. Michael Albert and Robin Hahnel, *Looking Forward: Participatory Economics for the Twenty-first Century* (Boston: South End Press, 1991).

11. The Amalgamated Bank became a prime source of loans for clothing manufacturing and used that role for such purposes as stabilizing employment by reducing seasonal variations in the industry.

12. Jeremy Brecher, "Connecticut Community Economic Development Program," in *Jobs and the Economy: A Survey of 1993 New England Legislation* (Cambridge, Mass.: Progressive Policy Initiative, 1994).

13. Such programs provide a mechanism for redistribution of investment flows that partially counter the necessity to maximize enterprise growth while continuing to utilize the price system as a vehicle for rational choice. In effect, such approaches adjust the supply or price of capital (or both) to correct for market failures at the point in the reproduction cycle where investments are determined.

14. It should be recalled that this was also the original purpose of the savings and loan system.

15. Filipiak, interview. For the history and current implementations of the service credit idea, see http://www.timedollar.org.

16. These are extensively documented in Clark Kerr, "Productive Enterprises of the Unemployed, 1931–38" (Ph.D. diss., University of California, 1939).

17. Arthur M. Schlesinger, *The Coming of the New Deal* (Boston: Houghton-Mifflin, 2003), 279.

18. These approaches create capital whose ownership is social but whose control is decentralized. Such an approach can be promoted by public policy. The Italian law for

cooperatives, for example, provides a significant tax benefit for profits put in an "indivisible reserve." These funds in effect create capital that can be used for the co-op's investment but cannot be used for any other purpose. If a co-op is liquidated, any remaining funds must be donated to other co-ops or co-op federations.

19. This is known as the "isolation problem" in economics and as the "fetishism of commodities" in Marxist theory.

20. Whyte and Whyte's *Making Mondragon* (see chap. 2, n. 18) makes clear the extent to which the Mondragon cooperative movement is less a collection of individual co-ops than a central entrepreneurial structure generating self-managing but still dependent subsidiary units. This was not always clear to American advocates of the Mondragon model, however.

21. See Glasser and Brecher, *We Are the Roots* (see chap. 8, n. 3).

22. The NVP's more recent anti-predatory-lending campaign, described in the next chapter, represents another approach to reforming the housing market.

23. See John Logue, "Economics, Cooperation, and Employee Ownership: The Emilia-Romagna Model," http://www.kent.edu/oeoc/OEOCLibrary/EmiliaRomagnaLong.htm; and Matt Hancock, *Compete to Cooperate: The Cooperative District of Imola* (Imola, Italy: Bacchilega Editore, 2007).

24. See Diane Elson, "Market Socialism or Socialization of Markets," *New Left Review* 1, no. 172 (1988), for a discussion of the need for open access to information if markets are to serve as effective vehicles for coordinating self-managed firms.

25. Juan Forero, "Chavez Restyles Venezuela with '21st-Century Socialism,'" *New York Times*, October 30, 2005.

Chapter 12: Afterstories

1. This section draws on extensive research conducted by the author for the Mattatuck Museum during 2002–5 and compiled in the unpublished report "Brass Roots, New Shoots: Research for Revision of the Brass Roots Exhibit," on file at the Mattatuck Museum, Waterbury, Conn.

2. "CNV Regional Plan, 1998," 21, NVP Collection, Mattatuck Museum, Waterbury, Conn.

3. Historical data used in this section are not always consistent because of differences between the data-processing techniques of different agencies, such as the Connecticut Department of Labor and the U.S. Census, and due to repeated changes in data definitions and processing over time.

4. "Waterbury among Worst Cities for Jobs," *Waterbury Republican-American,* May 1, 2010.

5. The course was cotaught with longtime Waterbury resident and Columbia University professor of urban studies Peter Marcuse.

6. Robyn Adams, "Coalition Serves Pancakes by Candlelight," *Waterbury Republican-American,* October 9, 2005.

7. Ben Conery, "State Settles Suit against 'Predatory' Home Brokers," *Waterbury Republican-American,* April 25, 2006.

8. Naugatuck Valley Project, *Naugatuck Valley Project: History Project Exhibit* (Water-

bury, Conn.: NVP, 2010), includes material from the exhibit and reunion. Visit http://www.brassvalley.org for additional material from the exhibit.

9. For more on the Merrimack Valley Project, see Allen N. Fairfax, "Challenging the Rules: The Merrimack Valley Project and the Construction of Public Space" (Ph.D. diss., Boston College, 2006).

10. For comparative information on the problems of New England cities, see New England Futures at http://www.newenglandfutures.org, especially material there by journalists Neil Peirce and Curtis Johnson.

11. Memorial service for Theresa Francis, May 20, 1994, transcript in NVP Collection, Mattatuck Museum, Waterbury, Conn. The following quotes also come from this source.

12. ICA, "Taking Care of Business" (see chap. 8, n. 2).

Interviews

Interviews are deposited at the Mattatuck Museum in Waterbury, Connecticut, unless otherwise indicated.

Anonymous office worker. December 8, 1987. Seymour.
Anonymous Seymour worker. May 27, 1986. Seymour.
Bean, Kevin. April 9, 1990. Waterbury.
———. May 11, 2009. Waterbury.
Beck, James. September 23, 2009. Waterbury.
Benson, Rev. Tim. May 12, 1986. Seymour.
Burkhart, Carol. May 29, 1986. Waterbury.
Burkhart-Lyons, Carol. May 20, 1994. Memorial service for Theresa Francis.
Cline, Roland. May 12, 1986. Waterbury.
———. May 20, 1986. Waterbury.
Crowe, Agnes O'Brien. Audio recording and transcript in "Keeping Time: An Oral History of Clockmaking" collection, Thomaston Public Library, Thomaston, Connecticut.
D'Agostino, Attilio. Video. Waterbury.
Diorio, Pat. April 14, 1999. Waterbury.
———. August 4, 1999. Waterbury.
Drescher, Carl, Jr. December 8, 1987. Seymour.
Duke, David. November 14, 1994. Seymour.
Filipiak, Doreen. June 16, 1999. Waterbury.
Francis, Theresa. May 19, 1986. Waterbury.
———. VCC slide-show script. Waterbury.
———. Video. Waterbury.
Galdston, Ken. November 19, 1985. Waterbury.
———. December 18, 1985. Waterbury.
———. April 14, 1986. Waterbury.
———. October 16, 1987. Waterbury.
———. February 24, 1988. Waterbury.

———. March 23, 1988. Waterbury.

———. May 25, 1988. Waterbury.

———. October 26, 1989. Waterbury.

———. May 20, 1994. Memorial service for Theresa Francis.

Gay, Merrill. December 3, 1990. Waterbury.

Gerard, Maria. VCC slide-show script. Waterbury.

González, Lillian. May 13, 1999. Waterbury.

Harrington, Jerry. April 30, 1995. Waterbury.

Kane, Francis. Audio recording and transcript in "Keeping Time: An Oral History of Clockmaking" collection, Thomaston Public Library, Thomaston, Connecticut.

Kearney, Mike. May 12, 1986. Seymour.

———. November 16, 1987. Seymour.

———. June 1, 1990. Seymour.

———. September 27, 1991. Seymour.

———. December 6, 1991. Seymour.

———. December 29, 1992. Seymour.

———. Video. Seymour.

Kwochka, Sam. Seymour.

Labacz, Ed. October 16, 1980. Seymour.

Lovett, Campbell. May 7, 1991. Waterbury.

Monahan, Matthew. Audio recording and transcript in "Keeping Time: An Oral History of Clockmaking" collection, Thomaston Public Library, Thomaston, Connecticut.

Muller, Faith. VCC slide-show script. Waterbury.

Norman, Henrietta. VCC slide-show script. Waterbury.

Parker, Derricia. September 23, 2009. Waterbury.

Perella, Fred. Video. Waterbury.

Ploman, Howard. Video. Waterbury.

Rosati, Margie. April 23, 1999. Waterbury.

Rosazza, Peter. March 21, 1986. Waterbury.

———. Video. Waterbury.

Tycenski, Mary. Audio recording and transcript in "Keeping Time: An Oral History of Clockmaking" collection, Thomaston Public Library, Thomaston, Connecticut.

Wilson, James. Audio recording and transcript in "Keeping Time: An Oral History of Clockmaking" collection, Thomaston Public Library, Thomaston, Connecticut.

Index

accountability, xxiii, 187–89
"accountability sessions," 201
ACORN, 194
"Adopt a House Fund," 211
Adrian Dominican Sisters, 118, 134
Advanced Leadership Institutes, 213
Alinsky, Saul, 23–24, 27, 57
Amalgamated Clothing Workers bank, 193, 238n11
American Brass Company, 4
AMF Alcort, 60
Ansonia, CT, 60
Anthony, Richard, 211
Aviles, Victor, 180

"Badder Homes and Gardens Tour," 208
Baldridge, Malcolm, 67
Baldridge, Margaret, 173
Barbieri, Richard, 181
Bean, Kevin, 174, 175, 177, 181–83, 185
Beck, James, 183
Bell, Drummond, 41
Benson, Tim: on churches' role in Naugatuck Valley Project (NVP), 58–59; first reaction to Naugatuck Valley Project (NVP), 27; on grassroots nature of Naugatuck Valley Project (NVP), 60; on local ownership, 57–58; on Naugatuck Valley Project (NVP) goals, 57–58; on Naugatuck Valley Project (NVP) independence, 53; Naugatuck Valley Project (NVP) steering committee co-chairmanship, 60; on Naugatuck Valley Project (NVP) success, 66; on people's commitment to Naugatuck Valley Project (NVP), 34; on results of Seymour buyout and Seymour Specialty Wire, 48; role in Seymour buyout, 38–39; on Seymour buyout and Naugatuck Valley Project (NVP) power shift, 40–41; on Seymour buyout process, 38
Bergin, Edward, 71, 74
Blumenthal, Richard, 168
brass industry, 3–5
Brass Mill Mall, 80
Brass Valley Music Festival, 216, 217
Brass Workers History Project, 28, xi
Bridgeport Brass, 84, 86
Brookside Housing Cooperative: accomplishments, 184–85; author participation, 179; current problems and achievements, 183; development process, 178–79; Fort Hill roots, 170–78; groundbreaking, 180; housing environment surrounding development, 164–65; membership/qualification criteria, 179–80; Naugatuck Valley Project (NVP) research and experience, 178–79; ongoing organizing needs, 182–83; Shamrock Ridge roots, 165–70; sweat equity requirement, 179
brownfield sites, 198, 200, 209
Brownfields Job Training and Development Demonstration Pilot, 209
"bundle of rights," 189–90, 237–38n7, 238n8, 238n9

Burkhart, Carol, 60–61, 62, 71, 77, 171
Burkhart-Lyons, Carol, 208, 210. *See also* Burkhart, Carol
button and hardware manufacturing, 2–3

The Capitalist Manifesto: How to Turn 80 Million Workers into Capitalists on Borrowed Money (Kelso), 44
Carroll, Robert, 29–30
Carson, John, 40
Castellani, Father, 30–31
Catholic Archdiocese of Hartford, 10, 21–22, 175, 198, 209
Catholic Campaign for Human Development, 125
Catholic social doctrine, 21–22, 58
Center/Edge Project, 198, 209
Central Naugatuck Valley Planning Agency, 203–7
Century Brass: bankruptcy filing, 72; buyout feasibility research, 70, 74–75; conflicts during buyout investigations, 78–80; corporate history, 67–68; initial involvement of Naugatuck Valley Project (NVP), 60; management corruption investigation, 75–78; summary of Naugatuck Valley Project involvement, 81–83; wage freeze, 68; worker rejection of concessions, 68–69; workforce cuts, 68
Chase Brass Company, 4
Chase Forge, 30–31
Chubat, John, 85
CIO (Congress of Industrial Organizations), 7–8
"civic capitalism" tradition, 14
Clergy Association of Thomaston, 29–30
Cline, Roland, 41–43, 45, 70, 78–79, 80
Cody, Henry, x, xxiii
Coleman, James, 77
Collins, Chuck, 169
Commerford, Donald Jr., 89
Community Economic Development Fund (CEDF), 194, 195, 196, 209
Community/Labor Support Committee, 12
community land trusts (CLTs), 167–69
community organizing. *See* organizing methodology
Community Reinvestment Act (CRA), 193, 202
condominium conversion, 164, 165–66
Congress of Industrial Organizations (CIO), 7–8

Connecticut Association for Home Care (CAHC), 163–64
Connecticut Business and Industry Association, 11
Connecticut Citizen Action Group (CCAG), 12, 21, 64, 75, 171–73
Connecticut Community Care, Inc., 114, 117
Connecticut Department of Economic Development, 39–40
Connecticut Development Authority, 12, 68, 99
Connecticut Magazine, 10
Connor, Lucille, 180
consciousness-raising, 60–61
Cooney, John, 212
Cooperative Home Care Associates (CHCA), 112, 113, 133, 197, 198
Co-Opportunity, 171, 173
corporations, 14–15, 19, 20, 222n34. *See also* deindustrialization
"Create Jobs that Save Our Environment," 208
CREDO, 173
Cumbler, John, 14
Curtin, Tom, 36

D'Agostino, Attilio, 69–70, 80
David, Ray, 77
Day, Berry, and Howard, 39
deindustrialization: accountability, 14–15, 187–89, 222n31; early responses, 11–13; economic crises and solutions, xxi; extended authority of management, 222n30; failure of traditional political representation, 19–20; financial restructuring, 8–9; as first phase of economic globalization, 18–19; industrial dominance decline, 8–9; "market forces," 16–19; Naugatuck Valley negative effects, 9–11; power of ownership, 14–15; relationship to economic globalization, xiv–xx; side effects, 111; speculative investment irresponsibility, 15; statistics for Naugatuck Valley, xxi; unionism, 187; workplace culture, 15–16. *See also* corporations; economic globalization
DelBianco, Doreen, 174
Deloitte, Haskins, and Sells, 39–40
democratization. *See* economic democratization
Dillon, Reed investment bank, 40
Diorio, Pat: on closing ValleyCare Coop-

erative, 158; on diversity of ValleyCare Cooperative staff and workers, 132; experience and training, 116; on home health care scheduling, 144; on home health care worker challenges, 137; on job improvement challenges, 145–46; on racial balance problems in staffing ValleyCare Cooperative, 151; on salary limitations, 145; on staff expansion at ValleyCare Cooperative, 144; on staffing needs unfulfilled, 150–51; on ValleyCare Cooperative accomplishments, 119, 159–60; ValleyCare Cooperative consensus- and team-building, 124; on ValleyCare Cooperative financial problems, 160–61; on ValleyCare Cooperative problems after restructuring, 157; on ValleyCare Cooperative worker turnover, 147; on worker attitudes about ownership, 127; on worker-owner numbers at ValleyCare Cooperative, 154

Dolan, Dick, 177

Downs, Tim, 31

Drabek, Geraldine, 164–65

Drescher, Carl: buyout approval, 38, 42; experience and training, 45–46; firing, 98; management difficulties, 91, 93–94; transition role at Seymour Specialty Wire, 100

Duke, David, 109–10

DuPont, Debby, 182

Dwyer, Thomas, 71

economic democratization: accountability, 187–88; alternative efforts, xxii, 220n8; complexity, 201–2; essential elements, xix; government role, 199–201; grassroots character, xxi–xxii; market changes, 196–99; Naugatuck Valley Project (NVP) as effort toward, xviii–xx, 186–87, 202; ownership forms and methods, 189–91; resources supporting, 192–96; workplace culture, 191–92

economic globalization, xix–xx, xxii, 220n8

economic powerlessness, 19–20. *See also* deindustrialization

Eigen, Richard, 174

Emhart, 60

employee ownership, 189–91

Employee Stock Option Plan (ESOP): Seymour Specialty Wire, 42, 45, 91–95, 105, 189–90; ValleyCare Cooperative, 125–28, 190–91

empowerment. *See* economic democratization; victim transformation

Environmental Protection Agency (EPA), 209

Environmental Remediation Technician Training Program, 209

Episcopal Diocese of Connecticut, 118

ESOP. *See* Employee Stock Option Plan (ESOP)

Evans, Seth, 112, 113

Fair Rent Commission for Waterbury, 176

Farrell factory, 60

Father Nadolny Good News Fund (GNF), 170–71, 177, 178, 182. *See also* Nadolny, Edmund

Fedak, Robert, 165, 166, 170

Federal HOME (Home Ownership Made Easy) Funds, 211

Fernandez, Marita, 182

Filipiak, Doreen, 111–12, 117, 128, 158–59, 163, 195

Financial Democracy Campaign, 194

financial support, 193–96. *See also* Naugatuck Valley Project (NVP) and specific related projects

Flynn, John, 26

Foothill Capital Corporation of Los Angeles, 100, 104

Ford, Ray, 80

Formica, Jerry, 80

Fort Hill, 170–78, 181. *See also* Brookside Housing Cooperative

Fox, Stanley, 169, 176–77, 178, 179

Francis, Kathy, 214–15

Francis, Theresa: on Century Brass, 74–75, 77, 82–83; character traits, 214–15, 217; on co-creation vs. victimization, xxiii, 76; on Fort Hill, 175, 177; on grassroots organizing, 216–17; leadership role in Naugatuck Valley Project (NVP), 72, 78–79, 182; Naugatuck Valley Project (NVP) colleagues on, 213–17; on Naugatuck Valley Project (NVP) role, 82–83; as organizer, 179; overview, 72–74; remembered, 213–17; on ValleyCare Cooperative, 131, 217

funding, 193–96. *See also* Naugatuck Valley Project (NVP) and specific related projects

Galdston, Ken: affordable housing research, 166–69; on Century Brass, 79–80, 81;

Century Brass buyout initiation, 71; on diversity of preexisting relationships in Naugatuck Valley Project (NVP), 56–57; on early meetings with corporate executives, 30; education and experience, 22–25; on educator role, 51–52; employee buyout informational presentations, 36–38; on Evelyn Lush, 166; home care business concept, 111; on leadership training, 50; Massachusetts relocation, 174; on Naugatuck Valley Project (NVP) and housing, 164, 169; on Naugatuck Valley Project (NVP) goal, xii; on Naugatuck Valley Project (NVP) member commitment, 33, 34, 64; on Naugatuck Valley Project (NVP) membership struggles, 64; on Naugatuck Valley Project (NVP) organizer role, 65–66; on need for deviation from Alinsky model strategy, 54–55; organizer and researcher, 32–33, 53–54, 64–66; Perella on, 22; post-Naugatuck Valley Project organizing, 212–13; on power structure in housing industry, 166–67; recent and current activity, 208; on Seymour buyout, 39, 41–43, 43–44; on team development, 52; on Theresa Francis, 72–74; on tradition and solidarity, 38; vision, 25; on Waterbury, 69
Gardiner, David M., 88
Gaumer, Rick, 168
Gay, Merrill, 171–73, 174, 177–78, 178–79, 180
General Time Controls, 29
Gerard, Maria, 127, 138, 141, 144, 159
Giacomi, Robert, 177
Giroux, Andre, 180, 216
globalization. *See* deindustrialization; economic globalization
González, Lilian, 124, 127, 139, 154
Good News Fund (GNF), 170–71, 177, 178, 182. *See also* Nadolny, Edmund
Goodyear, Charles, 3
government, 162–63, 167–68, 199–201
Granite State Organizing Project, 213
Grasso, Ella, 68
grassroots organization overview, xxi–xxii
Great Depression, 195
Greater London Enterprise Board, 195
Green Community Services of Waterbury, 165, 170–71, 173

Hanlon, Roger, 39
Harlor, John, 102, 103, 230n68

Harrington, Jerry, 98–104, 108
Hartford Catholic Archdiocese, 175, 198, 209
Hartford Courant, 70
Health Care Committee, 111–16, 112, 132. *See also* ValleyCare Cooperative
Health Care Interpretation Project, 210
Hogar del Futur, 173
Holy Cross Fathers, 118
Humphrey, Carolyn, 112, 116

IAF (Industrial Area Foundation), 23–24
ICA. *See* Industrial Cooperative Association (ICA)
Independence Care System, 198
individual powerlessness, xx. *See also* deindustrialization
Industrial Area Foundation (IAF), 23–24
Industrial Cooperative Association (ICA): experience and expertise, 32; Seymour buyout involvement, 37, 41–43; Seymour Specialty Wire involvement, 94; ValleyCare Cooperative involvement, 112, 113, 118, 124
industrialization, 17
"industrial-sector service centers," 198
Institute for Community Economics (ICE), 167, 169
"institution-based organizing," 53–54
Intervalley Project, 212

Johnson, Helen, 55–56

Kane, Francis, x
Kearney, Mike: Century Brass buyout research, 78–79; employee ownership expertise, 228n19; on Harrington and Seymour Specialty Wire, 99, 100, 101, 104, 231n93; on housing problems for workers, 164; on labor-management conflict at Seymour Specialty Wire, 90–91, 93–94; Naugatuck Valley Project (NVP) steering committee co-chairmanship, 60; on reactions to Seymour Manufacturing Company closing and buyout possibilities, 36, 37; Seymour buyout role, 46–47, 228n19; on Seymour Specialty Wire board of directors election, 45; on Seymour Specialty Wire workplace culture, 86; on Theresa Francis, 213–14, 217; on Universal Scheduling systems problems, 95–97; on wage concessions, 97

Kelso, Louis, 44
Kennebec Valley Organization, 213
Klimovich, Tom, 37, 96
Knight, Jo, 117
Knights of Labor, 7
Kwochka, Sam, 85

Labacz, Eddie, 35, 36, 38, 85
land trusts, 167–69
Latino Hispanic Resource Center, 209–10
leadership identification and training,
    49–50, 52
LEAP (Legislative Election Action Pro-
    gram), 26
Lebron, Luz, 210
Legislative Election Action Program
    (LEAP), 26
Leviticus Fund, 118
Lilly Foundation, 112, 118, 119, 125, 126, 134
limited liability, 14–15
"listening meetings," 201
Lombard, Charles, 29
Lombardo, Joe, 98, 99
Lovett, Campbell: on Century Brass, 76, 80,
    81, 82; on early power lessons, 31; on Nau-
    gatuck Valley Project (NVP) and Century
    Brass management, 77–78; on Waterbury
    Fair Rent Commission, 176
Lush, Evelyn, 165–66, 170, 180

Maloney, Mary Ann, 164, 182
Mankowski, John, 38, 55
Marianist Sharing Fund, 118
"market forces," 16–19
markets, 196–99
Matthei, Chuck, 167, 170
Matthews, Robert, 165
Matthies family, 84
Matutuck Museum, 211
McAlenney, Paul, 39, 45, 70
Merrimack Valley Project, 213
Methodist Church, 32
Monahan, Thomas, viii
Mondragon cooperatives, 196, 197, 202,
    239n20
Money Magazine, 10
Motel, Larry, 98–104, 104, 230n68
Ms. Collaborative, 118, 134
Mt. Auburn Associates, 198
Muller, Faith, 143, 145
Multi-Metals Training Center, 208
multinational corporations, 9

Murphy, Clayton, 169
Murray, Hank, 21, 25

Nadolny, Edmund, 164, 170–71, 173, 177, 183.
    See also Good News Fund (GNF)
Napoli, Ron, 62, 176
National Association for Home Care
    (NAHC), 163–64
National Distillers and Chemical Corpora-
    tion, 36, 39–40, 44–45, 86–87, 100
National Labor Relations Act, 188, 237n4
National Labor Relations Board (NLRB),
    104
National Westminster Bank (NatWest), 46,
    98, 100
Naugatuck, CT, 61
Naugatuck Valley, 1–8, 28–30, 203–7. *See
    also* Naugatuck Valley history
Naugatuck Valley history: African Ameri-
    cans, 6; colonial era, 1–2; conservatism,
    13–14; corporations, 4; deindustrializa-
    tion, 9–11; entrepreneurial elite, 4; ethnic
    tensions, 6; homogeneity, 5; immigration
    and industrialization demographics, 5–7;
    labor movement, 7–8; nineteenth century,
    2–5; pre-colonial, 1; recent, 203–7; as
    revealed by Galdston interview process,
    32–33; Roman Catholicism predomi-
    nance, 6; social evolution, 5–7; subsidiar-
    ization by large national corporations, 4;
    twentieth century, 4–5; unionization, 7–8;
    World War effects, 4–6
Naugatuck Valley Housing Development
    Corporation (NVHDC), 168–70, 182
Naugatuck Valley Project (NVP): accom-
    plishments list, xvi–xviii; author rela-
    tionship and role, xv, xviii–xix; Century
    Brass workers' support efforts, 70–72; as
    coalition of diverse organizations, 55–56;
    community history v. contemporary
    reality, 57–58; connections and roots dis-
    covered early, 32–33; convention, 62–64;
    credibility, 41; deindustrialization impact
    as unifying force, 54, 56–57; as developer
    of people, 65–66; diversity of participants,
    187–88; early goals and strategies, 24–28;
    early reactions of potential participants,
    27; as economic democratizer from
    below, 186–201; economic institution
    formation overview, xxi; economic rela-
    tionships and power challenge motive,
    54–55; as educator, xxii–xxiii; environ-

mental efforts, 198, 200; expansion into six chapters, 60; first valley wide meeting, 33; fledgling victories, 30–33; focus, 54–55; funding sources, 193–94, 195; Galdston research prior to launching, 26–28; Galdston role, 65–66; goals, xiv–xv, 27–28; grassroots organization overview, xxi–xxii; history committee, 211–12; housing approach, 171–73; housing committee formation, 164–65; independence from political and other organizations, 56; initial confrontations with corporate executives, 30; local community support, 33–34; as maximization of local power potential, 66; membership struggles, 63–64; as new form of organization, 64–66; nonpartisan nature, 200–201; organization development process, 59–64; organizing basis, 54; original sponsors, 28; overview, xiii–xxiii; ownership forms attempted, 189–91, 237nn5–6; pioneers, 24–28; plant closings as organization basis, 54, 56–57; potential leadership interviews, 28; public policy support overview, xxi; recent and current activity, 204, 207–12; resources other than financial, 195–96; "service credit" program, 195; as social learning process, 201–2; steering committee, 60; strategic focus, 54–55; strategies to impact markets, 197–98, 199; as "structured network," 188; uniqueness, 64–66; uses of pressure, 187–88. *See also* specific individuals; specific projects
Neighborhood Housing Services, 211
Nevins, George, 174
New England Joint Action (NEJA) Campaign, 213
New Milford, CT, 60
Norieka, Tim, 210
Norman, Henrietta: biographical and hiring information, 139; on challenges of home health care work for ValleyCare Cooperative, 140; on educational experiences as ValleyCare Cooperative home health worker, 141; as Naugatuck Valley Project (NVP) leader, 182; on problems emerging at ValleyCare Cooperative with growth, 151; on racial balance problems in staffing ValleyCare Cooperative, 153; on transportation challenges at ValleyCare Cooperative, 144; on work atmosphere at

ValleyCare Cooperative, 145; on worker ownership at ValleyCare Cooperative, 127

Office of Urban Affairs of the Catholic Archdiocese of Hartford, 10, 21–22, 175, 198, 209
O'Neill, William, 68, 174
organizing. *See* organizing methodology
organizing methodology: action identification and practice, 51; Alinsky influence, 49–54; commonality of community history v. contemporary reality, 57–58; consciousness-raising, 60–61; first convention, 62–64; independence from political and other organizations, 52–53; Industrial Areas Foundation (IAF) influence, 49–54; Industrial Areas Foundation (IAF) technique deviations, 54–59; institution building, 53–54; interviewing, 49–50; issue selection, 50–51; leadership identification and training, 49–50, 52; local identity and character, 59–60; powerlessness as motivator, 51–52; relationship development, 50; team development, 52–53; uniqueness of Naugatuck Valley Project (NVP), 64–66; visible economic reality motivation, 59–60
ownership, 189–92, 237nn5–6, 238–39n18

Papandrea, John, 174, 177
Parker, Derricia, 183–84
Parsons, Shepard, 168, 174, 175, 215–16
"participatory economics," 192
Perella, Fred: on deindustrialization impact on Naugatuck Valley, 10; on economic crises and solutions, xx; education and experience, 21–22; on Naugatuck Valley Project (NVP) and Catholic social doctrine, 58; Naugatuck Valley Project (NVP) involvement in Shamrock Ridge, 165; as Naugatuck Valley Project (NVP) pioneer, 25; on Naugatuck Valley Project (NVP) significance, 186
Peter Paul-Cadbury, 61–62
Piscotti, Arnold, 175
Plant Closing Coalition, 11
Plume and Atwood mill, vii
Pochron, Frank, 84–85
Porter brothers, 2
Poverty in American Democracy: A Study of Social Power (Perella), xx, 21–22

powerlessness. *See* economic powerlessness

predatory-lending campaign, 210–11

Purchasing magazine, 87–89, 97, 100

Quantum. *See* National Distillers and Chemical Corporation

Quebec Solidarity Fund, 194

Rapoport, Miles, 22, 25

Reagan Democrats, 12

"Reaganomics," xiv, xx

real estate and housing, 164–65

relationship development, 50

resources, 193–96

Reymond Bakery, 192

Rhode Island Organizing Project, 213

Rhodes, Irv, 171

Rosa, Elizabeth, 209

Rosado, Evelia, 180

Rosati, Margie: on confidentiality challenges of home health care workers, 142; on early days of ValleyCare Cooperative, 143–44; on ethics of worker ownership, 125; experience and training, 115–16; on experience of ValleyCare Cooperative, 163; on hiring home health care workers for ValleyCare Cooperative, 133–34; on home health care worker training at ValleyCare Cooperative, 134–37; multiplicity of early ValleyCare Cooperative functions, 144; on Naugatuck Valley Project (NVP) and connections, 132; on nurturing limitations, 142; *Poverty in American Democracy: A Study of Social Power* (Perella), 126; on racial balance problems in staffing ValleyCare Cooperative, 152–53; on reputation and ethics, 142–43; on small v. large organizations, 116; on solidarity of worker-owners at ValleyCare Cooperative, 153; on team development, 134; on ValleyCare Cooperative participatory environment, 122–24; on worker ownership and nature of cooperative, 126, 128–29

Rosazza, Peter, 26–27, 32–33, 40, 47–48, 50, 118

Rose City Land Trust, 167, 168

Rothberg, Ellen, 158

Rowland, John, 169

rubber industry, 3–4

Rubenstein, Charles, 67

Saglio, Janet, 32, 37, 40, 212

Sanford, Earle, 210

Santaguida, Frank, 78–79, 80

Santana, Elida, 132, 180

Santopietro, Joseph J., 175, 176, 181

Schuyler, John, 39–40, 70

"scientific management," 15–16

Scovill Manufacturing Company, 2–4, 12, 67–68

Scully, William, 74

Security Savings and Loan, 181

Segal, Lewis, 71, 77–78

Seth Thomas Clock Company, ix–x, 4, 9

Seymour buyout: Benson role, 38–39; community pressure campaign, 41; feasibility study, 41–43; financing methodology, 44–45; governing solutions, 45–46; leadership struggles, 43–45; management selection process, 45; Naugatuck Valley Project (NVP) connection, 38–39; political connection, 39; power shift, 40–41; state government support, 39–40; steering committee, 45–46; union role, 46–47. *See also* Seymour Specialty Wire

Seymour Congregational Church, 38

Seymour Manufacturing Company: early signs of plant closing, 36; foremen, 85–86, 228n4; history, 35–36; history and habits of workers and management, 84–87; management-worker division, 86–87; power structure, 87; unionism, 85, 87; worker contact with Naugatuck Valley Project (NVP), 36–37. *See also* Seymour buyout

Seymour Specialty Wire: accomplishments, 110; bonuses, 90–91; brass industry turmoil impacting, 87–89; business cycle impact, 89–90, 92, 97; closing, 104; conflict of interest allegations, 103–4; consulting for management systems, 95–97; delayed birth, 46–47; employee pay cut, 90–91; global forces against, 109; historical legacy, 84–87; labor-management conflict, 90–91; layoffs, 103; leadership change, 98–100; mistrust and suspicion, 102–4; Naugatuck Valley Project (NVP) strategic relationship, 48; overview, 84; power structure difficulties, 104–7; problems, 104–8; product and markets, 89; production and management changes, 100–104; production problems, 96, 97–98, 229n35;

quality and delivery problems, 100, 230n59; shutdowns, 102; strike threats, 97; training and skills problems, 108–9; union role problems, 108; wage concessions, 97; worker slowdown, 91; Workers Solving Problems (WSP), 91–92, 94–95; work roles problems, 107–8. *See also* Seymour buyout

Shamrock Ridge, 165–70. *See also* Brookside Housing Cooperative

Shamrock Ridge Tenants Association, 166, 169–70, 176–77. *See also* Brookside Housing Cooperative; Fort Hill

Shrag, Steve, 209

Silano, Anthony, 170–71, 177

Sisters of Charity, 118

Skowronski, Eugene, 39

Smith, Adam, 17

social learning process, 201–2

South Side Bank, 194

Spellman, Ed, 111–12

Spellman, Ethel, 111–12, 158–59

Spring, Pat, 171

State Plan of Conservation and Development, 194, 238n13

Steel Valley Authority, 194, 195

Stockton, Edward, 74

"structured network," 188

Summerset Hills, 165

Surpin, Rick, 112

sweat equity, 179

Talley Industries, ix, xiv–xv, 9, 29–30

tariffs, 17–18

Taylor, Frederick Winslow, 15–16, 192

Taylor, Vance, 64

team development, 52–53

Temporary Workers Association, 213

Thomaston, CT, ix–x

Torin Company, 60

Torrington, CT, 60

Torrington Chamber of Commerce, 64

Tremaine, Burton G., 88

Turner, Linda, x

Tycenski, Mary, ix

UAW. *See* United Auto Workers (UAW)

UAW Amalgamated Local 1827, 35

UAW Local 1064, 69–70

UAW Region 9A, 21, 28–30

Unemployment Information Centers, 12

United Auto Workers (UAW), 12, 21, 28–30, 35, 69–70

United Church of Christ, 32

Universal Scheduling, 95–97

University of Connecticut in Torrington, 31

Upper Connecticut River Valley organization, 213

usufruct, 189–90

Valley Brownfields Pilot Program, 209

ValleyCare Cooperative: accomplishments, 129, 147–48, 158–60, 162–63, 163; advisory committee, 118–19; author experience, 131; Catholic Campaign for Human Development role, 125; certification, 118, 134; closing, 158; conceptualization, 111–12; Connecticut Community Care, Inc. role, 117; decline in earnings, 150; diversity of staff hired, 118; early achievements, 118, 119–21; feasibility study, 113–14; financial difficulties, 153–55; financing for start-up, 118; goals, 114; governance methodology and philosophy, 121–22; government policy changes and funding cuts, 149–50, 162–63; high labor turnover, 130; incorporation and opening, 116–17; interviewing and hiring models, 133; job improvement challenges, 145–47; as job provider, 119–20, 163; Naugatuck Valley Project (NVP) roles, 112–16, 117–18, 131–32; office challenges, 143–45; organization, 114; ownership methodology, 121; participatory environment, 123–25; restructuring of 1998, 155; "service credit" program, 195; structure, 114; training home health care workers, 134–37; as VNA Healthcare subcontractor, 155–58; worker challenges, 137–43; worker-owners, 126–28; worker ownership training, 125–27; worker participation goals and policies, 122–24; worker wage challenges, 147

Valleycast, 42–43

van-pool system, 111–12

Vernovai, Mike, 68

victim transformation, 210–11

Visiting Nurse Associations (VNAs), 114, 155–58

Wagner Act, 202. *See also* National Labor Relations Act

Waterbury, CT, 60
Waterbury American, 176
Waterbury Area Council of Churches, 31
Waterbury Board of Realtors, 175
Waterbury Economic Development Department, 31
Waterbury Foundation, 175
Waterbury Progressive Coalition, 75
Waterbury Republican, 64, 177, 181
Waterbury Republican-American, 177
Whealon, John, 58
White, Patty, 215
Williams, Dick, 29–30

Wilson, James, x, 9
Worker Adjustment and Retraining Notification (WARN) Act, 14–15
worker ownership, 189–91. *See also* Employee Stock Option Plan (ESOP)
"worker self-management," 192
Workers Solving Problems (WSP), 94–95
workplace culture and power structure, 191–92

"Yankee peddlers," 2, 17

Zorilla, Norberto, 210–11

The Working Class in American History

Worker City, Company Town: Iron and Cotton-Worker Protest in Troy and Cohoes, New York, 1855–84   *Daniel J. Walkowitz*

Life, Work, and Rebellion in the Coal Fields: The Southern West Virginia Miners, 1880–1922   *David Alan Corbin*

Women and American Socialism, 1870–1920   *Mari Jo Buhle*

Lives of Their Own: Blacks, Italians, and Poles in Pittsburgh, 1900–1960   *John Bodnar, Roger Simon, and Michael P. Weber*

Working-Class America: Essays on Labor, Community, and American Society   *Edited by Michael H. Frisch and Daniel J. Walkowitz*

Eugene V. Debs: Citizen and Socialist   *Nick Salvatore*

American Labor and Immigration History, 1877–1920s: Recent European Research   *Edited by Dirk Hoerder*

Workingmen's Democracy: The Knights of Labor and American Politics   *Leon Fink*

The Electrical Workers: A History of Labor at General Electric and Westinghouse, 1923–60   *Ronald W. Schatz*

The Mechanics of Baltimore: Workers and Politics in the Age of Revolution, 1763–1812   *Charles G. Steffen*

The Practice of Solidarity: American Hat Finishers in the Nineteenth Century   *David Bensman*

The Labor History Reader   *Edited by Daniel J. Leab*

Solidarity and Fragmentation: Working People and Class Consciousness in Detroit, 1875–1900   *Richard Oestreicher*

Counter Cultures: Saleswomen, Managers, and Customers in American Department Stores, 1890–1940   *Susan Porter Benson*

The New England Working Class and the New Labor History   *Edited by Herbert G. Gutman and Donald H. Bell*

Labor Leaders in America   *Edited by Melvyn Dubofsky and Warren Van Tine*

Barons of Labor: The San Francisco Building Trades and Union Power in the Progressive Era   *Michael Kazin*

Gender at Work: The Dynamics of Job Segregation by Sex during World War II   *Ruth Milkman*

Once a Cigar Maker: Men, Women, and Work Culture in American Cigar Factories, 1900–1919   *Patricia A. Cooper*

A Generation of Boomers: The Pattern of Railroad Labor Conflict in Nineteenth-Century America   *Shelton Stromquist*

Work and Community in the Jungle: Chicago's Packinghouse Workers, 1894–1922   *James R. Barrett*

Workers, Managers, and Welfare Capitalism: The Shoeworkers and Tanners of Endicott Johnson, 1890–1950   *Gerald Zahavi*

Men, Women, and Work: Class, Gender, and Protest in the New England Shoe Industry, 1780–1910   *Mary Blewett*

Workers on the Waterfront: Seamen, Longshoremen, and Unionism in the 1930s   *Bruce Nelson*

German Workers in Chicago: A Documentary History of Working-Class Culture from 1850 to World War I   *Edited by Hartmut Keil and John B. Jentz*

On the Line: Essays in the History of Auto Work   *Edited by Nelson Lichtenstein and Stephen Meyer III*

Labor's Flaming Youth: Telephone Operators and Worker Militancy, 1878–1923   *Stephen H. Norwood*

Another Civil War: Labor, Capital, and the State in the Anthracite Regions of Pennsylvania, 1840–68   *Grace Palladino*

Coal, Class, and Color: Blacks in Southern West Virginia, 1915–32   *Joe William Trotter Jr.*

For Democracy, Workers, and God: Labor Song-Poems and Labor Protest, 1865–95   *Clark D. Halker*

Dishing It Out: Waitresses and Their Unions in the Twentieth Century   *Dorothy Sue Cobble*

The Spirit of 1848: German Immigrants, Labor Conflict, and the Coming of the Civil War   *Bruce Levine*

Working Women of Collar City: Gender, Class, and Community in Troy, New York, 1864–86   *Carole Turbin*

Southern Labor and Black Civil Rights: Organizing Memphis Workers   *Michael K. Honey*

Radicals of the Worst Sort: Laboring Women in Lawrence, Massachusetts, 1860–1912   *Ardis Cameron*

Producers, Proletarians, and Politicians: Workers and Party Politics in Evansville and New Albany, Indiana, 1850–87   *Lawrence M. Lipin*

The New Left and Labor in the 1960s   *Peter B. Levy*

The Making of Western Labor Radicalism: Denver's Organized Workers, 1878–1905   *David Brundage*

In Search of the Working Class: Essays in American Labor History and Political Culture   *Leon Fink*

Lawyers against Labor: From Individual Rights to Corporate Liberalism   *Daniel R. Ernst*

"We Are All Leaders": The Alternative Unionism of the Early 1930s   *Edited by Staughton Lynd*

The Female Economy: The Millinery and Dressmaking Trades, 1860–1930   *Wendy Gamber*

"Negro and White, Unite and Fight!": A Social History of Industrial Unionism in Meatpacking, 1930–90   *Roger Horowitz*

Power at Odds: The 1922 National Railroad Shopmen's Strike   *Colin J. Davis*

The Common Ground of Womanhood: Class, Gender, and Working Girls' Clubs, 1884–1928   *Priscilla Murolo*

Marching Together: Women of the Brotherhood of Sleeping Car Porters   *Melinda Chateauvert*

Down on the Killing Floor: Black and White Workers in Chicago's Packinghouses, 1904–54   *Rick Halpern*

Labor and Urban Politics: Class Conflict and the Origins of Modern Liberalism in Chicago, 1864–97   *Richard Schneirov*

All That Glitters: Class, Conflict, and Community in Cripple Creek   *Elizabeth Jameson*

Waterfront Workers: New Perspectives on Race and Class   *Edited by Calvin Winslow*

Labor Histories: Class, Politics, and the Working-Class Experience   *Edited by Eric Arnesen, Julie Greene, and Bruce Laurie*

The Pullman Strike and the Crisis of the 1890s: Essays on Labor and Politics   *Edited by Richard Schneirov, Shelton Stromquist, and Nick Salvatore*

AlabamaNorth: African-American Migrants, Community, and Working-Class Activism in Cleveland, 1914–45   *Kimberley L. Phillips*

Imagining Internationalism in American and British Labor, 1939–49   *Victor Silverman*

William Z. Foster and the Tragedy of American Radicalism   *James R. Barrett*

Colliers across the Sea: A Comparative Study of Class Formation in Scotland and the American Midwest, 1830–1924   *John H. M. Laslett*

"Rights, Not Roses": Unions and the Rise of Working-Class Feminism, 1945–80   *Dennis A. Deslippe*

Testing the New Deal: The General Textile Strike of 1934 in the American South   *Janet Irons*

Hard Work: The Making of Labor History   *Melvyn Dubofsky*

Southern Workers and the Search for Community: Spartanburg County, South Carolina   *G. C. Waldrep III*

We Shall Be All: A History of the Industrial Workers of the World (abridged edition)   *Melvyn Dubofsky, ed. Joseph A. McCartin*

Race, Class, and Power in the Alabama Coalfields, 1908–21   *Brian Kelly*

Duquesne and the Rise of Steel Unionism   *James D. Rose*

Anaconda: Labor, Community, and Culture in Montana's Smelter City   *Laurie Mercier*

Bridgeport's Socialist New Deal, 1915–36   *Cecelia Bucki*

Indispensable Outcasts: Hobo Workers and Community in the American Midwest, 1880–1930   *Frank Tobias Higbie*

After the Strike: A Century of Labor Struggle at Pullman   *Susan Eleanor Hirsch*

Corruption and Reform in the Teamsters Union   *David Witwer*

Waterfront Revolts: New York and London Dockworkers, 1946–61   *Colin J. Davis*

Black Workers' Struggle for Equality in Birmingham   *Horace Huntley and David Montgomery*

The Tribe of Black Ulysses: African American Men in the Industrial South   *William P. Jones*

City of Clerks: Office and Sales Workers in Philadelphia, 1870–1920   *Jerome P. Bjelopera*

Reinventing "The People": The Progressive Movement, the Class Problem, and the Origins of Modern Liberalism   *Shelton Stromquist*

Radical Unionism in the Midwest, 1900–1950   *Rosemary Feurer*

Gendering Labor History   *Alice Kessler-Harris*

James P. Cannon and the Origins of the American Revolutionary Left, 1890–1928   *Bryan D. Palmer*

Glass Towns: Industry, Labor, and Political Economy in Appalachia, 1890–1930s   *Ken Fones-Wolf*

Workers and the Wild: Conservation, Consumerism, and Labor in Oregon, 1910–30
  Lawrence M. Lipin
Wobblies on the Waterfront: Interracial Unionism in Progressive-Era Philadelphia
  Peter Cole
Red Chicago: American Communism at Its Grassroots, 1928–35   *Randi Storch*
Labor's Cold War: Local Politics in a Global Context   *Edited by Shelton Stromquist*
Bessie Abramowitz Hillman and the Making of the Amalgamated Clothing Workers
  of America   *Karen Pastorello*
The Great Strikes of 1877   *Edited by David O. Stowell*
Union-Free America: Workers and Antiunion Culture   *Lawrence Richards*
Race against Liberalism: Black Workers and the UAW in Detroit
  David M. Lewis-Colman
Teachers and Reform: Chicago Public Education, 1929–70   *John F. Lyons*
Upheaval in the Quiet Zone: 1199/SEIU and the Politics of Healthcare Unionism
  Leon Fink and Brian Greenberg
Shadow of the Racketeer: Scandal in Organized Labor   *David Witwer*
Sweet Tyranny: Migrant Labor, Industrial Agriculture, and Imperial Politics
  Kathleen Mapes
Staley: The Fight for a New American Labor Movement   *Steven K. Ashby and
  C. J. Hawking*
On the Ground: Labor Struggles in the American Airline Industry   *Liesl Miller Orenic*
NAFTA and Labor in North America   *Norman Caulfield*
Making Capitalism Safe: Work Safety and Health Regulation in America, 1880–1940
  Donald W. Rogers
Good, Reliable, White Men: Railroad Brotherhoods, 1877–1917   *Paul Michel Taillon*
Spirit of Rebellion: Labor and Religion in the New Cotton South   *Jarod Heath Roll*
The Labor Question in America: Economic Democracy in the Gilded Age
  Rosanne Currarino
Banded Together: Economic Democratization in the Brass Valley   *Jeremy Brecher*

JEREMY BRECHER is an award-winning documentary film-
maker, historian, activist, and writer. His other books include
Strike! and *Globalization from Below: The Power of Solidarity.*
He lives in western Connecticut.

The University of Illinois Press
is a founding member of the
Association of American University Presses.

Composed in 10.5/13 Adobe Minion Pro
at the University of Illinois Press
Manufactured by Sheridan Books, Inc.

University of Illinois Press
1325 South Oak Street
Champaign, IL 61820-6903
www.press.uillinois.edu